Paramount

CITY OF DREAMS

Paramount

CITY OF DREAMS

Steven Bingen

with Marc Wanamaker, Bison Archives

LYONS PRESS

Guilford, Connecticut

An imprint of The Rowman & Littlefield Publishing Group, Inc.

4501 Forbes Blvd., Ste. 200

Lanham, MD 20706

www.rowman.com

Distributed by NATIONAL BOOK NETWORK

British Library Cataloguing in Publication Information available

Library of Congress Cataloging-in-Publication Data available

ISBN 978-1-4930-5568-5 (paper : alk. paper)

ISBN 978-1-63076-201-8 (e-book)

♾™ The paper used in this publication meets the minimum requirements of American National Standard for Information Sciences—Permanence of Paper for Printed Library Materials, ANSI/NISO Z39.48-1992.

★ Table of Contents ★

Introduction

I've been to Paris, France, and I've been to Paris Paramount. Paris Paramount is better.

—Ernst Lubitsch

Hollywood is quite probably the most haunted place in the world. This is not surprising. So many people have come to Hollywood with outsized dreams and outsized ambitions; so much passion and frustration and creativity have been siphoned into the abstraction that is the entertainment business that it would be surprising if there were not echoes and whispers absorbed into the very walls of the studios and the terra-cotta sidewalks on the Boulevard. Both Marilyn Monroe and Montgomery Clift allegedly haunt the Roosevelt Hotel. The old Ozzie and Harriet Nelson house, Hollywood Forever Cemetery, Grauman's Chinese Theatre, the Warner Pacific Theater, and the Pantages Theatre all allegedly have their ghosts as well.

Every movie studio has its ghosts, of course. Whether a person believes in the supernatural or not, the proliferation of stories about haunted soundstages and spectral presences flitting through lonely backlots is hardly surprising. When you think about it, movies—the very product which these factories assemble—are nothing but ghostly projections of long-gone pantomimes. The movies themselves are the ghosts.

Which brings us to Paramount. Could there be any more haunted spot in the world than Paramount Studios? The lot was built on the site of an old cemetery, after all!

But this book is not meant to be a meditation on ghosts or the nature of filmmaking, or even about cinema itself. Rather, it is a book about a location—a physical place where the real and the unreal, the physical and the metaphysical, meet and intermingle. However, it should be mentioned, because no one else has ever done so, that *Sight and Sound* magazine's 2012 critics' poll of the greatest movies of all time placed *Vertigo* (1958) and *Citizen Kane* (RKO, 1941) at the top of the list. Both films were created at Paramount.

Paramount likes to call itself the "only major classic studio still in Hollywood." Technically, this is true. Of the seven sister studios that constitute the American film industry, Paramount is the only one whose corporate and production headquarters are still located inside the Hollywood district proper, the other six having long ago fled to suburbs. Although all seven of the studios, along with independent producers, still shoot or base productions inside the warren of "rental" studios which honeycomb Hollywood's media district, and both Warner Bros. and Twentieth Century Fox still had annex studio complexes in the neighborhood until very recently.

Interestingly, Paramount's current lot is not even the studio's original California site. Paramount didn't put their name above the gate until 1926. Yet they were the first of the still-surviving film companies to settle in Hollywood, in 1913. They have occupied their current lot longer than nearly all of the other majors; only Universal, whose storied factory dates back to 1915, has utilized a single studio property continuously for more years.

More so than any other film company, Paramount is associated with their lot. The company's logo has long been a mountain, but it is their iconic gate on Bronson Avenue that is one of the world's most recognized places. For decades there has been a tradition among actors to touch the gate and whisper "I'm ready for my close-up, Mr. DeMille," for good luck. Much of the popular culture of the twentieth century and beyond was milled on the lot behind these very gates. The soundstages of Paramount have hosted thousands of the world's most famous and successful film and television programs. All of the world's biggest stars have worked at Paramount.

The story of the studio resonates far beyond the physical lot, and affects us as individuals in ways which we will never be able to count or comprehend. Many of our ideas about the world, about history and geography and gender, were shaped by Hollywood, and by Paramount. For most of us, our ideas about history, culture, and religion were shaped less by our parents and peers than by Cecil B. DeMille. Ghosts indeed.

As I've done in my previous "studio tour" volumes—*MGM: Hollywood's Greatest Backlot* and *Warner Bros.: Hollywood's Ultimate Backlot*—I've told the story of the Paramount lot from the perspective of the 1960s. The decision wasn't really a choice at all. In the 1960s, Paramount, like its sister studios, was very much like it had been in the 1930s, and earlier. All of the iconic sets and stages were in place. Any earlier period could not have included all of these locations. And as "new Hollywood" swept in later in the decade, many of the most interesting and evocative places in the studio would soon be replaced by more-mundane offices and parking lots. I have, however, taken the liberty of moving forward and backward in time to tell the whole story of the property and its bizarre history. A map has been provided. Feel free to refer to it as we cross the lot and explore its many mysteries together.

I've also taken the perhaps infuriating tactic of breaking up the flow of the narrative by providing a list, of sorts, of films shot on the stages and backlots of Paramount within the chapters or sections describing these places. I fully realize that this material would perhaps be more welcome in an appendix, or even as a reference volume of its own. But in order to understand Paramount as a place, I've come to believe that one has to occasionally shake one's head at the sheer magnitude of the product, both familiar and forgotten, that this place has produced.

Sometimes the notes following the titles for a specific stage or set are idiosyncratic, to say the least. These notes reflect my opinion based upon interviews, or a viewing of the films, or upon original production records. If a description is in quotation marks, this means that the wording is lifted directly from these records. Of course, there are multiple interpretations as to what exactly that overworked clerk in that long-ago production office may have been referring to in those records.

So I invite my readers to indulge me by poring over this admittedly somewhat confounding minutiae, this cryptic haiku of the Paramount lot's strange, day-to-day job of impersonating our world.

Let's go inside, then, and find those ghosts.

—Steven Bingen
Hollywood, California, 2016

Acknowledgments

Movies are collaborations. Cinematic art—or cinematic dreck, for that matter—is never created alone by a single impassioned genius. A visit to any movie set will immediately confirm that it takes dozens—hundreds—of geniuses, or at least hundreds of people who *think* they are geniuses, to make a movie.

The above is, in a manner of speaking, the single unifying theme that resides at the very center of this book. Regardless of what some film schools and some film scholars would have us believe, "director" is not the first word that should come up to describe what is required to create a Hollywood movie. Who knows what the future will bring, but for the last hundred-plus years, it has taken a studio to make a studio picture.

My point? Well, it would be a fine thing, I think, if there was a Hollywood-style assembly line in place to help write a book.

There is not.

I suppose it's possible to author a book single-handedly. Perhaps a novelist or a poet might be able to create and color and contrast within a vacuum. Sadly, I'm not that person. In fact, I am indebted to all kinds of people for all kinds of reasons. The following is a list of those who I relied upon the most (or have stolen from the most). Thank you, one and all.

First and foremost, I have to admit that my collaborator and partner, Marc Wanamaker, is the only one who knows all the answers to all of the questions about Hollywood. Any errors in the text are mine; Marc's only error was in not catching them for me.

The staff and volunteers at Hollywood Heritage, Richard Adkins, in particular, were all so very helpful in throwing the doors open to their archives and the Lasky-DeMille barn, where our story, Hollywood's story, and modern American pop culture was born. Thanks, guys.

I owe the usual debt of gratitude to many of Hollywood's top historians and archivists. First off, I'd like to thank Rob Klein, who contributed both physically and thematically to the final book. Also, Stephen X. Sylvester, my frequent collaborator and coauthor. And Stan Taffel, who has always been there when I needed him, and will hopefully continue to be. The late Robert S. Birchard patiently set me straight, and straightened out my text, on some early Hollywood maneuverings. John Bengston, the great historical detective of filmmaking, certainly pointed me in the right direction. Thanks to Mike Greco, who knows many of Paramount's secrets and was happy to share (Just wait until *his* book comes out!). Ron Barbagallo, Gary DeVaughn, Greg Dyro, John Cox, Stuart Galbraith IV, Richard B. Jewell, Leonard Maltin, Mary Mallory, Ray Morton, Jon Primrose, E. J. Stephens, Troy Taylor, Frank Thompson, Jeffrey Thompson, and Bill Warren all shared stories and research and ideas, which I can now pretend I came up with myself.

My agent Marilyn Allen again made the deal for me. Likewise, Robert Lane again contributed to this book's architectural aspects. If you enjoy the maps of Paramount contained within, join me in thanking Rob for his efforts.

A special thank-you to my friends at the George Lucas Research Library, in particular, Jo Donaldson. And to Debbie Fine for her valiant and successful rescue of the Paramount Research Library, which we, and future generations, can all be grateful for.

I'd also like to mention a few of the employees of Paramount, past and present, or their families, who were willing to go on the record about their experiences. First off, Helen Cohen, thank you for helping me to arrange an interview with Cecilia de Mille Presley, who shared priceless stories about growing up on the lot and about being Cecil B. DeMille's granddaughter; Cece, thanks for talking about C. B. with me. Likewise, thanks to Mark Penn for getting me in touch with Betty Lasky, Jesse Lasky's daughter, and a fine Hollywood historian herself. Barbara Jaffe Kohn, thank you for talking to me about Sam Jaffe.

Other studio veterans who contributed in big ways include Scott Billups, Billy Blackburn, Leonard Dawson, Larry Jensen, Richard Lindheim, Ed Phillips, Randall Thropp, Charles Ziarko, and director Randal Kleiser and his assistant, Mani Perezcarro.

Appreciation is due to Christopher Salvano of the Cal State Northridge Map Library, Julianna Jenkins and Lucinda Newsome of the UCLA Library Special Collections, and to Louise Hilton, and the rest of the staff at the Academy of Motion Picture Arts and Sciences Margaret Herrick Library. Yes, they were just doing their job, but they all do it so well.

Gratitude and love are owed to my parents, and to Beth and Zoe.

CHAPTER I
Outside the Gate

For indeed it was the most outrageous city in the world. Where anything could happen and always did. Ten thousand deaths had happened here, and when the deaths were done, the people got up, laughing, and strolled away. Whole tenement blocks were set afire and did not burn. Sirens shrieked and police cars careened around corners, only to have the officers peel off their blues, cold-cream their orange pancake makeup, and walk home to small bungalow court apartments out in that great and mostly boring world.

—Ray Bradbury, *A Graveyard for Lunatics*

One of the greatest ventures in theatrical history began during a bumpy ride on a New York subway.

Born in 1873, Adolph Zukor was a Hungarian immigrant who had been in America since the age of fifteen. He trained as a furniture upholsterer and furrier, and had found success in those fields. His entrance into motion pictures came when his cousin, Max Goldstein, asked him for a loan to buy into a penny arcade chain which featured flickering moving pictures viewed inside a wooden cabinet. Zukor, by this time already a consummate businessman, insisted on investigating the prospect firsthand. Peering into one of these magic boxes, he was intrigued—but not because of any artistic or professional interest in "the flickers," as they were sometimes called.

The first picture show. On December 29, 1913, Cecil B. DeMille, center, in boots, poses his ragtag company of outsiders and outlaws and real and make-believe cowboys and Indians in front of the little barn where American popular culture was about to be born.

In fact, he had seen his first film, *The Kiss*, in 1893, and hadn't been impressed. "I enjoyed the picture as a novelty," he remembered in 1958. "But it cannot be reported that a flash of lightning opened the heavens and revealed the future."[1]

What Zukor could appreciate, as a businessman, was the concept that the customer was paying for a product he would not be allowed to take home. Patrons were buying an item which the next audience would pay for as well. Remarkable. Max got his loan, and Zukor found himself another business venture.

Originally, Zukor was only a film exhibitor. They distributed work others had made. He and his partners opened arcades and, later, vaudeville houses, up and down the East Coast, which featured live performers alternating with his ghostly flickers. Edwin S. Porter's *The Great Train Robbery* (1903) was the outstanding success of this era. Zukor once estimated that he saw it a thousand times in his years in the exhibition business. But by 1912 he also realized that the lowbrow appeal of the medium was limiting the size of its audience. Most patrons were, at this time, poor factory workers, laborers, children, and immigrants who didn't speak English. He made a bold decision: Adolph Zukor,

Photo by J.A.Ramsey
Dingman Studio
L.A.

himself an immigrant a mere twenty years earlier, was going to be the man to bring "culture" to the flickers.

Sarah Bernhardt was the most popular actress of her era, even though in 1912, "the Divine Sarah" was sixty-eight years old and had only one leg. Nonetheless, Zukor was certain the prestige of her famous name would be enough to get middle- and upper-class audiences into theaters, or perhaps even opera houses, where films had not played before. Zukor had tried this tactic the year before with a filmed passion play, with some success. He was certain that the Bernhardt name would make for the first "event" picture ever seen in America. The film he envisioned was to be called *Les Amours de la Reine Élisabeth*, or *The Loves of Queen Elizabeth*.

As it happened, Bernhardt was already filming a picture with that very title, or something like it, in France. But the expensive production had been beset with financial difficulties. The company making it eventually was forced to declare bankruptcy. So Zukor's offer of financial aid—reportedly between $18,000 and $20,000, in exchange for the American distribution rights—was eagerly accepted. Adolph Zukor, film exhibitor, would now become Adolph Zukor, film producer.

A new title, and a new company, would require a new name. In June of 1912 on that jostling subway, he envisioned yet more roles for famous players like Bernhardt, in famous plays like his recently acquired *Queen Elizabeth*; famous players in famous plays. So the Famous Players Film Company was born, made official on June 7, 1912. The incorporation documents list the company as possessing a capital stock of $250.000.

Queen Elizabeth would be every bit the success Zukor had imagined. It premiered not in a vaudeville house but on Broadway, at the Lyceum, and at nearly an hour long, was one of the silver screen's first successful epics. The film would also be one of the first films ever made to have its own original score, performed in the theater by a live orchestra.

The fledgling company made their first films entirely on their own; *The Count of Monte Cristo* (1913) and *The Prisoner of Zenda* (also 1913) lived up to *Queen Elizabeth*'s lofty example. The budget for each, according to Zukor, was between $40,000 and $50,000, which he claimed was three or four times the budget of any picture made in America up to that time. Eager for a follow-up to his success with Bernhardt, Zukor cast another older, but legendary, actress: Lilly Langtry, remembered today as the unrequited obsession of frontier judge Roy Bean, in *His Neighbor's Wife* (1913). Ironically, Edwin S. Porter, who had started it all with *The Great Train Robbery*, was the director or co-director on all of these projects.

These films were shot in a converted armory at 213–227 West Twenty-Sixth Street in New York. The facility is still standing, and happily, is still a studio. Today it is called Chelsea Studios and currently houses *The Rachael Ray Show* (TV 2006–).

While Zukor was dreaming of prestige for his chosen industry, his future partner, Jesse L. Lasky, was dreaming of it for himself. Lasky was not initially a businessman at all, but rather a performer. His later reputation would suggest that he had been an unsuccessful vaudevillian. But his daughter Betty, as well as playbills and press clippings from the time, insist convincingly that Lasky was, at least in the show business circles he moved within, part of the big time. In fact, the later success of *The Squaw Man* (1914) could well have been due, in part, to Lasky's connections on the vaudeville and theatrical circuits, which ensured that the film would be booked and promoted properly.

All we know for certain is that Lasky had toured in vaudeville with his sister, and had played the cornet professionally as part of something called the Royal Hawaiian Band. His affection for the instrument is reflected in the title of his 1957 memoir, *I Blow My Own Horn*. Among the men who built Hollywood, he was the only one native to California.

Born in 1880 in San Francisco, Lasky apparently first became interested in movies around 1910, through his sister Blanche's marriage to one Sam Goldfish (an Americanization of the original Polish "Szmuel Gelbfisz"). About the same time Lasky and Goldfish met one Cecil B. DeMille.

Born in 1881, DeMille was, at the time, the less successful brother of playwright William deMille (sic). But, like Lasky, he was eager and ambitious, and those ambitions involved vague dreams of fame on, or at least near, the stage. It was DeMille who convinced Lasky in 1913 to form a partnership with him and Goldfish, and Goldfish's pal, lawyer Arthur Friend, to make films. (They also approached "established" director D. W. Griffith, who unceremoniously turned the young upstarts down.) And so the Jesse L. Lasky Feature Play Company was born. Lasky was to be president; Goldfish, the general manager; and DeMille, the director general (whatever that meant).

Oscar Apfel was to be the actual director of their first film, an adaptation of a 1905 Western play called *The Squaw Man*, starring Dustin Farnum. Farnum, whose first name was later chosen by the parents of actor Dustin Hoffman, for their son, had previously starred in a 1911 revival of the same play, which (perhaps ominously) had not been a success. Their leading man, despite his rocky track record, was offered a quarter share in what would become Paramount Pictures, which the actor turned down in exchange for a flat $250 a week.

J. L. Lasky Feature Play Company was incorporated under the laws of New York on November 26, 1913, with a capital listing of $50,000.

At the time, most movies were still being made in New York. Location scenes were usually shot in the nearby wilderness of Fort Lee, New Jersey. Even Westerns like the venerated *Great Train Robbery* had been shot in nearby Milltown, New Jersey—which makes the Lasky Feature Play Company's decision even more surprising.

Before joining the quixotic venture with his friends, DeMille had been mumbling about going down to Mexico to witness the revolution there. Perhaps it was the adventure-struck DeMille who then convinced his partners to shoot their Western in the actual American West. Movies had been made in the wilderness before, but this was the first time a New York company had shot on such a distant location for the sake of the story's authenticity.

Another factor lurking behind this bold, and expensive, decision allegedly involved Thomas Edison's Motion Picture Patents Company, which, because of its patents on the equipment and film stock used to produce films during this era, could make it difficult, and expensive, for those outside of Edison's syndicate, or "trust," to operate—at least on the East Coast. This would not have been an issue in the Wild West, however. This "patents factor" was probably not as important as later accounts have indicated. In fact, the power of the trust, already weakened in 1913, would soon evaporate entirely, thanks to court decisions, enforcement issues, and expirations of the patents themselves, which had given Edison his power over the industry to begin with.

Where in the West would this epic be realized? Edwin Milton Royle, who had written the play, had set the action in Utah, and in fact early publicity implied that this was where the film would be realized. DeMille however, in his autobiography, mused that: "Well, we thought, Arizona might be good. It was a western. Some motion picture companies had been going to California, we knew; but California was still farther west than Arizona, and railroad companies had the unpleasant habit of charging by the mile. Arizona it was.[2]

In December 1913, DeMille and his crew of five boarded the train for Arizona. The director general had stowed a pistol in his luggage as insurance against a wild Indian or a trust enforcer attack on the other side.

Legend has it that it was raining; sometimes the story even holds that it was snowing in Flagstaff, Arizona, when DeMille's train puffed into the station. These legends also assert that, as DeMille had no desire to get his feet wet, he and his crew decided to stay on the train. But according to C. B. himself in his autobiography, Arizona was actually dry at this time, but they found it unsuitable because Flagstaff is forested and green—certainly not the West that

Easterners like DeMille had expected to see through their train window and camera viewfinders.

DeMille, remembering that California had been used as a location before, with pleasant results, decided to risk the company's ever-dwindling funds and stay on the train to the end of the line. Eventually DeMille wired his anxious partners the following cable: "Flagstaff no good for our purposes. Have proceeded to California. Want authority to rent a barn in a place called Hollywood for $75 a month. Regards to Sam. Cecil." Out of such trivia, empires are born.

Or perhaps not. Perhaps the entire Flagstaff story is a fallacy in itself. A look at the tickets, which astonishingly, still exist, DeMille and his company purchased for the trip, at a cost of $307.45 for the five-person party, show Los Angeles as being the destination all along. Years later, actor Henry Wilcoxon, later a close friend and associate of the director, remembered that upon meeting DeMille in 1934, he was quizzed by the director, who asked "What do you know of me?"

"I know we might be sitting in Arizona except it was raining in 1913," Wilcoxon said. To which DeMille 'fessed up that the story, at least that part of it, was "just publicity."[3]

A biography of Zukor, *The House That Shadows Built*, published just fifteen years after this event, reasonably surmises that Los Angeles had been their destination, but that Flagstaff was a place whose name and location they liked the sound of, and that they did take a glance at it through the train window on the way out. No one was impressed. Zukor, of course, was not there, so could only have been told about this after the fact.

So, Hollywood it was.

Later, in December of 1913, when Lasky finally went out to Los Angeles to monitor what was going on, he asked his cabdriver at the rail station to take him to Hollywood. The cabbie had no idea where Hollywood was, let alone the barn DeMille referred to in his fateful (perhaps apocryphal) telegram.

The community, six miles north of Los Angeles, had been founded by Daeida Wilcox and her husband Harvey, who in 1887 filed a deed and parcel map with

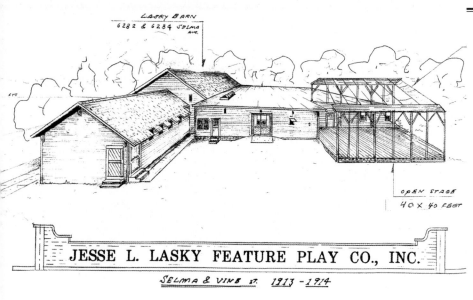

LASKY BARN
6282 & 6284 SELMA AVE.

OPEN STAGE
40 X 40 FEET

JESSE L. LASKY FEATURE PLAY CO., INC.

SELMA & VINE ST. 1913 - 1914

A promotional sketch of the Lasky-DeMille barn as it looked in 1914.

the Los Angeles County Recorder's office which had used that name to describe the community. Hollywood become a municipality in 1906 but had been annexed into Los Angeles in 1910 in order to take advantage of that city's water supply and sewage system.

The origin of the word "Hollywood" has been long-disputed. H.J. Whitley, a real estate developer known as the "Father of Hollywood," very possibly also gave the community its name, although the word is also said to have originated from a phrase Mrs. Wilcox had heard on the train coming west, which supposedly referred to a community in Illinois. American holly does not occur naturally in either California or in Illinois. And although it can grow to an impressive size, it is often classified as a plant and not a tree, so holly is not actually a wood at all. Hollywood as a place of myth, or lies, seems to have existed even before the movies got there.

The barn which DeMille referred to was actually as close to a studio as Hollywood could then offer. Built near the end of the nineteenth century on the current corner of Selma and Vine, the structure was not being used as a barn at all at the time DeMille showed up. A Sanborn fire insurance map of the building, dated January 1913, shows the structure listed as a "Carriage & Auto Ho" but it was in fact being subleased by two small-time producers, L. L. Burns and Harry Revier, for area productions and as a film laboratory. DeMille, like these earlier producers, used the building as a location, office, and base of operations.

What made *The Squaw Man* different from these earlier productions is that, at seventy-four minutes (or seventy-eight minutes, depending on which print you clock), it was the first feature film ever made in Hollywood. The picture allegedly, and legendarily, cost only $15,000 to make, which would have been a

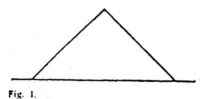

bargain even in 1913. But that figure, accepted as fact by generations of Hollywood sleuths, makes no sense; the rights to the original play cost that much. The actual negative cost was probably closer to $47,000.

No matter, *The Squaw Man* was, to everyone's surprise, an outstanding success, opening on February 7, 1914, in New York, and ultimately grossing an estimated $250,000.

It was back in New York, and at about the same time (well, May of that year, actually), that one William Wadsworth (W. W.) Hodkinson founded the Paramount Distributing Corporation. Hodkinson was the first film distributor to operate on a national rather than a territorial or statewide basis. The name "Paramount" allegedly came from an office building in New York, which Hodkinson observed on the way to a meeting with a group of film producers, including both Lasky and Zukor (even though no building in New York is known to have used that name during this period). Intriguingly, and perhaps significantly, there *was* a Paramount Apartment Building on West Ninety-Ninth Street in 1914, but whether or not this was the structure Hodkinson remembered seeing is debatable—especially since that mysterious building has also long since been demolished.

Equally mysterious is the origin and inspiration for the Paramount logo, one of the most recognized corporate emblems in history. Hodkinson sketched a mountain on a pad of paper during the aforementioned meeting and showed it to his business partners. This oft-repeated story begs the obvious question of whether or not this mountain—sometimes called, without explanation, "Mount Majestic"—ever actually existed, apart from Hodkinson's imagination and notepad.

ABOVE: A 1914 Moving Picture World announcement regarding the formation of "Gigantic Paramount Pictures." RIGHT: W.W. Hodkinson's "mountain" sketch, 1914.

So what exactly was the inspiration for this history-changing doodle? Was Hodkinson inspired by an actual mountain? Was it a real place? Did he get the idea for a mountain from a sign on that mysterious Paramount Building?

No one knows, but there are several interesting theories. Hodkinson was from Utah. Ben Lomond Mountain, outside Ogden, has been credited as his inspiration, although the resemblance to our Mount Majestic is vague, to say the least. Hodkinson had also lived in Colorado—Rocky Mountain country. And yes, the Paramount logo does bear a certain resemblance to certain spires in that region's Wasatch range, specifically to the famous Pikes Peak. DeMille seems to have favored this particular theory. (Although he was not there, and he never let that detail get in the way of dramatizing historical events.)

Oregon's Mount Hood and other precipices in California's Sierra Nevada, as well as far-flung Peru, Switzerland, and Scotland, have also been suggested as the inspiration. Sugarloaf Mountain, visible from the Paramount Ranch property in the Santa Monica Mountains, bears a certain resemblance to the on-screen logo, and since Paramount produced hundreds of films in the shadow of that spire, it would make sense that this was the source of the insignia. But as historian Marc Wanamaker has pointed out, the emblem was designed nearly a decade before the studio started filming in the region. It is believed that the original on-screen logo was designed by a studio matte artist, Jan Domela, although the only thing we know for certain is that Domela designed the first *color* version, for *The Trail of the Lonesome Pine* (1936).

Sometimes a mountain is just a mountain.

The three-quarter circle of stars encircling that mountain are slightly less mysterious. All of the parties that were there agree that the twenty-four stars represented the number of stars Paramount and its subsidiaries had under contact in 1914, although the names of those hallowed two dozen have been forgotten, rewritten, and disputed in the decades since. The number of stars has also fluctuated since then, depending on which graphic designer was tinkering with the logo during which decade. The number of five-point stars depicted in the

The 1916 merger. Jesse Lasky looks worried, Adolph Zukor calm. Samuel Goldfish, Cecil B. DeMille, and Zukor's brother-in-law, Al Kaufman, are there to bear witness to it all.

current logo stands at twenty-two, although Paramount does not have a single star under exclusive contact anymore.

Lasky and Zukor—still operating independently of one another, but certainly sizing one another up from across assorted boardroom tables—enlisted Paramount to distribute their product and became members of the board of directors for the new company. It was while operating in this capacity that the two decided to team up. This happened officially in June of 1916 with the creation of the Famous Players–Lasky Corporation. Zukor would be the president, Lasky, second in command, Goldfish, chairman of the board, and DeMille, head of production. Whatever happened to Arthur Friend is a subject for another volume.

Their immediate success bound the trio together, at least temporarily. Although Zukor looked at his partners and had other ideas. To Zukor's calculating mind, the "Feature Plays triumvirate ranged from the likeable (Lasky), and endurable (Cecil B. DeMille), to intolerable (Sam Goldfish)," writer Bernard F. Dick once reflected.[4]

Hollywood boom town. The backlot on the Selma-Vine lot was actually across the road on Argyle Street, 1922.

So Zukor would wait and see. But not for long.

In 1914 Zukor had purchased 10 percent of Paramount, but he and Lasky quickly realized that the distributor was doing a minority of the work and taking a majority of the profits, so the two of them quickly bought out the rest of the Paramount's stock to become their own distributor. Hodkinson would go on to found another powerful distribution syndicate, the W.W. Hodkinson Company. Leaving the motion picture industry in 1929, in later life he would became an aviation executive. Hodkinson, the man behind the mountain, died in 1971.

This new entity was, as noted by historian A. J. Stephens, "immediately the biggest in Hollywood."[5] Hollywood, of course, was still a provincial city, and movie production was still, in 1916, a provincial business. And those two words—*Hollywood* and *movies*—were yet to merge and entwine into a single definition. Yet it immediately became obvious to anyone involved in either the physical place, or the business around which that place was becoming associated, that a new era was beginning, and that a new, prototypical monarchy was emerging. Nothing would ever be the same again. By 1919 there were more than a hundred studios operating in the Hollywood area. Astonishing, considering that *The Squaw Man* had been made only six years before. Likewise, the population of the district itself had leapfrogged from 12,000 to 35,000.

Samuel Goldfish resigned his chairmanship of the board in 1916. His dervish-like personality reportedly rankled the nerves of the other partners, and not insignificantly rankled the valuable nerves of Mary Pickford, the new company's biggest star. Unlike Arthur Friend, however, Goldfish would enjoy a second, and even a third, act in the story of Hollywood. In 1916, he partnered with Edgar Selwyn and Selwyn's brother, and the three of them combined their two names, Selwyn and Goldfish, to create Goldwyn Pictures. In 1924, Goldwyn was acquired by Metro Pictures and Louis B. Mayer Productions. The resultant company, Metro-Goldwyn-Mayer, would quickly become the largest studio in the world. Although Goldfish had no part, no say, and no association with that company, he did manage to have his name included on the new company's letterhead and logo, and as part of its legacy.

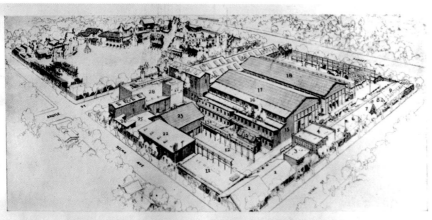

Here we have the Lasky Studio in Hollywood, California, where
the Western productions of Paramount and Arteraft are made

1. Property room.
2. Outgoing property room.
3. Star dressing room building.
4. Wardrobe building.
5. Engaging department.
6. Executive offices.
7. Cecil B. deMille's office.
8. Directors' offices.
9. Scenario department
10. Mary Pickford's dressing room.
11. Incoming property room.
12. Stage No. 1.
13. Wilfred Buckland's office over
     dressing room used by Geraldine
     Farrar.
13a. Title department, and printing
     plant, and electrical department.

13b. Projection room No. 2.
14. Extra dressing room.
15. Scene docks.
16. Principal dressing rooms
17. Stage No. 2.
18. Stage No. 3.
18a. Company dressing rooms, entire
     length of stage.
19. Stage No. 4.
20. Scene docks, entire length of
     Stage No. 4.
21. Sail boat in tank.
22. Dark stage.
23. Small glass stage.
24. Extra dressing rooms—and hos-
    pital.
25. Stock room.

26. Purchasing department. Press
    photographer's rooms.
27. Old paint frame now upholstering
    and wall papering department.
28. Laboratory. Frame building under
    number now removed and ad
    dition to laboratory erected.
29. Paint frame
30. Fitting room.
31. Carpenter shops.
32. Planing mills.
33. Property construction department
34. Plaster shops and blacksmith shop.
35. Garages.
36. Douglas Fairbanks' offices and
    dressing rooms.
37. Exterior sets built for productions

ABOVE: The Selma-Vine studio as it was. Or as its owners wished it was, in 1918. The
Lasky-DeMille barn, then being used for prop storage is at the bottom of the page.
RIGHT: A Selma-Vine studio fire Department map, undated but probably from the early
1920s.

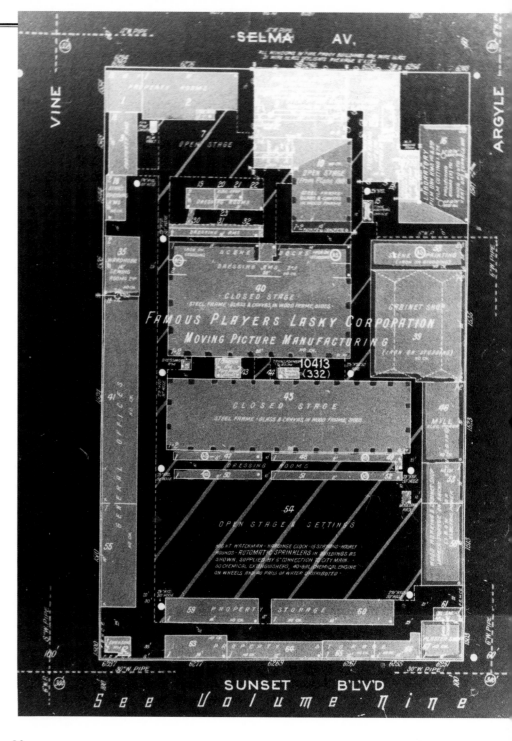

That name, by this time, was not Goldfish at all, but rather the much classier-sounding "Goldwyn," which he had decided to take for himself, legally changing his name in 1918. In 1923 he formed a company under that moniker. After that, and against all conventional wisdom, Goldwyn produced scores of prestigious pictures under that inspiring, majestic-sounding name and through his own independent production company.

Very few people have ever founded a Hollywood studio. Sam Goldwyn/Goldfish/Gelbfisz was responsible for, or associated with, the founding of three.

During this era the Famous Players–Lasky Corporation—this unseemly name would undergo several variations and alterations in these early years*— continued to operate out of a second New York studio, built in 1920 in Astoria, for most of Zukor's films, and at *The Squaw Man*'s barn site in California. DeMille bought out Burns and Revier and negotiated a permanent lease, and then an outright sale with owner Jacob Stern for the property. The studio eventually covered two city blocks around the original Selma and Vine location.

In 1918, the company leased the Oak Crest Ranch in Burbank. Originally part of the old Providencia Ranch abutting the Hollywood Hills, the property already had a cinematic résumé of sorts, having previously served as the backlot for the Nestor Film Company. Nestor, established in 1907, had been sold in 1912 to the Universal Film Manufacturing Company (now Universal Studios), which was created out of the merger of several small studios. Universal quickly outgrew this seemingly spacious movie lot, and in 1915 moved to its new (and current) Universal City location a few blocks away, on Lankershim Boulevard.

*DeMille bemusedly kept track of the name changes: "From 1927 to 1930 it was called Paramount Famous Lasky. Then it became Paramount Publix, recognizing the importance of the Publix theaters which it had acquired. In 1932 it was to become Paramount Productions, Inc. I might as well bring the list of changes up-to-date: In 1936 it became Paramount Pictures, Inc., and in 1950 returned to the name it began with in 1914, Paramount Pictures Corporation. Joining in the reader's sigh of relief, I can simply call it Paramount from now on" (Cecil B. DeMille, *The Autobiography of Cecil B. DeMille*, New Jersey: Prentice Hall, 1959).

RIGHT: DeMille in his office. Note the stuffed rattlesnake on the table in the foreground. 1918. FAR RIGHT: The Lasky Ranch as it looked in 1923. Forest Lawn Cemetery now occupies the site.

The battle scenes for D. W. Griffith's monumental Civil War drama, *The Birth of a Nation*, had been shot on this property in late 1914.

When Paramount acquired the lot, which they renamed the Lasky Ranch, they announced that their first film to shoot on the site would be a remake of *The Squaw Man*, again directed by Cecil B. DeMille (C. B. would return to the subject a third time in 1931). In fact, they had already rented the property on numerous occasions. Some scenes for the first *Squaw Man* had been lensed on the site. The studio would stop using the real estate in 1927. By then known as the Providencia Ranch, the property would, however, continue to be used by the industry as a location until 1952 when it would become Forest Lawn Memorial Park, Hollywood Hills, which today overlooks both Warner Bros. and Disney Studios.

Following Goldwyn's example, DeMille himself would leave the company in 1925 to become an independent producer/director. The rift with the company

LEFT: By 1920 the Selma-Vine lot was a busy factory. But in less than a decade it would all be gone. RIGHT: Map of the Brunton Studios in 1919. The property at the time still fronted Melrose Avenue, which would not happen again for decades.

he had helped to create had come about after a disagreement with Zukor over the budget on DeMille's gargantuan *The Ten Commandments* (1923). C. B. eventually entered into an unhappy marriage with MGM, but the old autocrat would return to the studio he helped found in 1932, after which his power, prestige, and box-office sense would never be questioned again.

In 1925 Paramount acquired producer B.P. Schulberg's Preferred Pictures. With this newest acquisition Paramount acquired both the talented Schulberg and a young production manager who wanted to be a producer, Sam Jaffe. Seventy years later, a still-sharp Jaffe, who did indeed become a producer, and later an agent, remembered how the current studio came to be in April 1926: "I spent all of my waking moments at the studio, and I soon saw how its limitations were draining us. Since we had no storage space, we had to rent props for each new production and dismantle the sets after each film was finished. Our roofless stage wasted us more time than the savings in electric lights was worth.[6] "So I told Schulberg, 'This studio is costing us too much; we rent everything over and over. So he arranged for me to go to New York and meet with our chairman, Adolph Zukor. I was only 28, and I was really frightened when I entered the boardroom. But Mr. Zukor gave me the go-ahead to buy this studio located in the heart of Hollywood, directly across from an old graveyard. So we moved to Paramount's present location."[7]

The property originally included most of the land between Marathon and Melrose, which Zukor quickly sold off. The studio would later have to buy this real estate back in the 1980s and '90s, at great expense. This lot, which reportedly cost Zukor $1 million, was built in 1917–1918 as the Paralta Studio, out of an eighteen-acre section of Hollywood Memorial Cemetery. Now known (as of 1998) as Hollywood Forever Cemetery, which had been founded in 1899. Apparently when the land to be used for the studio was sold, it had not yet been used for any interments.

The original construction included five glass stages (meaning, they had glass walls, to accommodate sunlight), as was the style of the time, and a dozen crafts and administration structures. The original lot ran above Melrose Avenue close

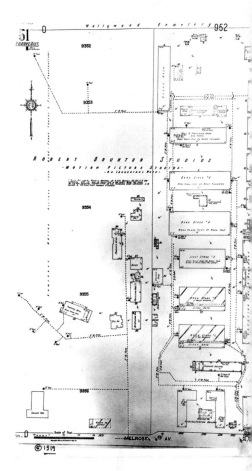

to the center of the current studio. Open land for backlot construction stood on either side. "The small portions of the grounds not occupied by buildings are being laid out in formal gardens of the French and Italian type,"[8] a contemporary article crowed, although these gardens, not surprisingly, have yet to be realized.

Paralta Studios, sometimes called "Paralta Plays," was founded in March 1917. The original idea was to use the plant as the production arm for a syndicate of former exhibitors. But company product, what there was of it, ended up being distributed, ironically, by W. W. Hodkinson, who had started his own, ultimately short-lived corporation for that purpose.

Originally, while the new lot was being purchased and constructed, some of the Paralta product was shot on leased property across the street, at the Clune Studio. That lot, built in 1914–1915, was named after one William H. Clune, who died in 1927 (but is still nearby at, what is now the Hollywood Forever Cemetery). Zukor's Fiction Players Studios, purchased in 1915, pre-Lasky and pre-Paramount, was an establishing tenant at Clune. Famed theatrical producer Charles Frohman, who had two hanger-on brothers, produced a Mary Pickford vehicle, *A Girl of Yesterday* (1915) there for Zukor (although one of those brothers, Daniel, took the credit). An article in the *Motion Picture News*, dated May 15, 1915, intriguingly indicated that the Zukor company was already in the process of buying the lot. Frohman, however, had perished a week before that article on the *Lusitania*. Frohman's death, it was speculated at the time, could have led to a destabilization of the company, so Zukor ultimately retreated back to New York until things could be sorted out. Had the ship not gone down, America might have had a different World War I experience, and Paramount might have had a different home. In 1979 the old Clune lot became Raleigh Studios, which it remains today.

The executive director at Paralta, one of the only actual filmmakers associated with that organization, was the smart and ambitious Robert Brunton. The board of

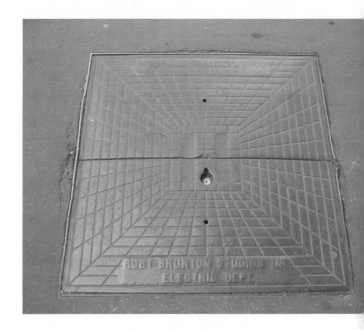

FAR LEFT: The Future Paramount studios as it looked in 1919. **ABOVE:** Ghosts of the distant past. A manhole cover still labeled "Rbt. Brunton Studios" still exists on the lot today.

LEFT: The new Paramount studio as it looked in 1927, shortly after the purchase. ABOVE: Paramount proudly crows about their "100% Production Plant" in a 1927 trade publication. (Photo courtesy Hollywood Heritage)

directors in New York apparently didn't know just how smart and ambitious Brunton was. In 1918 he took over the company, dissolved Paralta, and renamed the lot the Brunton Studios, which he ran as a rental facility. To this day, a manhole cover on the Paramount lot bears the ghostly ROBT. BRUNTON STUDIOS moniker.

In 1919 Brunton had five stages. Two of them were open, to take advantage of the plentiful California sunshine. One was a "light" stage, which means that it had a roof, but glass walls, and two were enclosed, or "dark," stages. The administration building, actually two L-shaped structures which bear little similarity to anything on the lot today, was practically on Melrose Avenue. The original property building was also south of Marathon Street.

Michael Charles (M. C.) Levee, who had managed the studio for Brunton just as Brunton had for Paralta, bought out his boss's interest in the studio in 1921 and renamed it United Studios. In 1922 Joseph M. Schenck bought the company. Levee left after the buyout, but would return in 1932 as executive manager at Paramount. The new company, and the new studio, was once again operated as a rental facility for independent producers, and for majors needing additional production space. First National, which was later absorbed into Warner Bros., was a major tenant during this era.

Of those majors, none was larger during this period than Paramount, or Paramount–Famous Lasky Corporation. Nothing in the history of popular entertainment compares to the influence this single entity wielded from the end of World War I to 1929. Paramount at the time had the most stars (including Rudolph Valentino and Gloria Swanson), the most theaters (over 1,000), the most pictures (as many as 156 a year), the greatest production values in those pictures, and the largest audiences for those pictures in the world. And with the acquisition of United Studios by Sam Jaffe in March of 1926, they were about to build the greatest and most storied factory-city for the production of motion pictures anyone had ever seen.

[1] Adolph Zukor, with Dale Kramer. *The Public Is Never Wrong: The Autobiography of Adolph Zukor.* New York: G. P. Putnam's Sons, 1953.
[2] Cecil B. DeMille. *The Autobiography of Cecil B. DeMille.* New Jersey: Prentice Hall, 1959.
[3] Cecilia DeMille Presley and Mark A. Vieira. *Cecil B. DeMille: The Art of the Hollywood Epic.* Philadelphia: Running Press, 2014.
[4] Bernard F. Dick. *Engulfed: The Death of Paramount Pictures and the Birth of Corporate Hollywood.* Lexington: University Press of Kentucky, 2001.
[5] E. J. Stephens, Michael Christaldi, and Marc Wanamaker. *Images of America: Early Paramount Studios.* Charleston, SC: Arcadia Publishing, 2013.
[6] Sam Jaffe, as told to Sam Locke. "The Night Paramount Burned," *Los Angeles Magazine* (October 1990).
[7] Donna Mungon. "Sam Jaffe: Looking Back at Hollywood by One Present at the Creation," *Los Angeles Times*, March 19, 1995.
[8] "New Paralta Studios Near Completion," *Motography*, April 20, 1918.

CHAPTER 2
Inside the Gate

Hollywood is an extraordinary kind of temporary place.
—John Schlesinger

On October 30, 1929, a *Variety* headline famously proclaimed that "Wall Street Lays an Egg." And officially, the good times were over.

The mighty Paramount was clobbered particularly hard. No one had seen the downswing in the economy coming, and once it arrived, no one would have predicted that it would last for as long as it did. Suddenly Paramount owned too many theaters, for which there were suddenly too few patrons, and the studio was making too many films to feed into those now-empty theaters. In fact, of all the majors, Paramount was the most vertically integrated, with a circuit more than 1,000 screens strong across the United States. By contrast, Warner Bros. and Fox controlled only 500 theaters each, RKO, 175, and MGM, 150.

The obvious fall guy for all of this overbuying was Lasky, who would be removed from the company he had cofounded in 1932. He went to Fox, and later partnered with Mary Pickford as an independent producer, and eventually made successful movies for other studios, most notably *Sergeant York* (1941) for Warner Bros. He died in 1958, and is buried behind the Paramount backlot at what is now the Hollywood Forever Cemetery.

Lasky's blood was not enough to save the company. In 1933, the Paramount-Publix company, as it was called at the time, toppled into receivership. A bank

Paramount's global influence was such that in 1919 the company could boast of having a film exchange office even in Hong Kong, China. In 1929, however, it would all come crashing down.

committee, led by Otto Kahn, who had been the inspiration for the "mayor" figure in the Monopoly board game, came onto the lot to try to save the company. Zukor must have been sure that he would be the next to be ousted, but Kahn and his fellow bankers instead kept him in his office, and under their thumbs, even after a second bankruptcy procedure in 1935.

The following year, Barney Balaban, who had joined the company through the purchase of his theater chain, Balaban and Katz, would become president of the newly reorganized company, finally named Paramount Pictures, Inc. Zukor was diplomatically moved to a chairman of the board position; later, his title became honorary chairman, and finally, it was modified to the even more remote yet impressive-sounding "chairman emeritus," a title he would hold for the rest of his extraordinarily long life.

The other volley in the one-two-punch combination that sent the studio reeling was the sound revolution. Talking pictures had been in the works since at least the time of Edison, but a practical way of projecting properly amplified and synchronized sound into an auditorium had eluded engineers until Warner Bros., using something called the Vitaphone system, had scored a riotous hit with *The Jazz Singer* (1927). In 1928 Paramount laid out plans to build four "sound" stages inside a single building, featuring an exterior sound-recording facility interconnected through the walls, as was the custom at the time.

Early movies had been shot in roofless glass buildings so as to take advantage of natural light. But with Hollywood's new assembly-line process, producers eventually agreed that the savings realized in utilizing sunshine (rather than electricity), even in California, was offset by that sunshine's inconsistency, making it hard to match shots taken in the morning with those filmed in the afternoon. So large windowless stages were constructed and electric lights replaced the natural light which had brought many cinema pioneers out west to begin with. Because originally there was no sound being recorded, multiple sets and movies could be shot on the same stage, at the same time. This system would no longer work with talkies, however. Sound and picture could only be

The Paramount Camera Department was as affected by the sound revolution as any department on the lot. This 1930 publicity photo shows the various sound buffers, booths, and blimps used to keep the whir of their noisy machines off the soundtrack. Actor Neil Hamilton, who decades later would portray Alfred the butler on the *Batman* TV series, pretends to record them all with a handheld camera, 1930.

recorded on one stage at a time, and those stages would have to be soundproofed, as noise from the outside would otherwise find its way onto the soundtrack of the picture being made inside.

The Paramount sound complex was to be built on the northwestern side of the lot as Stages 11 through 14. (Stage 13, usually considered unlucky, was included this time.) Unfortunately—or perhaps, unluckily?—all four of the new soundproofed stages burned on January 16, 1929, the same day they were completed. Stage 14 was completely destroyed; the other three were so badly damaged that it would take weeks to make them usable again. Zukor told Sam Jaffe, "Paramount will be out of business in six months."

That night Jaffe took a worried walk across the backlot and into the cemetery. "I took note of the remarkable peace and quiet among the graves," he recalled. "Out of nowhere like a noiseless bombshell came the thought: No soundstage could be quieter than this! If we filmed at night we wouldn't need soundstages. We could use our old stages and put twelve talking pictures into production right away. Plus we would have an advantage over the other studios, whose production of sound pictures would have to be limited to the number of soundstages they could build. By the time I was back in bed, I'd worked it all out. We would film on our old stages from nine at night until dawn. During the day construction of the soundstages could proceed at full speed. I fell asleep feeling like I had crawled out from under a giant iron wheel."[1]

Jaffe's technicians discovered that the old silent stages were indeed acceptable for recording sound after hours, although the high ceilings in those stages tended to cause the dialogue to echo, a problem eventually solved by hanging blankets above and around the sets. While the technical details were being worked out, Paramount added sound effects to completed silent films like *Warming Up* (1928) and *Loves of an Actress* (1928). They even added limited dialogue to *Beggars of Life* (1928) to fulfill obligations to their theaters for "sound" pictures, while they prepared their first actual talkie: *Interference* (1928). Ultimately, even with the delays and bad luck, Paramount was still one of the first studios to be successfully wired for sound. In fact, MGM, which was financially surviving the Depression much better than Paramount was, had to rent one of Jaffe's new stages for their initial talkie, *Alias Jimmy Valentine* (1928).

In 1928 Schulberg hired David O. Selznick, the son of pioneer film producer Lewis J. Selznick, whose career had been destroyed by the ascent of studios like Paramount. Schulberg hired Selznick in spite of his personal belief that the younger man was ambitious and arrogant, and that he believed that he knew everything about the picture business. In fact, Selznick *was* ambitious and *was* arrogant, and he did, in fact, know everything about the motion picture business. Selznick would leave for RKO in 1931, having made little impact on Paramount artistically, or as a studio.

Selznick did, however, contribute to the sound revolution. *Beggars of Life* special-effects man Roy Pomeroy—who suddenly found himself in charge of the newly created Sound Department at Paramount by virtue of the fact that he had once taken a walk-through tour of Western Electric's laboratories—insisted to director William Wellman that Wallace Beery stand motionless so that a stationary microphone could record his dialogue, a bawdy bar song. Wellman, according to his own version of the story, frustrated that he was being forced to keep his camera still in order to record dialogue, fought to put the camera on a pole that would follow Beery as he walked. Selznick had to be called down to the set to settle the argument. His decision was that the microphone would be hung from the pole, resulting in the first words ever recorded for a Paramount film, or on a mic boom anywhere—although, sadly, only the silent version of this scene exists today.

Like everyone else in Hollywood, Ricardo Cortez, then busy shooting *Not So Long Ago,* could not have contemplated how much more difficult releasing films in foreign versions would be after the arrival of sound, 1925.

During this period the Astoria, New York, studio was vital to the company's output, if not to its bottom line. In the 1920s several of the other majors had shut down their East Coast production activities, but at Astoria—perhaps in deference to Zukor, at least at first—a respectable amount of Paramount product, including newsreels and short subjects, continued to be developed and shot. Astoria would not close until 1932.

Paramount, for a brief time, also was in possession of a studio complex in Joinville, France. Again, the impetus behind this ambitious experiment was sound. With the coming of sound a question arose: If movies talk, and they talk in English, then what about other countries where English is not spoken? Suddenly vast markets all over the world would no longer be able to enjoy Paramount product.

In 1929 Paramount was in possession of frozen funds in France, which could not be taken home. The solution was the purchase of the Aubert Studio at Joinville-St. Maurice, which, exactly as was happening in America, had to be completely rebuilt for sound. Robert T. Kane, the former general manager of the Astoria studio, came over to manage the facility, which was intended to be the home base for productions, usually remakes of American pictures, shot in non-English languages. Not just in French, either, but also as many as fourteen other languages, simultaneously.

ABOVE: Paramount's first venture into sustained international production resulted in the Joinville, France, studio facility pictured here. *Avec regret*, it was not a success. 1931. RIGHT: As Paramount expanded across their new, more spacious lot, pedestrians outside the fence at the corner of Melrose Avenue and North Irving Boulevard, must have wondered at the juxtaposition of the prehistoric and the technological. The dinosaur skeleton is from *The Lost World* (First National. 1925), the rest of it, well, who knows? 1927.

Well, it didn't work out that way. Eventually, because of the logistical and linguistic problems inherent in such an awkward, Tower of Babel enterprise, most films ended up being shot only in Spanish, French, and German, or only in French. The Depression and the concept of dubbing (or subtitling) movies further doomed the experiment. Moreover, an average picture made at Joinville could cost $150,000, a not-insubstantial amount to earn back in some territories.

Ultimately, however, it was the star system which doomed the idea of producing local films using the Hollywood factory process. Gary Cooper was a star in *Morocco* (1930), but he was also a star in Morocco. No one, not even in Morocco, wanted to hear a French Cooper stand-in speaking Cooper's words in Moroccan.

That said, Joinville produced over three hundred pictures in the three years of its existence (1930–1933). Many of them are lost. In some cases, even the *titles* have been lost. So Joinville, and Kane's strange experiment, remains a strange, lost, Gallic chapter in "Hollywood's" story.

With the entirety of Paramount's production needs suddenly coming out of one location, the twenty-six-acre property was renovated and enlarged, and not just for sound production. A new administration building, known as the Sumner Redstone Building from 2012 on, was constructed in 1926. Placed reverently under its cornerstone, if a press release is to be believed, was a print of *Queen Elizabeth*, the film that started it all. The famous Paramount Studio gate, at the end of Bronson Avenue, was built in 1926. New stages were built and old ones were retrofitted for sound. A more or less permanent backlot arose near the current center of the studio.

Paramount has always suffered somewhat in that their location, right in the center of Hollywood, became valuable quicker than the outlying suburbs of Culver City and Burbank. With the movie boom of the 1910s and '20s came escalating real estate prices, and so relatively early on in the game, the studios with the most desirable and centralized locations, responsible for the sudden local growth to begin with, found themselves with no place to expand beyond their current locations. Paramount's lot was big enough for this to not be as much of a problem as it was for neighboring studios RKO and Columbia, but they never had the space for the sprawling backlots which could be found at some of the other, outlying studios.

A look at the Paramount product tends to bear this out. Most of the studio's pictures are rather stage-bound. There are few exteriors, and these are often soundstage exteriors, with painted backdrops and process screens substituting for the real thing. Artistically, this somewhat artificial *mise-en-scène* gave the studio's pictures a definite and recognizable "house style." And yet this look was definitely a practical choice rather than an artistic one. To alleviate their lack of suitable exteriors, Paramount purchased a 2,400-acre ranch near Malibu in 1927, although perhaps due to its somewhat distant location, it wasn't used as much as other studios' more-accessible backlots.

On the main lot the architectural style of the studio, if not its product, has always been something of a hodgepodge. The lack of a consistent or stable management team meant that improvements to the studio were made in good years, which would be ignored, minimalized, removed, or cannibalized during quarters when the profits were less bountiful. While one building would be spacious and beautiful, its neighbor might be shabby and ramshackle, or luxurious, but in an entirely different style. Often production would adapt these buildings to suit the needs of whatever was shooting, putting Tudor-style patterns on the exteriors of an office, for example, which would then be left up for decades. "It was not

a pretty lot," recalled television executive Richard Lindheim. "It was functional, just a bunch of buildings. There was hardly any grass outside, just old sheds, parts of sets. And inside was hardly any better. The buildings had been retrofitted so many times. They had hallways going nowhere, floors that dropped away."[2]

In the 1930s, any improvements to the lot, when they came at all, were financed by a new type of star, one created to be heard as well as to be seen. The influx of actors from the stage, as well as from the music business, changed the character of the lot and of the movies made there. During this era the studio made stars, or star directors, of New York imports like the Marx Brothers, Clara Bow, Mae West, and W. C. Fields, along with German imports Marlene Dietrich, Josef von Sternberg, Erich von Stroheim, Hans Dreier, Ernst Lubitsch, and later, Billy Wilder. Also causing changes at the studio were others of uncertain Midwestern or Mid-Atlantic origin, like Cary Grant, Bing Crosby, Gary Cooper, Carole Lombard, Claudette Colbert, and director William Wellman. These were actors who could speak and directors who could direct for a new medium and a new era. Some in this new era were on the way up—and some were on the way out.

Bob Hope arrived in 1938. His comedies and especially his unexpected chemistry with Crosby, beginning with *The Road to Singapore* (1940), proved popular with audiences, if not critics. Preston Sturges started out as a screenwriter, rapidly becoming a popular director who then bolted from the studio after a dispute with producer Buddy DeSylva—all in the course of four breathless years. Wilder, who also began as a screenwriter and became a director, would remain with the studio until 1954. "The creative atmosphere at Paramount was absolutely marvelous," Wilder remembered decades later. "You just walked across the lot and there they were; von Sternberg and Gary Cooper and Dietrich and Leo McCarey and Lubitsch. It was an atmosphere of creativity: We made pictures then."[3]

In 1936 Paramount's board of directors was able to boast of a $3 million profit in its first post-receivership year. In the late 1930s, however, the box office started to drop off again, partially due to the gradual loss of foreign markets as World War II rolled across the globe.

LEFT: Paramount stars Fredric March, Gary Cooper and Marian Hopkins, circa 1932. ABOVE: Bing Crosby and Bob Hope in front of the Production Building in 1936 — although, oddly enough, they would not be paired on-screen until 1940's *Road to Singapore*.

When it finally reached America in 1941, the war itself proved to be a good thing for the company, and for Hollywood in general. War-weary, entertainment-craving audiences led the company into posted profits of $13 million that year, and when the war ended, the profits continued to climb. What's more, Paramount was actually making fewer movies during this era. In 1935, for example, the studio released fifty-eight pictures. In 1936 the number was seventy-one. By contrast, in 1945 they only released twenty-three, and in 1946, only nineteen.

In 1944 Hal B. Wallis moved to the studio as an independent producer. Dean Martin and Jerry Lewis were Wallis discoveries. Elvis Presley became a movie star working for Wallis (although his 1957 movie debut had been in Fox's *Love Me Tender*). Wallis would remain on the lot until 1969.

Star Spangled Rhythm (1942), released in the darkest days of World War II, was, from the standpoint of the studio lot, the high point of its era, the quintessential war-era representation of the studio as itself. The plot involves the son of a studio guard (Eddie Bracken), whom Paramount telephone operator Betty Hutton convinces everyone is actually the head of the studio. Astonishingly, the picture includes virtually no "behind the scenes" look at the studio lot. At the time Hollywood apparently did not mean lights and soundstages at all, but rather the stars that stood on those soundstages and under those lights. The film was almost entirely set (and filmed) on the lot, yet the focus was on the people working there rather than the place itself. The picture even neglected to give us the perfunctory view of the famous Bronson Gate, even though seemingly half the plot concerned itself with getting over or around that very entrance. At the time, it should be noted, Paramount was not a place separate from "Hollywood." Its edifices and landscapes were not yet as recognizable as Hope and Crosby, or even as the featured filmmakers DeMille and Sturges—who, of course, played themselves. It would take the war and its carnage to make places more permanent and immovable than the people who occupied them.

Star Spangled Rhythm was a bit of a landmark in another way. The studio had used its own name in short subjects and promotional films, but this was the first time that the lot played itself in a feature film. In earlier (and many later) cinematic visits to Hollywood, Paramount worked under an alias. For example, in *Make Me a Star* (1932), the studio played "Majestic Studios"; in *Sitting Pretty* (1933), it was "World Attractions"; in *The Preview Murder Mystery* (1936), it was "Acme Pictures;" in *The Perils of Pauline* (1947), it was Artcraft Studios. In *Murder in Hollywood* (1929) and Sturges's *Sullivan's Travels* (1942), the place remained coyly unnamed throughout, although in the latter, Ernst Lubitsch and Cecil B. DeMille, both then in residence behind the Paramount gate, are name-dropped.

Sunset Boulevard (1950) introduced the Bronson gate to audiences who had never been to Hollywood. Here a stand-in for Erich von Stroheim, who could not drive, makes his entrance; William Holden and Gloria Swanson, presumably, are in the back seat, 1949.

All that changed even more dramatically, of course, with Wilder's *Sunset Boulevard* (1950). Here the identification with a specific place goes even further than in *Star Spangled Rhythm*. Former actress Norma Desmond, played by Gloria Swanson, once the studio's biggest star, drives up to that Bronson Gate and demands admittance. "They can't drive on the lot without a pass," a young security guard (John Cortay) complains.

"Miss Desmond can. Come on," replies an older guard, Jonesy (Robert Emmett O'Connor), who remembers another era. He opens the gate.

"Thank you, Jonesy. And teach your friend some manners. Tell him without me he wouldn't have any job, because without me there wouldn't be a Paramount Studios," Norma warns him. She doesn't say Paramount Pictures. She says Paramount *Studios*. The place is what is haunted. The place is Paramount.

Sunset Boulevard showed, for the first time, that life and the march of time could make stardom seem impermanent, even grotesque. Suddenly the studio, again for the first time, was the iconic and inspirational monument. The stars, unlike in *Star Spangled Rhythm*, were now the ones trying to get through the gates of Paramount. The studio itself was now the star.

Only DeMille—who of course plays himself, just as he had as far back as *Hollywood* (1923)—was represented as being immune to the ravages and impermanence of Hollywood. The only familiar trope Wilder fails to indulge in, surprisingly, is that he does not dress the older director in his familiar boots and jodhpurs. (Actually, DeMille does wear the boots, but they are mostly covered up by conservative gray slacks.) Movie stars, Wilder seems to be saying, would come and go, but movies, Paramount, and perhaps Cecil B. DeMille were as permanent as the pyramids.

Kevin Brownlow, in his book *The Parade's Gone By*, mentions that DeMille directed movies "as if chosen by God for that one task." This was not condescension. There has never been another director about whom such a statement could have been issued without the faintest wisp of irony.

Some have remarked that Wilder was somehow mocking DeMille and his earlier style of filmmaking in *Sunset Boulevard*, even suggesting that the older director was somehow not in on the joke.

"Not true," asserts granddaughter Cecilia de Mille Presley. "Billy Wilder and he were *friends*; I still have my grandfather's copy of Wilder's script, with handwritten annotations regarding his dialogue. In fact, DeMille added the phrase 'young fellow' to his lines, in referring to Gloria Swanson—which is what he had always called her in real life. And Wilder encouraged him to do so! Remember that Billy Wilder never allowed anyone to tamper with his dialogue. But he trusted DeMille so much as to let him do that."[4]

Post–*Sunset Boulevard*, Paramount would still continue to use an alias on occasion. For example, Paramount played the "Famous Pictures" lot in *The Buster Keaton Story* (1957); in *The Errand Boy* (1961), it was "Paramutual Pictures." In *The Carpetbaggers* (1964), it was "Bernard B. Norman Studios," and in *Harlow* (1965), it was "Majestic Pictures." In *The Last Tycoon* (1975), it was "World International Films." In *The Godfather* (1972), it was "Woltz International Pictures." And so on. But more and more frequently other movies of the era would use the studio as a location, as a destination unto itself.

Dean Martin, Diana Lynn, John Lund, and Corinne Calvet crash Paramount for this publicity shot, if not for the film, *My Friend Irma Goes West* (1950).

Jerry Lewis, one of the studio's most popular stars, invaded the lot, on-screen, three times, although *My Friend Irma Goes West* (1950) somehow lost the scenes where Paramount plays itself to the cutting-room floor. In *Hollywood or Bust* (1956), Lewis's last film with partner Dean Martin, Dean carries Jerry, playing a "dummy," through the Bronson Gate, leading to a mad chase across the lot. In *The Errand Boy* (1961), Jerry wreaks havoc on the backlot as the title character.

The Errand Boy opens with the camera mounted on a helicopter, tracking across various studios before zooming down into Paramount, identified, as mentioned, as Paramutual Pictures. A spoken prologue assures us that "Yes, this is Hollywood, where for just the price of a ticket they will take you anyplace you want to go. Anyplace, that is, except one. Seldom will they let you inside one of those soundstages down there, where the magic potion is brewed. And we'll show you why . . ."

Lewis, who first worked at the studio in 1949's *My Friend Irma*, remarked that "the lot was warm and affectionate, and it started with the executives who ran it. I would visit others: MGM was as cold as ice. Fox was clinical; Columbia was shoddy; and Universal was a machine. There is a tendency for people to speak of studio lots as having been 'family'; well, don't believe the other guys. Paramount really was."[5]

Actress Arlene Dahl, who worked at Paramount in the 1950s, echoed Lewis's sentiments. "Paramount was a very down-to-earth lot, folksy. I was at MGM for seven years before I came to Paramount, and there, you would have a limousine take you from your dressing room to the set. At Paramount, people used bicycles."[6]

Angela Lansbury agreed. "We used to call MGM the factory. It was all very sterile at MGM. But Paramount, on the other hand, was a much friendlier, warm, family sort of place, and everybody used to run in and out of their dressing rooms. And in the evenings, after shooting, they would all get together in one or the other dressing rooms and have a drink before they went home. They knew one another and they fraternized with each other."[7]

The studio during this era was a city unto itself. Jack Senter, who worked in the art department, recalled that "nothing was outsourced. They were a compete entity, with the camera department, the art department, the effects department—all under the one roof."[8]

The good times started to end in 1948 when Paramount and the other studios were found guilty of antitrust violations regarding their longtime practice

of producing and distributing product into their own theaters. This meant all of those theaters and theater chains Zukor had acquired over the decades suddenly needed to be sold off. Even the beloved Paramount Theater in New York had to go.

Profits plummeted. The rising popularity of television, widespread and ruinous allegations of communist sympathies in the film industry, and the flight to the suburbs by postwar audiences changed the viewing habits of millions who had previously gone to the movies as their main source of recreation.

The figures tell the story. Movie attendance in the United States in 1946 was over 90 million people a week! This is particularly impressive when you consider that the population of the entire country was only 140 million people at the time. By 1950 the number of weekly attendees had dropped to 60 million. By 1960, the number would be just 40 million.

The studios responded by trying to give audiences spectacles they could not get at home. VistaVision was Paramount's answer to Twentieth Century Fox's successful CinemaScope process. Both formats offered audiences films projected in theaters on a wider screen and with stereo sound. Unlike CinemaScope, which squeezed the picture into a more or less conventional 35mm frame using lenses, VistaVision, which debuted in 1954 with *White Christmas*, used the same size film stock but a larger frame, made possible by shooting and projecting that frame horizontally rather than vertically, as other systems did. VistaVision was a success, publicity-wise, but only a few theaters could project images shot using the format, so most VistaVision pictures were ultimately printed on standard, vertically projected film stock. The system was abandoned in 1961, after *One-Eyed Jacks*.

A bigger image also meant bigger movies. DeMille, whose name had long been synonymous with large-scale epics, ended his career with three of his biggest, *Samson and Delilah* (1949), *The Greatest Show on Earth* (1952), and a VistaVision remake of *The Ten Commandments* (1956).

ABOVE: The beautiful, and long lost, Paramount Theater in New York, 1929.
RIGHT: Victor Mature and a lion in Samson and Delilah (1949), one of DeMille's biggest hits.

The Ten Commandments had a budget of $13 million, the largest amount ever allocated for a motion picture up to that point. It eventually, if briefly, overtook *Gone with the Wind* (MGM, 1939) as the all-time box-office champion. DeMille suffered a heart attack during production, but finished the film, which would be his last. He died in 1959. Like many other alumni, DeMille was buried in the cemetery behind the studio.

In 1957 Paramount was the recipient of a rare honor when a town was named after it. Two communities in south Los Angeles, Hynes and Clearwater, were merged, and the name "Paramount" was chosen for the combined communities—although hay and dairy products, not motion pictures, were the new town's chief exports to the world.

In February 1958, the studio sold most of its pre-1948 sound film library to the Music Corporation of America (MCA), which at the time was supplying, and soon would be producing, product for television. MCA eventually became the parent company of Universal Studios, which owns these 764 Paramount titles today.

The price for these priceless titles? Fifty million dollars. "An insanely bad deal for Paramount,"[9] as Scott Eyman put it. Another historian, David Thompson, agreed, calling the deal "madness," yet noted that the check was photocopied, framed, and put up to impress people.[10] Oddly, in the early 1980s, Paramount would also discuss an overall merger of facilities with Universal. They got as far as preparing a press release before the idea was abandoned.

With the dawn of the 1960s Paramount, perhaps even more than the other studios, seemed to be less a going concern than a moribund symbol of an industry increasingly out of touch with the public it was frantically trying to attract. Hits like *Psycho* (1960), *Breakfast at Tiffany's* (1961), *Hud* (1963), *The Carpetbaggers* (1964), *Alfie* (1966), and *Barefoot in the Park* (1967) hardly made up for dated, stale comedies and musicals like *Hey, Let's Twist* (1961), *The Pigeon That Took Rome* (1962), *Beach Ball* (1965), *The Last of the Secret Agents* (1966), *C'mon, Let's Live a Little* (1967), and *Skidoo* (1968).

ABOVE: Audrey Hepburn, shooting *Breakfast at Tiffany's* (1961) on the lot peddles herself and her dog, Mr. Famous, across the lot. Sadly, the much-loved Yorkshire Terrier would be killed in a car accident the same year.
RIGHT: Although this 1965 fire was very real, studio guests and some employees initially thought it was a special effect.

Much of the problem was due to the relative consistency in the studio's management over the decades. Zukor, ninety-one years old in 1964, still sat in the boardroom. It is difficult to imagine what the mogul who had once hired Sarah Bernhardt thought of Jerry Lewis, Elvis Presley, and Jane Fonda. Barney Balaban, only seventy-seven that year, was referred to by Zukor as "the boy."

Howard W. Koch, a producer and occasional director (he had directed something called *Frankenstein 1970*— in 1958), still in his late forties in 1964, was brought in as production head with the intent of injecting a measure of youthful vitality into the declining company. Koch only lasted two years.

On October 29, 1965, a fire started in a storage shed and spread into a lumber mill. From there the blaze ignited a gas line and jumped west across the fence to the adjacent RKO-Desilu Studios, and south onto a corner of a Western backlot, where an episode of TV's *Bonanza* (1959–1973) was filming, which was partially destroyed. The fire also disrupted a barbecue for theater owners being hosted by the studio on the set of an upcoming movie, *Nevada Smith* (1966). Steve McQueen, the star of the film, was among the guests at the event. One of the theater owners, Weldon Limmroth, apparently expecting a Hollywood spectacle, told the press that "at first I thought it was something added just to put a little zest into the party—then I realized it was real."[11]

RKO studios in 1931, before the construction of stages 11, 12, and 14, which would soon be built, and still stand, on the property.

Another sort of fire was about to ignite in the boardroom. In 1966, Paramount was "acquired" by Gulf+Western, a conglomerate of companies created by businessman Charles Bluhdorn in 1958. In February 1967, Bluhdorn also acquired Lucille Ball's Desilu Productions in a $17,000,000 stock exchange. Lucy's company, which would eventually become Paramount Television, marked Paramount's very late entry into the television game, after several aborted earlier attempts going back to 1929. The first Paramount in-house television programs would be *Love, American Style* (1969–1974) and *The Brady Bunch* (1969–1974), although many other TV shows had already been shot on Paramount and Desilu stages. More importantly for this narrative, the Desilu deal also included what had been for decades the old RKO lot, located next door to Paramount.

RKO's corporate history is somehow even more convoluted than Paramount's. Its origins can be traced to 1919, at least, when Robertson-Cole, a British distributor, was acquired by the Film Booking Offices of America (FBO), which opened a fourteen-acre studio at the corner of Melrose and Gower. In 1923, Joseph Kennedy, father of future president John F. Kennedy, joined the company, eventually buying it outright. FBO mostly produced low-budget Westerns, which ran in small towns, away from competition from the major studios.

The Radio Corporation of America (RCA) entered the picture with the coming of sound. RCA and Kennedy combined their interests and together purchased the Keith-Albee-Orpheum (KAO) vaudeville chain for their circuit of theaters. Cecil B. DeMille, during his independent producer phase, was one of the small distributors whose company was gobbled up during Kennedy's buying spree. In 1929, Kennedy consolidated FBO and RCA with KAO into Radio-Keith-Orpheum, or RKO, a new major studio, the first created after the advent of sound, and with a ready-made chain of theaters and sound-production facilities.

The RKO studio in Hollywood was one of two lots controlled by RKO, the other being a one-time DeMille lot in Culver City known as Pathé. Many RKO pictures—and there would be over a thousand of them over the next quarter-century—would be shot in both studios, as well as at the RKO Ranch in Encino.

In January 1929 RKO announced in the *Hollywood Citizen News* that a new soundproof stage would be built (actually, the future Stages 5 and 6), and that all of the other stages would be soundproofed as well. In addition, three projection rooms would be constructed. The cost for these improvements was announced at $250,000, but would ultimately cost the company about half a million dollars. In fact, according to historian Richard B. Jewell, the cost of outfitting the twelve-and-a-half-acre lot on Gower Street was ultimately even more than that. "When the expansion program concluded," Jewell wrote, "the company had spent two million. The studio lot now contained ten production stages, an administration building, an office building, a dressing room building, an editing and projection building, plus four other buildings and a restaurant."[12]

In spite of RKO's undeniable pedigree and power, the studio would ultimately wrangle with nearly constant financial and management problems over the course of its life. Unlike its next-door neighbor, Paramount—which was, during the same period, relatively stable—whatever executive was unlucky enough to be a part of RKO's upper management team could expect to face a near-constant blitz of bad decisions, unsuccessful pictures, suspensions, firings, and, probably, ulcers, practically on an hourly basis.

What is surprising about RKO is that during this near-constant turmoil, the studio somehow produced or distributed some of the most enduring films in Hollywood history, including *Cimarron* (1931), *King Kong* (1933), *The Lost Patrol* (1934), *The Informer* (1935), *Gunga Din* (1939), *Citizen Kane* (1941), *It's a Wonderful Life*

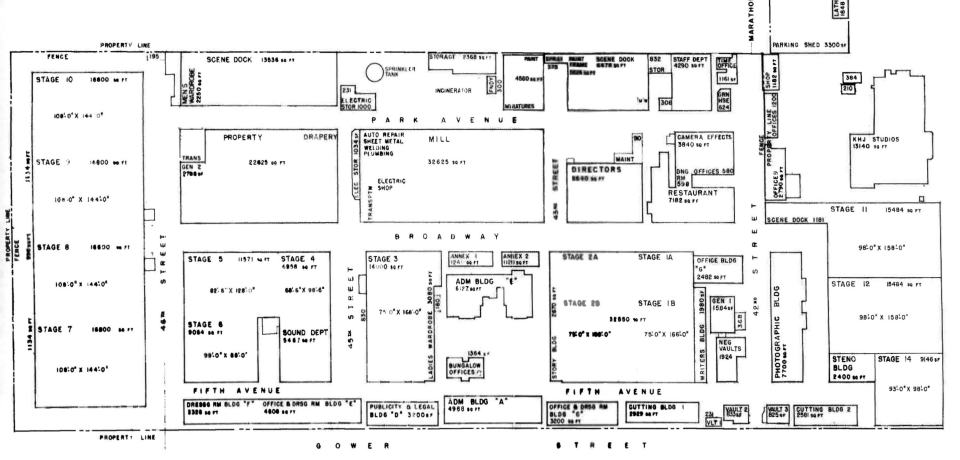

RKO RADIO PICTURES INC
HOLLYWOOD STUDIO

KEY SITE PLAN F
COST SURVEY
W. L. PEREIRA A.
MAY 19

NOTE: FIGURES INDICATE GROSS FLOOR AREAS

LEFT: The RKO lot in 1947, the year before Howard Hughes acquired the property. RIGHT: Unlikely moguls Lucille Ball and Desi Arnaz at the door to their new empire, 1957.

(1946), *The Hunchback of Notre Dame* (1939), *Out of the Past* (1947), and *Rashomon* (1952). Other famous productions and important Hollywood figures that make up the RKO canon include the Fred Astaire and Ginger Rogers musicals, the Val Lewton horror films, many of Walt Disney's and Samuel Goldwyn's classics, as well as major films by directors John Ford, Jean Renoir, Orson Welles, Fritz Lang, Robert Wise, Edward Dmytryk, Anthony Mann, Nicholas Ray, and Alfred Hitchcock, and stars like Cary Grant, John Wayne, Katharine Hepburn, Ingrid Bergman, Randolph Scott, Boris Karloff, Robert Mitchum, Dolores del Rio, Maureen O'Hara, Jane Russell, Irene Dunne, Richard Dix, Charles Laughton, Robert Ryan, Victor McLaglen, and, significantly, Lucille Ball.

In the 1950s however, the whole erratic, misfiring, three-ring circus that was RKO finally started to implode. Tycoon Howard Hughes had acquired control of the company in 1948, and his eccentric management style, even by the standards of RKO, dealt the company a nearly fatal blow. In 1955 Hughes sold RKO to General Tire and Rubber Company for $25 million. Two years later the studio and its two lots were acquired by Desilu at the fire-sale price of $6,150,000. Desilu, of course, was owned by Lucille Ball and her husband, Desi Arnaz, who had become major stars on TV's *I Love Lucy* (1951–1957). Ball had been a contract player at RKO in the late 1930s. "I regret the passing of the studio system," Lucy said years later. "I was very appreciative of it because I had no talent."

Upon acquiring the property, Lucy moved into Ginger Rogers's dressing room and took a tour of the gigantic RKO wardrobe department. Her friend, character actress Mary Wickes, said that "it took her back to when she was a contract player, and to see all those furs and things that suddenly were hers. She couldn't believe it. God knows, she didn't need them anymore, but it was a giant look backward."[13]

With the purchase of Desilu, Paramount gained control of valuable TV properties like *The Untouchables* (1959–1963), *Mission: Impossible* (1966–1973), and *Mannix* (1967–1975), along with less-successful programs (at the time), like *Star Trek* (1966–1969). The studio also gained control of the old RKO lot(s). Gulf+Western quickly sold the Culver City plant, as well as other Desilu properties, as ordered by a federal government consent decree. But an article in the *Los Angeles Times* mentioned that "the other studio on Gower Street in Hollywood and adjoining Gult+Western's Paramount Studio would be retained. The wall separating the studios will be torn down, officials said."[14] "Toward the back of the lot there was only a wire fence separating the two studios,"[15] recalled producer A. C. Lyles.

That fence came down with a ceremonial ribbon cutting. The ribbon was made of film, and cut by Lucy, with Bluhdorn looking on. With one slice of those scissors the forty-two-year-old barrier between the two properties was erased. Lucy told the smiling reporters on the lot, "I've been smiling since I first met Charlie because I knew he was the man to do it right." This made Bluhdorn wonder who had acquired whom. "I think Lucy has taken us over," he said."[16]

Merging the two properties was not as easy as cutting a piece of film, however. Ed Phillips, CEO of Matthews Studio Equipment, and a studio electrician in 1967, wryly referred to the barrier as the "Great Wall." "Before the Great Wall came down Desilu was a boutique studio with a family atmosphere, which almost

LEFT: Charles Bluhdorn and Lucille Ball cut the film ribbon joining the Desilu studio lot with that of Paramount, 1967. ABOVE: Traces of RKO can be seen on the Paramount lot to this day, although this RKO manhole cover has recently been obscured by an access ramp, 2011.

immediately changed after the Paramount acquisition . . . things moved much more slowly before. Production was at a slower pace, and there was more time for more fun."[17]

Suddenly many of the departments—property, construction, and administration buildings—were duplicated, so the studio had to decide which one to utilize. Paramount even had two commissaries. Sadly, Paramount also found themselves with duplicate staffs for these departments, so many RKO/Desilu employees were laid off and sent home. The new influx of fourteen RKO soundstages was certainly welcome, although for several months the original numbers were retained, meaning Paramount found itself in the confusing position of having a "Paramount Stage 4," for example, and a separate "Gower Stage 4," just a few yards away.

A few other vestiges of RKO continued to exist for decades. As recently as 1982, on the western wall of Stage 28 there could still be seen, faintly, the painted lightning bolts of the RKO logo looking out onto Gower Avenue. Film critic Leonard Maltin, working there in the 1980s on *Entertainment Tonight*, remembers looking at the logo and marveling that it had not been painted over in all those years. (It has since then.) There is also an RKO-labeled manhole cover on the studio streets to this day, although it has recently been covered over with an accessible walkway. Stage 21 has the original RKO corporate globe on its roof to this day. It looks down upon a very different world.

At the same time the studio was expanding, the animation division was shutting down. Paramount Cartoons had originally been produced externally by the East Coast–based Fleischer Studios, and included the popular *Popeye* and *Superman* series. Upon seizing control of Fleischer in 1941, Paramount had renamed the division Famous Studios, and from 1956 on, Famous Cartoon Studios. Most of the animation, however, was still not produced on the lot— although producer George Pal did create a charming series of stop-motion "Puppetoons" for the Short Subject Department in-house during World War II. In 1967

Robert Evans and Jack Nicholson, on the set of *Chinatown*, here seem to have a lot to smile about, 1974.

Gulf+Western, along with most other studios during the era, realized that the market for theatrical animated shorts was withering away, and closed the cartoon department for good.

Like the cartoons, the Paramount newsreel division came from the "more serious" East Coast. It was established in September 1927 as "Paramount News." The logo depicted the Paramount Mountain with those words in the center. Their motto was "The Eyes of the World," and post-talkies, "The Eyes and Ears of the World." Two newsreels were released per month as part of a program, which could also include two features, trailers, short subjects, and a cartoon. Paramount News lasted until February 1957, by which time television, and television news, had long since made newsreels, cartoons, and the other short subjects on the bill a redundancy. In 1963 Wolper Productions acquired the Paramount newsreel library.

To the surprise of everyone, in 1966 Bluhdorn hired Robert Evans as head of production. Evans had, in another life, been an actor. In fact, he had portrayed legendary producer Irving Thalberg in *Man of a Thousand Faces* (Universal, 1957). Apparently Bluhdorn had read an article in the *New York Times* about an Evans-acquired, not-yet-released Frank Sinatra vehicle, *The Detective* (Twentieth Century Fox, 1968), and subsequently decided to give him the top spot.

During this era a *Life* magazine article quoted Stanley R. Jaffe, the twenty-nine-year-old chief operating officer in charge of "streamlining company functions," as saying, "[A]s for the studio, we're going to get rid of it. That delights me personally. Without that tremendous overhead we will have flexibility. It's like the army. A general can move ten men more easily than a thousand. In the future we can be more receptive to changes in the marketplace without the studio hanging around our necks."[18]

Statements like this would indicate that during this era, the prognosis for the company—and, particularly, for the studio—was very bleak indeed.

[1] Sam Jaffe, as told to Sam Locke. "The Night Paramount Burned," *Los Angeles Magazine*, October, 1990.
[2] Interview: Richard Lindheim, April, 2016.
[3] Charles Higham and Joel Greenberg. *The Celluloid Muse: Hollywood Directors Speak*. Chicago: Henry Regency Company, 1969.
[4] Interview: Cecilia de Mille Presley, January, 2016.
[5] Alan Leigh. "Gated Community," *The Hollywood Reporter, Special Issue*, July 2002.
[6] Ibid.
[7] Scott Eyman. *Empire of Dreams: The Epic Life of Cecil B. DeMille*. New York: Simon & Schuster, 2010.
[8] DVD: *The War of the Worlds—Special Collector's Edition* (1953).
[9] Eyman, Empire of Dreams.
[10] David Thompson. *The Whole Equation: A History of Hollywood*. New York: Alfred A. Knopf, 2005.
[11] "Flames Damage Desilu and Paramount Studios," *Los Angeles Times*, October 30, 1965.
[12] Richard B. Jewell. *RKO Radio Pictures: A Titan Is Born*. Los Angeles: University of California Press, 2012.
[13] Coyne Steven Sanders and Tom Gilbert. *Desilu: The Story of Lucille Ball and Desi Arnaz*. New York: Quill, William Morrow, 1993.
[14] "Federal OK Limits Gulf & Western's Desilu Acquisition," *Los Angeles Times*, July 26, 1967.
[15] Leigh, "Gated Community."
[16] Arelo Sederberg. "Gulf & Western's Chairman Admits He Loves Lucy, Too," *Los Angeles Times*, July 27, 1967.
[17] Interview: Ed Phillips, February, 2016.
[18] "The Day the Dream Factories Woke Up," *Life*, February 27, 1970.

CHAPTER 3
Behind the Gate

*Look at this street. All cardboard, all phony, all done with
mirrors. I like it better than any street in the world.*
—Betty (played by Nancy Olson) in *Sunset Boulevard* (1950)

Our survey of Paramount is a snapshot of how the studio would have
looked in 1968. The date probably could have been 1938, or even 1988,
but 1968 was chosen instead because this was a transitional era for
the studio. During this period, Paramount was a reflection of old Hollywood—
which was dying in front of its creators' eyes, even though they may not have
comprehended the magnitude of those death throes at the time—and new Hollywood,
which was taking root in the cracks. In our review of the lot, we can see
the newly combined Desilu/RKO and Paramount lots. We can see the original
backlot, before it was compromised and destroyed by bulldozers and by bullshit.
We can see traces of the original studio, and traces of the studio to come. A perfect storm.

In 1968 the studio encompassed fifty-four acres. The official address at the
time was 5451 Marathon Street; the current address, 5555 Melrose Avenue, did
not come about until the company expanded outward to that street in 1988. Paramount
boasted thirty-two soundstages in 1968, 363,544 square feet of indoor
shooting space in total. Of these stages, eighteen were original Paramount
structures, with the remaining fourteen having been RKO stages. There were
also nine rentable backlot districts on the lot at the time. Although they were

Paramount from the northeast in 1976.

FAR RIGHT: Paramount as it looked in 1967 at the time of our survey of the lot. The numbers correspond to specific stops on our virtual studio tour of the property.

1. BRONSON GATE
2. ADMINISTRATION BUILDING
3. WAR MEMORIAL
4. WARDROBE AND CASTING BUILDING
5. DRESSING-ROOM BUILDING (AND MAKEUP DEPARTMENT)
6. PRODUCTION BUILDING AND PARK
7. DIRECTORS-WRITERS BUILDING
8. STAGE 1
9. STAGE 2
10. SPECIAL PHOTO STAGE
11. CAMERA DEPARTMENT
12. STAGE 4
13. STUDIO HOSPITAL
14. SECURITY DEPARTMENT
15. POWERHOUSE
16. GRIP/LIGHTING DEPARTMENT
17. VAN NESS GATE
18. LEMON GROVE GATE
19. STILL DEPARTMENT
20. STAGE 17
21. PROPERTY BUILDING
22. STAGE 18
23. THE MILL
24. SPECIAL EFFECTS
25. FIRE DEPARTMENT
26. STAGE 10
27. MUSIC DEPARTMENT
28. STAGE 8
29. STAGE 9
30. ART DEPARTMENT
31. STAGE 7
32. STAGE 6
33. STAGE 5

all variations on their European street, which included a park, New York Street, encompassing McFadden Street, Boston Street, Brownstone Street, and Modern Street, the names tended to change often, along with Western Street, made up of Upper and Lower Western Streets and a Mexican village.

The borders of Paramount at the time were Lemon Grove Avenue on the north (a residential street which did not actually border the lot at all, the actual northern border being the wall between Paramount and the cemetery), Van Ness Avenue on the east, Gower Street on the west, and Melrose on the south—which the studio thus far had only lapped against on one (RKO) corner. At the time, the company employed a total of three thousand people, including three hundred permanent employees in the studio's production, servicing, and administrative departments.

Included is a map of Paramount as it looked during this period. The reader is encouraged to consult this map, to crawl inside of it and walk its streets, exploring its mysterious alleys and dark corners. Numbers have been attached to all of the major sets, stages, departments, and historic sites that will be encountered on our journey. The building names correspond to what those buildings were called during the 1960s, but earlier departments, names, numbers, movies, and people who passed through these buildings are noted and remarked upon as well, including those of later bureaucrats and barbarians who had an impact on the studio.

The soundstages have presented a particular logistical problem. In 1968 the blending of Paramount and Desilu was far from complete. In fact, for many months the studio listed their stages as those on the "Paramount Lot" and the "Gower Lot," as the departments were combined and intermingled. So both numbers are included, as well as any other names that the stage has had painted upon its vast elephant doors over the decades.

Welcome to Paramount, city of dreams.

34. TEST STAGE AND STAGE 3
35. SCREENING ROOM (S)
36. BARBERSHOP
37. DEMILLE OFFICES AND GATE
38. FILM VAULTS
39. EDITORIAL
40. COMMISSARY
41. LASKY-DEMILLE BARN
42. MAILROOM/MESSINGER DEPARTMENT
43. STAGE 14
44. STAGE 12
45. STAGE 13
46. STAGE 11
47. STAGE 15
48. SOUND DEPARTMENT
49. STAGE 16
50. NEW YORK STREET
51. SCENIC ARTS
52. B-TANK
53. WESTERN STREET
54. EUROPEAN STREET
55. SCENE DOCKS
56. WATER TOWER
57. STAGE 29
58. STAGE 30
59. STAGE 31
60. STAGE 32
61. NORTH GOWER GATE
62. STAGE 28
63. STAGE 27
64. STAGE 26
65. RESEARCH DEPARTMENT
66. TRANSPORTATION DEPARTMENT
67. STAGE 25
68. GOWER ENTRANCE
69. (LUCY) PARK
70. STAGE 24
71. STAGES 22 AND 23
72. STAGE 21
73. STAGE 20
74. STAGE 19

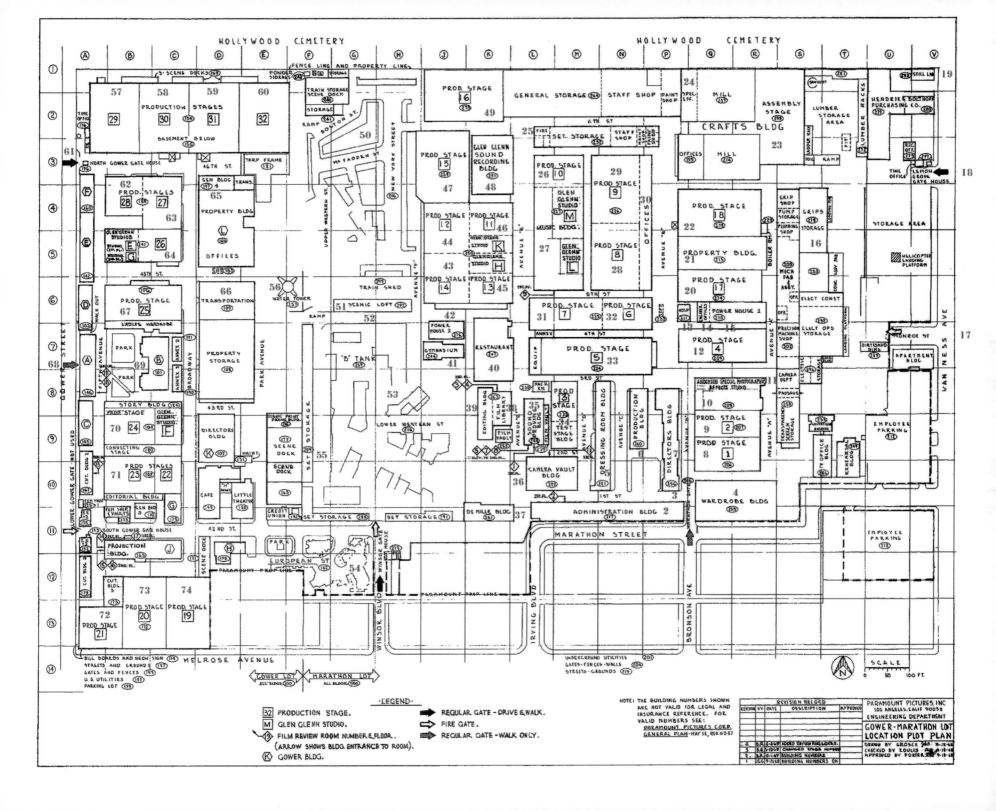

GOWER-MARATHON LOT LOCATION PLOT PLAN — Paramount Pictures, Inc., Los Angeles, Calif. 90038, Engineering Department

I BRONSON GATE

The most famous gate in the world, Hollywood's Arc de Triomphe, was designed by Ruth E. Morris and built between August 26 and September 10 in 1926. Some printed accounts have insisted that the original belfry above the arch was built to detour female fans hoping to climb over in pursuit of their idol, Rudolph Valentino. Seeing that the great lover had died on August 23 of that year, three days before construction of the gate commenced, this is doubtful. We do know that this same belfry was removed in 1936 because of the possibility of its being toppled by earthquakes. Fortunately, post-Valentino, there have been few reported attempts of fans trying to crawl over the now-flattened tile top.

The gate perhaps first attracted attention outside of Hollywood when a 1937 labor strike that took place in front of the entrance brought newsreel cameras out to cover the disturbance. These pictures and moving images of picketing IATSE (International Alliance of Theatrical Stage Employees) staffers in front of the gates did more to publicize Paramount as a physical place than as an abstraction, than anything the studio itself was attempting at the time.

Interestingly, although much has been made of the gate and its distinctive look, this Mission Revival–style, arched-and-columned theme was popular in the 1920s, and can be seen in many other less-heralded buildings from the era. In fact, few seem to have noticed that just a few yards down to the east, a smaller entrance into the wardrobe building can be seen sporting nearly identical architecture. At the administration building to the west (also designed by Ruth Morris), the same motif can be viewed again, under the oft-changed "Paramount Pictures, Inc." sign.

The motif was aped yet again on the new (1988) Melrose Gate (sometimes referred to as the Windsor Gate), named in honor of the street leading into it. Many tourists now assume this is *the* Paramount gate, which it was intentionally designed to mimic. In fact, the original Bronson Gate is not open to motor traffic at all anymore, modern vehicles being too large to safely enter through it.

RIGHT: The Bronson gate, arguably the most famous entrance to anything, anywhere in the world, under construction, 1926. FAR RIGHT: 1937 labor dispute brought picketers, and reporters, to the Bronson Gate, and inadvertently first introduced the general public to its iconography as well.

So anyone who talks about driving though the Bronson Gate is either lying, very old, or referring to the Melrose Gate instead.

It has long been a tradition for actors first visiting the Paramount lot to touch the iron gates and whisper "I'm ready for my close-up, Mr. DeMille," for good luck, a reference to the famous line in *Sunset Boulevard*, although that line was not uttered in this or any other film in this location. The tradition probably originated due to the fact that the casting department was located next to the Bronson Gate for many years, and undoubtedly throngs of hopefuls would have stood there for hours, looking through the wrought-iron entryway, awaiting their big break.

One actor, Richard Arlen, literally did get his big break at the Bronson Gate. He was a motorcycle messenger for a film lab who crashed into those gates while entering the lot and fractured his leg. The studio, fearful of a lawsuit, gave him a job, which led to a starring role in William A. Wellman's *Wings* (1927). "I crashed the movies by breaking my leg," Arlen said.

Several celebrities, after their own (acting) breaks, have reflected publicly about the effect of entering the studio through those gates and working inside. "I felt like a man in a sketch, this British creature driving a Ford Mustang convertible through the gates of Paramount. I was actually living the fantasy I'd had as a boy in Belfast movie theaters," said actor Kenneth Branagh, who was on the lot to make *Dead Again* in 1981. "One day someone mentioned we were on the same lot where Orson Welles had filmed parts of *Citizen Kane*. I felt very romantic about that, like here I was, truly in 'The Land of Movies.' "[1]

Similarly, film critics Gene Siskel and Roger Ebert mused once on their long-running (1986–2010) TV program what it must be like for the cast of the *Star Trek* franchise to still be driving through those gates after all those years.

Jerry Zucker and his brother David, who with Jim Abrahams later wrote and directed the classic comedy *Airplane* (1980), never had any problem getting through those gates. Jerry once recalled that "Paramount was a great lot for David and I because they always thought we were Adolph Zukor's grandsons. Security never gave us trouble at the gates even before we were successful. No one ever noticed that our name was spelled differently than his."[2]

Future movie tough guy Charles Bronson allegedly borrowed his screen name from the Bronson Gate. In 1954 Charles Buchinsky chose the name that he would carry with him to stardom, presumably while waiting outside Paramount's casting department. It's a good story, and Bronson himself used to like to tell it, although its credibility is not exactly enhanced by the fact that the first time the name "Charles Bronson" appeared in the credits for a movie was not for a Paramount picture at all, but for the Warner Bros. release, *Drum Beat* (1954).

To the left of the front of the Bronson Gate, highlighting the contrast

The Bronson Gate and the administration building with Marathon Street in the foreground and Paramount and RKO's water towers all in the background, 1936.

between art and commerce, was a window behind which was the studio's payroll department, until it moved to the directors' building in 1948.

Other studios have since hijacked the Bronson Gate's appearance in order to signify Hollywood and its environs. Universal Studios has something similar in front of the turnstiles to their amusement parks, for example.

Animation has often copied the look of the Bronson Gate because cartoonists would not have to pay Paramount for a drawing inspired (however closely) by a real place, So animated films, from *The Autograph Hound* (Disney, 1939), *Shrek 2* (DreamWorks SKG, 2004), and *Inside Out* (Disney, 2015) have blatantly borrowed the look of the gate, if not the name above it.

Live-action projects in which the Bronson Gate makes an appearance would be too numerous to catalog in full. A partial list could include feature films like *Murder in Hollywood* (1929)—which placed a clock at the crux of the arch, a true oddity never seen again—*Hollywood Extra Girl* (1935), *Henry Aldrich Gets Glamour* (1943), *Variety Girl* (1947), *Hollywood or Bust* (1956), *Career* (1958), *The Errand Boy* (1961), *The Carpetbaggers*, (1964), *Harlow* (1965)—seen from the rear only—*The Day of the Locust* (1975), *The Last Tycoon* (1975)—again, seen from the rear only—*W. C. Fields and Me* (Universal, 1976), *The World's Greatest Lover* (Twentieth Century Fox, 1977), *Movers & Shakers* (MGM, 1985), *The Muse* (October Films, 1999), *Man on the Moon* (Universal, 1999), *Crocodile Dundee in Los Angeles* (2001), *Mulholland Drive* (Universal, 2001), *SImOne* (New Line, 2002), *Austin Powers in Goldmember* (New Line, 2002), and *Hitchcock* (Twentieth Century Fox, 2012).

Television appearances include *Gomer Pyle, USMC* (for the 1968 episode, "A Star Is Not Born"), *Mission Impossible* (in the 1970 episode, "The Falcon, Part 3," redressed as "Arngrim Prison," and the 1971 episode, "Nerves"), *The Brady Bunch* (1974 episodes "The Driver's Seat" and "Welcome Aboard"), *The Odd Couple* (1974 episode, "The Hollywood Story"), *Happy Days* (1977 three-part episode, "Hollywood"), *Rescue from Gilligan's Island* (1978 TV movie), *Laverne & Shirley* (1980 episode, "Studio City"), *Growing Up Brady* (2000 TV movie), *Melrose Place* (2009 episode, "Windsor"), *Angel* (2001 episode, "Over the Rainbow"), *Entourage* (2008 episode, "Fire Sale"), and multiple episodes of *Episodes* (2011–).

Weirdly, in a 1975 TV special, *Paramount Presents*, Gloria Swanson was brought back for a curtain call to the Bronson Gate one last time to partially re-create her *Sunset Boulevard* entrance there, twenty-five years after the fact.

The original gate, almost as famous as Paramount itself, was closed and locked in 1962 because of the difficulties in keeping it maintained, and because the entrance served little practical purpose, except for symbolically. Two years later, however, it was officially reopened, with the wrought iron newly gilded and the arch restored. Howard W. Koch presided over the ceremony, which included actress Carroll Baker, who was then filming *Harlow* (1965) there, and any producers or executives who could be persuaded to pose for the cameras.

The gate, or rather its iconography, has also been used by the company as an on-screen logo for their Paramount Classics (later Paramount Vantage) specialty distribution label.

2 ADMINISTRATION BUILDING

The administration building was designed in-house by Ruth E. Morris and built between April and July of 1926. A slight jog in the interior corridors, noticeable to this day, is the result of a design error.

Located to the west of the Bronson Gate, the building has often been the administrative center of the studio in name only. The long, two-story structure has sometimes housed various leaders of the studio, but it has been used more often as dressing rooms, postproduction suites, and operations department annex office space. This was particularly true during long periods when the studio was run out of New York.

Further confusing its identity, the structure, today known as the (Sumner) Redstone Building, is Tudor-style on the back and somewhat Spanish on the front and near the front door. The facade above that front door has been engraved at various times with "Paramount Famous Lasky Corporation, West Coast Studios" (1920s), "Paramount Publix Corporation West Coast Studios" (early 1930s), "Paramount Productions" (1932–1936), and "Paramount Pictures, Inc." (1936–   ).

In the 1950s, Dick Martin, before his stint as half of the comic duo of *Rowan & Martin's Laugh-In* (TV, 1969–1973) spent some nights moonlighting in the administration building as a janitor. In 1962 he returned to the studio, this time during the day, to costar with Lucille Ball in the first season of *The Lucy Show* (TV, 1962–1968).

TOP: The administration building and the Bronson gate in 1977. ABOVE: The Paramount administration building, 1991.

3 WAR MEMORIAL

By the middle of 1944, according to the *Motion Picture Herald*, of the 19,600 people employed in the motion picture industry, 6,500 were in the armed services, joining the 12,000,000 US citizens in uniform. MGM led in total employee enlistments, with 908 serving, 1 killed, and as of April of that year, 1 captured. Twentieth Century Fox came in second, with 700 men in the service, and 7 fatalities. Warner Bros. was third, reporting 675 serving, of which 5 had been killed. The first Paramount casualty was Franklin C. Gilbert, a studio engineer who was killed in May of 1942 in a training accident in New Jersey. At the time of this survey, Paramount was fourth, and 2 employees had been killed of the 537 serving.

By war's end, however, August 15, 1945, after the final noble tally had been calculated, it was announced that 681 Paramount employees had served in the various branches of the armed services, and 11 had been killed. A bronze memorial was placed on the south wall of the directors' building in 1948, which remains there today—an oddly poignant reminder of the all-too-real drama which takes place outside of Hollywood's backlot battlefields.

4 WARDROBE AND CASTING BUILDING

"I used to sneak into the costume department," Cecilia de Mille Presley remembers. "It was the most amazing place."[3]

The wardrobe department, where the stars were dressed to look like beggars or cowboys or courtesans or kings, was officially opened in 1921 at the Selma-Vine studio. Howard Greer was the first significant Paramount wardrobe department head, but in 1925 he left Paramount to freelance and was replaced by Travis Banton. It was Banton who moved into this building next to the Bronson Gate, built circa 1925, when the studio relocated to its more-spacious digs. The costumes themselves were eventually stored all over the lot and even under the

LEFT: A World War II memorial plaque was dedicated in 1948—and remains on the lot even today. ABOVE: The racked clothing in the costume department once included the wardrobe of Hollywood's greatest stars. RIGHT: The wardrobe department tailor shop as it looked in 1968.

soundstages as the department expanded to include—no exaggeration—millions of pieces, encompassing the entire history of mankind's wardrobe.

In 1924 Banton hired Edith Head—an ambitious but inexperienced twenty-six-year-old with no costuming background—as a sketch artist, even though she could barely draw. She later admitted that the sketches she had submitted with her application had not even been hers. Unlike Banton, however, Head did know how to promote herself, and how to get stars to request her rather than her boss as their personal designer. In 1939 Banton, realizing he had been outmaneuvered by a subordinate, moved to Twentieth Century Fox, leaving Head with his title and his office.

Claudette Colbert, learning of Banton's downfall, complained in a 1940 studio memo that "[she] considers Edith Head an Art Student, [and] has no faith in her designing ability." Yet Edith Head would keep that title, and that office, for the next forty-three years. She eventually won a record eight Academy Awards for Best Costume Design, a category she was instrumental in creating and which, due to her repeated appearances on the Oscar podium and her penchant for self-publicity, made her a household name. In fact, for many people, Head is the only costume designer whose name means anything at all. In 2003 she was even featured on a US postage stamp.

One of the stars Head dressed was Mae West, whose bawdy, innuendo-laced comedies nearly saved Paramount. Head first worked with West in her second film, *She Done Him Wrong* (1933), and decades later, in her last, *Sextette* (Crown International Pictures, 1978)—a remarkable forty-five-year span. Head left Paramount for Universal in 1968, returning once for *Ash Wednesday* (1974). She died in 1981.

Her replacement was Walter Hoffman, who had already managed the department for Head. Hoffman retired in 1988.

In 1968 the wardrobe department included dying and aging rooms (for making clothes look used), a tailor shop, and a steam press. In 1974 Paramount films captured all five nominations for Best Costume Design, the only time that's ever happened. In 1985 costumes were moved into Stage 3, which officially became the Edith Head Wardrobe Building in 1987. It remains so today, although the modern Paramount only nominally has a costume department. Pieces are now stored in this building only as a service to on-lot productions.

Also in 1985, with wardrobe no longer actually there, the wardrobe building was gutted and the main entrance was moved from the northwest corner of the structure to the middle of the west wall. The resultant office building was named the Charles Bluhdorn building, after the longtime Gulf+Western chairman.

Fred Schuessler and then Milton Lewis were for many years the heads of the Paramount casting department, which was in one corner of the wardrobe building. According to actress Yvonne De Carlo, Lewis had a one-way mirror in the casting office where auditioning hopefuls would read their lines. "You never knew who was on the other side,"[4] she said.

Performers who survived the initial casting process in the 1930s and '40s and became contract players were usually paid between $75 and $250 a week. They were also schooled, tutored, manicured, dressed, tested under various conditions, and then asked to test with other contract players, or aspiring contract players. All of this was in hopes that something would happen during the contract period that would convince someone that the contractee would be a continuing asset to the studio.

OUR EADIE

A clever lass is Edith Head,
Whose costumes more than
earn her bread.
With a bolt of cloth and a
sketch or two
She could even make a Lombard
out of you!

LEFT: Edith Head ran the wardrobe department for generations. This affectionate caricature, and doggerel, from the 1938 studio newspaper captures her look almost better than a 1956 photograph does. ABOVE: The wardrobe and casting building faced the street, so the casting office in particular was prone to unwanted attention from the public, as seen here in a free-for-all casting session for *The Spoilers* (1930).

Because of its proximity to the street, and the tourist-attracting Bronson Gate, employees in the department were constantly besieged by hopefuls. In 1936 Schuessler's secretary, Rosalind Boerger, told the company newsletter that she kept a pair of sharpened scissors in her desk in case some "future star" should climb through the nearby window. She also confessed to never leaving Schuessler alone in his office in case of just such a happening.

In 1968 only Universal Studios still had contract players and a traditional casting department.

LEFT: The rear of the dressing room building as seen here in 1961, has long doubled as an impromptu set, a role it continues to play today. BOTTOM: Alan Ladd in his Paramount dressing room, which looks a bit like a Texas steak house, 1949.

5 DRESSING-ROOM BUILDING (AND MAKEUP DEPARTMENT)

This three-story building, built in 1926 at a cost of $16,603.56, illustrated very well the three-tier pecking system of the studio era. In the 1930s the first floor contained the nests of the "Famous Players," the biggest stars, including Mae West, Bing Crosby, W. C. Fields, and Carole Lombard. Marlene Dietrich, according to actor Richard Arlen, used to play football on the "Production Park" lawn across from her dressing room.

On the second floor could be found the dressing rooms of up-and-coming actors who aspired to move up but were not quite there yet. Supporting actors, character actors, and second leads on the way down had to walk up a second staircase to the third floor. Paramount employees used to joke that the dressing-room building was the only place in Hollywood where performers aspired to move down.

In early 1968 the dressing-room building (and an annex) was occupied by Robert Culp, Bill Cosby, Danny Thomas, Vince Edwards, Gale Gordon, Ronnie Jacobs, Peter Graves, William Shatner, Mike Connors, Leonard Nimoy, Barbara Bain, and Joe Campanella. A special suite was set aside for "Guest Star—*Lucy Show.*"

Sometimes the dressing rooms were used for grieving, and for hiding out. In 1969, after actress Sharon Tate and four others were murdered by cult leader Charles Manson and his "family" in Beverly Hills, director Roman Polanski, who had been married to the pregnant Tate, found solitude in a dressing room on the first floor, which had recently been vacated by Julie Andrews. Only his friend and employer, Robert Evans, and a few close associates knew where the grieving filmmaker was during the days following the murders.

In the 1960s portable dressing rooms (sheds on wheels, actually) were often carted across the lot and parked outside the soundstages or exterior sets for ease of access by the cast. According to author and historian Larry Jensen, who was on the set of *Bonanza* (TV 1959–1973) during this era, they "were six or seven feet wide, about ten feet deep, with a door on the front. I don't remember windows, but there must have been at least one. Lorne Greene apparently sat in it, smoked, and read between scenes. You could tell it from the others by an arc of cigarette butts radiating out several feet from the door; dozens of them, as if he used one to light another and then flicked it out the door."[5]

The makeup department, run by Walter "Wally" Westmore, was also located on the third floor of the dressing-room building. The Westmores were the undisputed masters of Hollywood makeup. George Westmore, Wally's father, had created the first specific makeup department at Selig Studios in 1917. His six sons, including Wally, a middle son, eventually managed the makeup departments for five of the seven studios, as well as for many smaller companies in classic Hollywood.

Wally's career at Paramount began in 1926 at the age of twenty-three. According to the family biography, he became head of the makeup department there "solely because his name was Westmore,"[6] but quickly earned his keep designing the grotesque makeup for *Dr. Jekyll and Mr. Hyde* (1931) and *Island of Lost Souls* (1932).

For many years the question of how handsome Dr. Jekyll was transformed into the monstrous Mr. Hyde, on-camera and seemingly without dissolves or other optical trickery, was speculated upon by both special-effects and makeup professionals. The answer was not revealed until the film's director, Rouben Mamoulian, admitted in 1969 that they had used colored filters which corresponded to the makeup that needed to be visible, or invisible, on camera. As the film was photographed in black and white, these gradations, if not their ultimate results, were invisible to astonished audiences of the era. "It was all rather primitive—the filters were hand-made," Mamoulian stated, "but it worked."[7]

Fredric March, who played both parts, worked out as well. Paramount hired him for $11,105.77 total compensation. And he won an Oscar.

During this era, stars had to be treated with deference in regards to even their slightest whims. Billie Burke, on the lot for *One Night in Lisbon* (1941), for some reason insisted that her makeup be applied at MGM, and that she then be transported over to Paramount only afterward for shooting. Paramount not only agreed, but promised to pay half of her MGM makeup artist's weekly salary during production.

Wally was often assisted by Charles Gemora, one of those jack-of-all-trades types so prevalent in Hollywood at the time, particularly before unions made it difficult to wear multiple hats. Gemora specialized in special makeup and hair appliances, as well as special effects, art department work, and costumes. He also climbed into his own appliances and played a gorilla in *Lost Souls* and countless other pictures for Paramount and other studios. He even patented a device to deflect water off of hair for use in the shower. Gemora, whose life was probably as interesting as those of many a star's, died in 1961.

For *The Ten Commandments* (1956), Wally and his team had to spray the thousands of extras involved with tan makeup to make them look Egyptian or Hebrew, and then apply beards to their newly tanned faces. Booths were created where spray guns could douse the chosen people with the right pigment. Unfortunately, these aerosol guns left a vapor hanging in the air which the extras nearly choked on. The solution was to put fans in the booths to blow the excess pigment away. Frank Westmore, Wally's brother, remembers what happened next. His description is worth reprinting:

> That seemed to solve the problem, until Wally called me to his office with a complaint. The windows in our spray booths overlooked Hollywood Cemetery, and the vaporized body makeup sucked out the windows by our fans was turning the nearby tombstones a lovely shade of tan. When we applied beards to the men, little pieces of wool also flew out the windows and stuck to the sullied monuments. The cemetery attendants had tried to clean the markers but had been unsuccessful. Studio laborers were sent out with buckets of detergent and wire brushes to do the job. Meanwhile we made canvas flumes, attached them to the fans, and then ran them down to the ground to spray there. And that was the end of the problem of the suntanned, bearded tombstones.[8]

Wally occasionally freelanced at other studios, but even with a series of crippling strokes in the 1960s, he stayed close to his makeup chair at Paramount until 1970. By that time most of the work on the lot was for television and outside companies, and Wally would not allow cast members of either to be made up in his office—which was, after all, meant for Paramount *movies*. Even the cast of *Bonanza*, an enormous steamroller of a television success, was not permitted, under any circumstances, to use his office for makeup application. His younger brother Frank had to utilize a shack on the backlot instead.

Sadly, but not surprisingly, Wally lost his job of more than forty years while on vacation in Hawaii, when a studio accountant realized that Wally had been billing television budgets for makeup services they were not allowed to utilize. Wally Westmore died in 1973.

In the 1930s character actor Jack Oakie took to playfully stealing hairpieces being used by follicle-challenged leading men and nailing them to the dressing-room ceilings of the stars who had most recently been wearing them. In the cash-hungry 1960s the makeup department listed the rental of (perhaps) some of these same hairpieces in their catalog of services available to producers, at a fee of $15 a week for the first week, and $7.50 a week after that.

Wally Westmore would be shocked to learn that in the twenty-first century, Paramount does not have a designated makeup department. Makeup artists are hired on a per-production and as-needed basis, and not by the studio, but by specific projects. Makeup is usually applied in portable trailers and inside unused soundstages, specifically inside the cavernous Stage 10.

In the 1990s the story department, responsible for "covering" reading and evaluating submitted screenplays, was also located in the dressing-room building.

This same structure, now entirely made over into office space, is still called the dressing-room building, even though no one gets dressed (or undressed) there anymore. No one, except for a few, usually female, executives puts on makeup there, either.

Like many buildings on the lot, this one has a schizoid nature that allows it to be filmed as more than one geographic place. It is partially wood-planked on the west side, looks comparatively modern on the east side, and is Tudor-style on its southern end, which matches the Norman look on that side of the nearby administration building—which itself is Spanish Colonial from the front.

A columnist for the *Los Angeles Herald Examiner* must have been talking about just this sort of thing when he described the Paramount lot as exhibiting a "playful elusive ambiguity between what is real and what is filmably real."[9]

6 PRODUCTION BUILDING AND PARK

Paramount always lacked the dynamic hands-on approach of moguls at rival studios like Warner Bros. and Twentieth Century Fox. Lasky was gone after 1932. Zukor became increasingly distant as the years passed, both

LEFT: The Jerry Lewis vehicle *The Delicate Delinquent* cast the production building as a police precinct, 1957.
ABOVE: The production building in 2016.

administratively and geographically. And DeMille preferred his megaphone and his soundstage to the life of an administrator. Even Balaban was actually an exhibitor, more interested in ideas and ideals than in maintaining a factory.

Therefore, the actual running of the studio was left not to one man, but rather to offices full of accountants and bureaucrats. In 1938 Balaban chose Y. Frank Freeman, a former soft-drink executive, as vice president of studio productions. Freeman would manage the company until 1959, but like Zukor and Balaban, he seldom could be bothered to venture from his paneled offices in Manhattan. So when the system was working and the films were making money, no one from New York appeared to ask questions in the studio conference rooms or hover ominously in the shadows behind the crackling klieg lights on the stages.

This laissez-faire system shouldn't have worked, but it actually ticked along remarkably well for a considerably longer time than it should have. The proper system of checks and balances, of creativity and commercialism, of independence and interdependence, and even of art and commerce, kept the stages and the theaters full for a long time. The alchemy that made it work was a happy and unexpected accident that no one really understood, but which many took credit for.

In this building, constructed in 1934, contracts were negotiated, deals were made, and teams of artisans and autocrats were assembled and shuffled and ignored and dismissed. Soundstages were booked and budgets were approved, looked over, and overlooked. And promises were honored or dishonored. Because of, and in spite of, all of this, thousands of movies, sometimes very good ones, were made.

The production building and park—the latter a sometimes-grassy area in front of it that did not become the permanent park it is today until 1983—was the nerve center of the studio. The place was not managed from this building; in fact, a case could be made that Paramount was not managed at all, only focused, sharpened, channeled, and released. But all of the practical considerations inherent in running a factory were attended to here.

For a good long time, Paramount managed to deal well with iconoclasts like W. C. Fields, Josef von Sternberg, and Ernst Lubitsch. In 1935 the Paramount machine even appointed Lubitsch as production manager for the whole teetering studio. Only Paramount, or rather, the unsupervised hole-punchers in this building, would ever have thought to make a director the manager of his own studio. In fact, to this day Lubitsch remains the only major director to achieve such a lofty, if dubious, honor. He lasted about a year.

The Marx Brothers were a good example of hothouse flowers which could only have bloomed on the stages of Paramount. Brought to Hollywood for *Monkey Business* (1931) after two films at Astoria, the manic, almost feral family of dervishes were supported financially by the studio and given vast soundstages full of props and playthings and straight men. No one in the production building, let alone the administration building, had any ideas about "civilizing" the Marx Brothers, or imposing any sort of structure upon their films. All the accountants wanted was to make pictures that would get paying customers into their theaters. In gratitude for all the support they were given, the brothers proceeded to moon Paramount, and the world, with three leering comic raspberries: *Monkey Business* (1931), *Horsefeathers* (1932), and *Duck Soup* (1933). None of these films could have been made at a studio where a "creative" executive would have imposed discipline or structure upon the anarchy. In fact, when the brothers eventually took their circus up the road to MGM, Irving Thalberg, undisputedly the most creative producer at any studio, quickly bleached their comedy of much of its prickliness, giving their stories cohesive plotlines and making the boys heroes, rather than hellions. Things would never be the same again.

The Marx Brothers; Harpo, Groucho, Chico and Zeppo, as seen while shooting a promotional film, *The House that Shadows Built* (1931). The person on the left is their equally eccentric father "Frenchie," visiting what must have been a very chaotic set.

The building where all of these good, bad, and indefensible decisions paid off, or didn't, has often been seen on-screen as a government, or public, building. Probably its earliest on-screen credits were as an apartment in *Thanks for the Memory* (1937) and a college in *Campus Confessions* (1938). It was also the "Pacific Institute of Science and Technology" in *The War of the Worlds* (1953), and a police station in *The Delicate Delinquent* (1957). Recently it was seen in *Hitchcock* (Twentieth Century Fox, 2013).

On television, this same exterior was seen in the 1968 *Star Trek* episode, "Patterns of Force," as an off-world Nazi headquarters, and in episodes of *Mission Impossible* (1966–1973), *Mannix* (1967–1975), *Family Ties* (1982–1989), *Webster* (1983–1989), and *The Bradys* (1990), among many, many others.

Today, the production building is known as the Schulberg Building. The dressing-room building (see #5) is to the east, and across that lawn to the west is the directors-writers building, now known as the Lubitsch Building, which was named, one must assume, after the director rather than the production manager.

ABOVE: The director's-writer's build-ing is on the left, Stage 2 is on the right. The *Love Story* poster is on the southern wall of Stage 4, 1968. RIGHT: The director's-writer's Building, left, has always housed all sorts of studio personnel, not just directors, and not just writers, 2014. FAR RIGHT: Jerry Lewis, on the camera crane, directs *The Errand Boy* in front of the "Para-mutual Pictures" gate. The director's-writer's Building is just beyond, on the left, 1961.

This long, narrow, grab-bag office building was known only as the directors' building in the 1930s when it was built, and then even into the 1960s, although by that time the name was an umbrella title for office space even then, regard-less of whoever was actually using those offices. Originally, the tenants here were lucky indeed to be assigned to this building. At the time of its construction, in 1930, it was the only three-story office building with an elevator inside a Holly-wood studio.

The writers at Paramount actually tended to float about the studio, which is perhaps indic-ative of how little respect screenwriters (or scribes, as *Variety* romantically likes to call them) are afforded in Hollywood. In 1950 alone there were three designated writers' "buildings" at Paramount. Only a bottom portion of the southern half of this particular building was originally designated for writers. Two additional, different buildings, since torn down, in the southeast corner of the lot near Van Ness were also set aside for writers in the 1930s and '40s. It didn't matter, as most writers tended to spend more of their time at Lucy's El Adobe Cafe up the road.

While working for Schulberg in 1930, David O. Selznick found the writers' department in such disarray that he and department head Vivian Moses tried, with little success, to rebuild the department based on the MGM model, where Selznick had recently worked. At MGM, writers were assigned to projects based on their previous credits and affinity for the material rather than on who hap-pened to be available when the assignment came in. Selznick would soon leave Paramount to start his own company, taking his ideas about writers with him.

8 STAGE 1 (1922)

WIDTH: 73 feet

LENGTH: 146 feet

HEIGHT: 25 feet

SQUARE FEET: 10,658

Soundstages are where most films continue to be made to this very day. For the purposes of this book we have provided the size of each stage, when available, as well as its square footage and other pertinent details. If the stage has been renamed, renumbered, reconfigured, or removed since 1968, this information is provided as well, with details about what transpired to bring about these changes.

Stages 1 and 2 are two of the first things a visitor sees upon entry into the lot, 2014.

Also included is a list of titles which shot within the stage—not comprehensive, by any means, but as close to that as anyone has ever compiled to show the breadth of American popular culture created within these walls. Dates for television series reflect the entire run of the show, not specifically when production was occurring inside that stage. Feature-film dates reflect that film's release date, not specifically when that film was in production inside that stage. All feature titles are Paramount films, unless otherwise noted.

Stage 1 was constructed in 1922 and remains, with its nearby sisters, one of the oldest on the lot, and is in fact one of the first things one sees when entering though the Bronson Gate.

Stage 1 was built as a single shooting space, along with Stages 2 and 3, by United Studios. At the time movies were shot in large enclosed areas, which had recently replaced the open, roofless stages which the film industry had originally embraced during the era when natural light was utilized. In these vast sheds multiple pictures could be shot at one time because there was no sound being recorded. (Although how an actor playing a love scene could concentrate on his performance with a knockabout comedy being pantomimed a few feet away and a saloon fight being staged behind that is a tribute to that actor's skills, or to that of his leading lady.) Sadly, there are apparently no surviving records of what specifically was shot inside these walls during this distant era.

Stage 1 was listed as "#10" during the earliest days of the studio. Paramount probably renamed it Stage 1 in 1929–1930, when it (and its sister stages) were soundproofed. Intriguingly, there are two small basements near the northern wall, although their intended usage and current existence has been long forgotten by most.

Shot on Stage 1:

Island of Lost Souls (1931) —assorted.

I Married a Witch (1942)—hotel lobby interiors; Susan Hayward's home.

The Uninvited (1944)—Dr. Scott's office.

The Virginian (1946)—Molly's hotel room.

Welcome Stranger (1947)—the McRory home.

A Foreign Affair (1948)—the Lorelei Club.

Samson and Delilah (1949)—Bar Simon's house; Samson's house.

Dark City (1950)—bookie joint for a scene with Jack Webb.

My Friend Irma Goes West (1950)— Grand Central Station sets.

Son of Paleface (1951)—assorted.

Ace in the Hole (1951)—cave set interiors.

The Greatest Show on Earth (1952)—"backyard haystack" for scenes with Betty Hutton.

Tropic Zone (1953)—assorted.

Houdini (1953)—Tony Pastor's place.

The Naked Jungle (1954)—Joanna's (Eleanor Parker) hut.

Strategic Air Command (1955)—the home of Dutch and Sally Holland (James Stewart and June Allyson).

The Delicate Delinquent (1956) —assorted.

The Man Who Knew Too Much (1956)—the McKenna suite set, where Doris Day first performs her lifetime anthem, "Whatever Will Be, Will Be (Que Sera Sera)."

Teacher's Pet (1957)—assorted; Clark Gable played the title role.

Vertigo (1957)—interiors of the Plaza Hotel and the Fairmont ballroom.

The Sad Sack (1957)—office of Major Shelton (Phyllis Kirk).

The Geisha Boy (1958)—office of Major Ridgley (Barton MacLane).

The Matchmaker (1958)—assorted.

King Creole (1958)—the drugstore and principal's office.

The Space Children (1958)—cave set interiors.

The Pleasure of His Company (1961) —assorted.

Blue Hawaii (1961)—Chapman's (Howard McNear) office; Island's Inn luau scenes.

The Man Who Shot Liberty Valance (1962)—assorted.

Love with the Proper Stranger (1963) —assorted.

McLintock! (1963)—parts of the famous mud-pit fight scene.

The Nutty Professor (1963)—Jerry Lewis's masterpiece; some exteriors shot in Tempe, Arizona.

Donovan's Reef (1963)—chapel set; much of the film shot in Kauai, Hawaii.

Who's Minding the Store? (1963) —assorted.

The Carpetbaggers (1964)—Jonas's (George Peppard) Los Angeles home.

El Dorado (1966)—Robert Mitchum's place and the cantina set.

Nevada Smith (1966)—the Whiskey Barrel and Sweetwater Saloons.

The Night of the Grizzly (1966)— interiors of the "Bald Eagle", and a bank.

The President's Analyst (1967) —assorted.

Paint Your Wagon (1969)—ten shooting days on the lot; mostly shot in Oregon.

The Sterile Cuckoo (1969)—assorted.

Darling Lili (1970)—assorted.

The New Odd Couple (TV, 1982– 1983)—Ron Glass and Demond Wilson were the new Felix and Oscar; some scripts from the original series were recycled.

Brothers (TV, 1984–1989)—also Stage 2; Robert Walden was the star of this early Showtime series.

MacGyver (TV, 1985–1992)—assorted.

Jade (1995)—assorted.

Vampire in Brooklyn (1995) —assorted.

Moesha (TV, 1996–2001) —assorted.

The Truman Show (1998) —assorted.

Roswell (TV, 1999–2002)— Max's room.

Resurrection Blvd. (TV, 2000–2002)—assorted.

Nip/Tuck (TV, 2003–2010) —assorted.

Rizzoli & Isles (TV, 2010–2016) —assorted.

Happy Endings (TV, 2011–2013) — assorted Chicago interiors.

9 STAGE 2 (1922)

WIDTH:	57 feet, 1 inch
LENGTH:	147 feet, 6 inches
HEIGHT:	26 feet
SQUARE FEET:	8,420

Like its sister stage (#1), Stage 2 was also built in 1922. It was originally referred to as Stage 9, and was probably renumbered in 1929–1930 when it was soundproofed.

Stage 2 was long designated a "transparency stage," sometimes called a "process stage." Whatever it was called, this stage was, in effect, where rear

Stage 2 was where many process shots involving rear projection were composed, as here, for Gary Cooper in *The Story of Dr. Wassell* (1944).

projected images shot elsewhere were combined with material shot live onstage. For example, if an actor was to be seen in the backseat of a car, an actual automobile cut in half in order to fit the camera and equipment would be towed onto the stage. The car would then be positioned in front of what was called a transparency screen, part of which was visible through the car's rear window. Pre-shot second-unit footage—in this case, taken from the rear window of a real car—would then be threaded into a projector. This projector, by the way, often had to be positioned outside the eastern door of Stage 2, and inside the adjacent transparency screen storage building, which was across the street, in order to avoid "hotspots" incurred by putting that projector too close to the screen. When the director called "Action!," this projector, its shutter synchronized with the shutter in the camera in order to avoid flutter, would project this image across the street and onto the back of, and then through this screen, so the projected material could be seen running behind the emoting actors while the camera recorded it all. Meanwhile, grips rotated tree branches off-screen in front of a light to simulate the car passing by trees, or whatever.

Virtually every Paramount picture for generations would contain such material, although process scenes were shot on other stages as well. In spite of the Rube Goldberg complexity inherent in making it all work, and the somewhat unconvincing nature of the finished result, for financial and logistic reasons it was almost always considered preferable to shoot these scenes here rather than going outside the gates to a real location.

The following list of titles shot on Stage 2 is a mixed bag of films actually shot on the stage, which did happen when no transparency (or process) shots were scheduled, along with those shot here beyond the 1970s, after which these sequences would become increasingly rare, and films which utilized these trick effects. Whenever possible, an attempt has been made to differentiate, although that has not always been possible.

Shot on Stage 2:

It's a Gift (1934)—process shots of a suburban street, a county hospital, and a Western town, to be seen in the window of W. C. Fields's Ford.

The Cat and the Canary (1939)—the house's cellar and garden, and the scenes in the secret passageway.

Beau Geste (1939)—Port Said bar; the film also shot at the Paramount Ranch, on recycled sets from *The Adventures of Marco Polo* (Goldwyn, 1938), at Busch Gardens in Pasadena, and in Yuma, Arizona.

Union Pacific (1939)—Mrs. Hogan's car (process).

Dr. Cyclops (1940)—The cumbersome three-strip Technicolor, and the story—about a scientist who shrinks his victims in size—made this one a technical challenge for Paramount. The "double-exposure shots," presumably referring to process and matte sequences, were done here, and on Stage 3.

The Lady Eve (1941)—undetermined; probably process sequences.

West Point Widow (1941)—ambulance-based process shots.

Sullivan's Travels (1941)—process shots for cars and boxcars.

The Palm Beach Story (1942)—process shots of the background as seen through an office window.

Star Spangled Rhythm (1942)—the boat rail for the Navy landing scene.

I Married a Witch (1942)—process shots involving, among other things, a flying taxi.

Double Indemnity (1944)—the sedan process shots.

Action Report (US Navy, 1945)—The studio often lent its facilities to the military during World War II. This Navy Department film, perhaps now lost or buried in a government archive, was never shown to the public, and because it came out so late in the conflict, was possibly never seen by the audience it was produced for, either. Apparently, the entire film, not just its process shots, was produced on this stage.

The Perils of Pauline (1947)—The carriage process scenes were shot here, with a horse on a treadmill in the foreground.

Welcome Stranger (1947)—Pullman car, and the McRory family car process shots.

The Emperor Waltz (1948)—process shots of the Tyrolean highway.

The Heiress (1948)—process shots.

Song of Surrender (1949)—process shots for hansom cab.

My Friend Irma Goes West (1950)— The call sheets for this early Dean Martin / Jerry Lewis vehicle list Stage 2 as being used for "dream room and train platform" scenes.

September Affair (1950)—Naples cafe/tavern process shots.

Son of Paleface (1951)—process shots.

Ace in the Hole (1951)—process shots from car windows.

When Worlds Collide (1951)—process shots involving cars, planes, and helicopters.

Road to Bali (1952)—process shots.

The Stars Are Singing (1953)—Washington, DC, phone-booth process shots.

The Naked Jungle (1954)—dugout for Leiningen (Charlton Heston) and the deserted Indian village scenes.

Secret of the Incas (1954)—process shots and the El Prado cafe set. Charlton Heston is costumed in this film *exactly* like Indiana Jones. Did Steven Spielberg see this one as a child?

Rear Window (1954)—process shots taken in Jeff's apartment and phone booth.

That Certain Feeling (1954)—taxi and limo process shots.

The Seven Little Foys (1955)—process shots.

The Trouble with Harry (1955)— undetermined sequences.

You're Never Too Young (1955)—car process shots for Dean Martin and Jerry Lewis's fourteenth film together.

The Rose Tattoo (1955)—process shots for sailboat.

Strategic Air Command (1955)— Dutch's (James Stewart) office.

The Desperate Hours (1955)—Walling family attic for process shots; the rest of the house was built on Stages 7 and 8.

That Certain Feeling (1956)—undetermined sequences.

The Delicate Delinquent (1956)— assorted scenes for Jerry Lewis's first film *without* Dean Martin.

The Man Who Knew Too Much (1956)—process shots involving the marketplace and a taxi.

Rock-a-Bye Baby (1957)—assorted.

The Sad Sack (1957)—the rifle range set and process shots for scenes in a station wagon.

Vertigo (1957)—rooftop gap.

The Joker Is Wild (1957)—assorted.

Funny Face (1957)—process shots for taxi interiors.

The Geisha Boy (1958)—process shots for police-car interiors.

Houseboat (1958)—process shots for convertible interiors.

King Creole (1958)—process shots for the boat and taxi interiors.

The Rat Race (1960)—process shots from inside of bus.

One-Eyed Jacks (1961)—undetermined sequences.

The Pleasure of His Company (1961)—undetermined sequences.

The Misfits (UA, 1961)—The process shots involving Gay's (Clark Gable) truck and Roslyn's (Marilyn Monroe) station wagon were shot here between October 24, and November 2, 1960. Gable died two weeks later. This was the last completed film for Monroe as well.

Blue Hawaii (1961)—process shots of road and pineapple fields.

The Man Who Shot Liberty Valance (1962)—process shots for stagecoaches and train interiors.

Hatari (1962)—"animal herding car" process shots.

Love with the Proper Stranger (1963)—assorted.

McLintock! (1963)—open countryside process shots.

Donovan's Reef (1963)—speedboat process shots.

Who's Been Sleeping in My Bed? (1963)—assorted.

Who's Minding the Store? (1963)—assorted.

It's a Mad, Mad, Mad, Mad World (UA, 1963)—Process and special-effects shots for this all-star comedy were created here. Perhaps significantly, considering the title, the film was released almost simultaneously with John F. Kennedy's assassination.

The Disorderly Orderly (1964)—undetermined sequences.

The Carpetbaggers (1964)—pilot's cockpit.

Paradise, Hawaiian Style (1966)—process shots for cable car and helicopter scenes.

Rosemary's Baby (1968)—unknown sequences.

The Molly Maguires (1968)—assorted.

Paint Your Wagon (1969)—ten shooting days on the lot, probably effects sequences; the film mostly shot in Oregon.

The Sterile Cuckoo (1969)—assorted.

Brothers (TV, 1984–1989)—main sets on this stage.

Vampire in Brooklyn (1995)—assorted.

The Truman Show (1996)—assorted.

Roswell (TV, 1999–2002)—Crashdown Cafe.

Growing Up Brady (TV, 2000)—Stage 2 here plays Stage 5, where the original Brady house interiors had been constructed.

Resurrection Blvd. (TV, 2000–2002)—assorted.

Nip/Tuck (TV, 2003–2010)—assorted.

Rizzoli & Isles (TV, 2010–2016)—assorted.

Happy Endings (TV, 2011–2013)—assorted.

10 SPECIAL PHOTO STAGE (1922)

The special photo stage was originally called Stage 3. It was often used for special photographic effects, trick shots, stunts, and miniature work. The building cost $61,480.54 to construct in 1922.

There are very few specific titles associated with this stage, and many assigned to it are incorrect because the current Stage 3, designated as such in 1968, is an entirely different building.

This Stage 3 was widely used for miniature and trick shots by the special-effects department. For example, this is the stage where the whiskey glass point-of-view special-effects sequences for *The Lost Weekend* (1945) were shot. It is where trick shots from *Dr. Cyclops* (1940) and *The Mountain* (1956) were completed. It is where train-wreck miniatures for *The Greatest Show on Earth* (1952), killer ant inserts in *The Naked Jungle* (1954), and alien vistas for *When Worlds Collide* (1951) and *The Conquest of Space* (1955) were composited. It is where a single shot of James Stewart falling into a mattress for the climax of *Rear Window* (1954), and the "Colossus of Seti" model for *The Ten Commandments* (1956), were recorded, as well.

Aptly enough, in 1968 this building was leased by the Howard A. Anderson special-effects company. (Anderson's story is told in section 24, Special Effects.)

In 1987, the building was adapted into the wardrobe department and rechristened the "Head Building," after Edith Head, a designation which it retains today, although the wardrobe department is no longer there, it is still largely used for costume storage.

‖ CAMERA DEPARTMENT

In the 1960s, the camera departments at the major studios were not really what they had been in the past. From 1921 on, those studios had owned Mitchell 35mm motion picture cameras and equipment. The cameras were durable and versatile, and unlike the earlier wooden boxes, which were once called film cameras, they were made of metal. At first, individual cameramen owned their own cameras, and Paramount would rent both the equipment and its owner contractually. Eventually the studio purchased or contracted the cameras and cameramen and accessories and maintained them in-house, in vast, well-stocked buildings like this one.

In the 1950s, as outsourcing became the norm at studios, Paramount started renting cameras from outside companies, like the German manufacturer Arri, and, starting in 1953, a Los Angeles company, Panavision. Today most cameras on Hollywood film sets, including digital ones, are from Panavision.

Eventually Paramount started using their in-house camera departments only as brokers for these outside companies, and as a place to store camera accessories, and, until recently, raw stock. In fact, in 1968, this building, built in 1931, and the camera department, then managed by one A. C. Winchester, was basically a place on-lot to store film and equipment. In 2006, a studio newsletter described how another department head, Rudy Pahoyo, would let guests on the studio tour "paw through empty film cans and select one from a show they particularly liked. 'People love anything Hollywood,'" said Rudy.[10]

LEFT and ABOVE: The Paramount camera department understandably liked to position its equipment next to the studio's lending ladies. Here Kay Johnson and Mae West effect near identical poses in the same year, 1934.

A dramatic view of the lot looking north up what was then Avenue B, and today is known as Avenue P. Stage 4, then and now, is on the right, 1953.

12 STAGE 4 (1918)

WIDTH: 195 feet, 3 inches

LENGTH: 70 feet, 10 inches

HEIGHT: 26 feet

SQUARE FEET: 13,830

Stage 4 was originally designated as Stage 7. It was converted for sound production in 1929–1930. The building contains four pits located under the floor. The largest one, 13.5 by 13.5 feet, is 7 feet deep; the three smaller ones are 11.5 by 11.5 feet, and are 9 feet deep. What the pits were first excavated for, and when, is unknown.

Shot on Stage 4:

Morocco (1930)—also shot at the Warner Ranch and the Guadalupe sand dunes.

Union Pacific (1939)—assorted.

The Way of All Flesh (1940)—the Kriza home, Europa Cafe interiors, and Joe's Place.

The Glass Key (1942)—Nick's (Joseph Calleia) office.

I Married a Witch (1942)—Fredric March and Veronica Lake's homes were constructed here. The atmosphere on the stage was apparently not harmonious. A call sheet for April 29, 1942, written by a concerned assistant director, mentions that "Miss Lake took two and a half hours for lunch and a change of hairdresser. Company closed at 6:15 due to Miss Lake walking off set and refusing to do one more shot, which would have killed set except for inserts."

The Palm Beach Story (1942)—department-store settings.

The Uninvited (1944)—lower and upper halls of the old house.

The Blue Dahlia (1946)—the Blue Dahlia's office.

Welcome Stranger (1947)—town meeting room.

A Foreign Affair (1948)—process shots involving an airplane and a town car.

Samson and Delilah (1949)—Tubal's house; Tubal was played by William Farnum, brother of Dustin Farnum, who DeMille had cast in *The Squaw Man* back in Hollywood's prehistory.

Song of Surrender (1949)—museum interiors, lodge, and Hunt house.

A Place in the Sun (1950)—assorted.

Union Station (1950)—railroad station and police headquarters sets.

Dark City (1950)—Union Station scenes.

Detective Story (1951)—assorted.

When Worlds Collide (1951)—clinic, underground offices, some rocket interiors.

Son of Paleface (1951)—assorted.

My Favorite Spy (1951)—interior of villa.

Road to Bali (1952)—assorted.

The War of the Worlds (1953)—"burned field."

Houdini (1953)—Houdini's death scene on a Detroit stage was lensed here.

The Caddy (1953)—assorted.

The Stars Are Singing (1953)—bedroom sets.

September Affair (1954)—living room and tavern sets.

That Certain Feeling (1954)—Norman's (pre–*Leave It to Beaver* Jerry Mathers) room, the TV studio, and offices of the senator, psychiatrist, and cartoonist Al Capp, who filmed a cameo here as himself.

The Seven Little Foys (1955) —assorted.

You're Never Too Young (1955) —assorted.

Strategic Air Command (1955)— plate of an "[aircraft's] nose going into a snowbank."

The Man Who Knew Too Much (1956)—Hitchcock filmed the ambassador's study and some London street scenes here.

Desire Under the Elms (1957) —assorted.

Rock-a-bye Baby (1957)—assorted.

The Joker Is Wild (1957)—assorted nightclub settings.

King Creole (1958)—home of Danny (Elvis Presley, in one of his best roles), and also Maxie's (Walter Matthau) apartment set.

Alias Jesse James (UA, 1959)— Duchess Room.

The Rat Race (1960)—Crystal Garden and rehearsal hall.

Visit to a Small Planet (1960)— "Hungry Brain."

The Errand Boy (1961)—Jerry Lewis is seen cavorting about both inside and in front of the stage.

Come Blow Your Horn (1963) —assorted.

Papa's Delicate Condition (1963) —assorted.

Who's Been Sleeping in My Bed? (1963) —assorted.

Who's Minding the Store? (1963) —assorted.

The Carpetbaggers (1964)—The movie set for a cowboy film was created here on an actual movie set.

Seven Days in May (1964)—assorted.

Where Love Has Gone (1964)—Mrs. Hayden's (Bette Davis) house.

The Patsy (1964)—assorted.

El Dorado (1966)—Maudie's place, and barn.

Nevada Smith (1966)—assorted.

Star Spangled Girl (1971)—Tests were shot here on February 25, 1971, for the purposes of casting. John Ritter, Tim McIntyre, and Stanley Kamel read for the role of Andy, although Tony Roberts ultimately played the part. Sandy Duncan, Lesley Ann Warren, and Jennifer O'Neill read for Sue, the role Duncan would play in the film.

The Last Tycoon (1975)—assorted.

Black Sunday (1977)—assorted.

Washington: Behind Closed Doors (TV, 1977)—For this fictionalized miniseries based on John Ehrlichman's book, a very detailed re-creation of the Oval Office was created here, which was retained and reused several times again over the next few years for projects like *The President's Mistress* (TV, 1978) and *Backstairs at the White House* (TV, 1979).

The Colbys (TV 1985–1987) —assorted.

Coming to America (1988)— assorted; also shot in New York and Simi Valley, California.

The Presidio (1988)—assorted.

Star Trek V: The Final Frontier (1989)—unknown.

Wayne's World (1992)—assorted.

Star Trek: Deep Space Nine (1993–1999)—interiors, living quarters, etc.

Roswell (TV 1999–2002)—assorted.

Andy Richter Controls the Universe (TV 2002–2003)—set for Andy's apartment.

Nip/Tuck (TV 2003–2010)—assorted.

Rizzoli & Isles (2010–2016) —assorted.

Bent (2012–2013)—assorted.

Veep (2012–   )—Camp David sequences, among others.

13 STUDIO HOSPITAL

First Aid as it looked in the 1980s. It looks very much like this today.

The studio hospital has always been adjacent to the security building and beneath the property department. Everything from bruised egos to broken bones were, and are, treated here on a daily basis. The department was founded at the Selma-Vine lot in April 1925 by Dr. Hugh J. Strathearn. In 1945, Dr. Strathearn estimated that his department was treating 20,000 patients a year.

Although the first-aid department no longer has a doctor on staff, fifteen registered nurses are on-site to this day, all of them still working out of the oldest studio hospital in Los Angeles.

The building, built in 1926, was used as a set in *Skippy* (1931), where Jackie Cooper takes a dose of castor oil from a nurse, and in *Top Gun* (1986), where it served as the back of Kelly McGillis's home.

The security department goes back to the earliest days of the studio, although, according to veteran security officer Fritz Hawkes, during the Roosevelt administration, "we were paid by petty cash vouchers, and they didn't keep any records at that time." Security work was on an as-needed basis. Again according to Hawkes, "[I]n those days, they didn't call you. You went and sat on the curb to get a job. Then when the unions got in, they started calling."[11] Hawkes, who celebrated his fiftieth year at the studio in 1983, was still on the lot, giving tours and working special projects, when he passed away in 1986.

Hawkes's boss in those salad days was Chief W. F. "Bill" Combs, who came to Paramount in 1936 after six years as house detective at the Ambassador Hotel in downtown Los Angeles.

Today Louis Lam is the executive director of security services at Paramount. Modern security concerns are about the same as Combs and his fellow officers faced in previous decades, "crowd control, potential stalking of celebrities, workplace violence, break-ins, and a new threat, terrorism."[12] To meet these demands, the department is a mix of in-house and contracted guard staff. The studio has also installed two hundred video-surveillance cameras across the lot. In addition, his department now deals with issues of potential film piracy.

The department, for decades located behind the first-aid department and alongside the powerhouse in the (Ray) Milland Building, was, in 2002, moved between Stages 11 and 12, and then out to Melrose Avenue adjacent to the (current) Stage 19. It shares real estate with the environmental health and safety department, the fire department, and the studio tour office, and is where all security clearances and lot passes are now issued from.

The building in which the security department is now located, not originally part of the lot, is the former home of KHJ and later KCAL television, which also leased Stage 21. Capitol Records at one time owned the building, as well.

LEFT: A member of the Paramount security department staff, pensive and unidentified, at the Bronson Gate. ABOVE: Also a studio sergeant's and an employee ID badges, circa 1930s.

15 POWERHOUSE

The studio powerhouse was not a replacement for electricity supplied by the city, but rather a supplement to those outside electrical sources. In 1945 it was reported that Paramount's electrical needs were approximately that of a city with a population of 20,000. Power was supplied at 44,000 volts by multiple Westinghouse DC power generators. The electrical requirements of a studio, especially after the advent of Technicolor after 1935, proved to be so massive that transformers, often hidden in underground vaults, were required to fulfill the DC requirements of production needs. And then, as now, outside crystal sync generators were required to boost the amperage available on the soundstages and factories. The powerhouse also supplied AC current to offices and departments.

As recently as the 1990s there were still four electrical substations on the lot. Today, none remain. The main one, next to the security department, has been repurposed—first, as a dance rehearsal hall for *Glee* (TV, 2009–2015), and later, as a conference room for television writers, although the massive ventilation output shafts from the building's previous life are still on the roof.

Paramount now gets all of its electricity from the city.

16 GRIP/LIGHTING DEPARTMENT

For most of the studio era, studios built their own lighting and electrical equipment. Likewise, "grip" equipment, used for rigging this gear, seemingly took its name from an archaic circus term for the stagehands and their tools during that pre-film era.

Equipment designed in-house tended to be heavy, cumbersome, and idiosyncratic. It was not practical for location shooting, seeing that a soundstage or a backlot was initially as far as it would need to be transported. This equipment also did not work well with similar machinery designed at other studios. The result was that a Paramount light stand only worked well with Paramount lights.

A 1929 study of one of several electrical substations once located on the lot. This particular building, if not the equipment inside, still stands today.

In 1927 a company named Mole-Richardson started manufacturing equipment designed specifically for film lighting. This equipment, practical, somewhat portable, and interchangeable, revolutionized life for technicians on the dark side of those glowing Fresnel lenses. Yet studios during this era were so insular that it took years for the wizards in the grip/lighting department to adapt their own lights, electrical equipment, and camera dollies to work according to the Mole-Richardson standard. There seemed to be little reason to change what had worked so faithfully for generations.

In 1968 Paramount let one of their grip department staffers, Ed Phillips, have access to a basement full of old lighting equipment, which he picked through, bought, and then refurbished into the first commercially available lightweight, 225-amp DC brute arc—in other words, the orig-

inal portable location light—which he ultimately sold back to Paramount. Phillips later created a company called Cinemobile Systems, along with cameraman Fouad Said and producer Sheldon Leonard, which built buses to carry this lightweight equipment, as well as mobile sound gear, smaller generators, and portable Arri cameras, instead of the Mitchell behemoths the studios had been using for decades.

Obviously an improvement, these renovations made location shooting easier, and tended to break down the walls between the studios even further. Suddenly a Paramount set only differed from a Warner Bros. set, or a set in England, because of the geography of their locations. Hollywood had somehow suddenly gotten larger. Or smaller.

The grip/lighting department actually consisted of half a dozen smaller departments housed in and around a massive complex near the studio's eastern wall, originally called the machine shop. It remains the set lighting and grip building even today. Photo circa 1933.

The Van Ness Gate, seen here in 1968, was, and is, primarily a heavy industry and employee entrance.

17 VAN NESS GATE

The Van Ness Gate, which was installed shortly after World War II, was, and is, primarily a studio truck entrance which leads into the heavy industry end of the studio, serving as the primary outside-access point for the grip, set lighting, and assorted construction departments.

18 LEMON GROVE GATE

This tiny, isolated, and easy-to-miss studio entrance and guardhouse also once housed the time office, which after 1939 tabulated the hours employees worked. In 1946 Paramount got the permission of the city to incorporate this part of Lemon Grove, the tiny street that the gate fed into, into the studio lot itself.

This Lemon Grove guardhouse was originally next to the transportation department, as it is today, but in the 1960s that department had been awkwardly shuffled to the other side of the lot, to its RKO equivalent, thus making the Lemon Grove Gate even more isolated than it already was.

Because of its lonely demeanor, the Lemon Grove Gate has long been reported by skittish security guards as being haunted. The gate is the closest entrance to the cemetery next door. According to author Troy Taylor in his book *Bloody Hollywood*, the most common type of spectral appearances here involve security personnel, always alone, and always at night, seeing figures moving through the studio wall and into the cemetery. To this day, many security personnel are nervous about taking this assignment in the lonely hours after sundown.

This gate, like all studio gates at every studio, has itself been in the

The lonely, and possibly haunted, Lemon Grove gate, as seen from inside the lot, 2016.

movies. *The Space Children* (1958) is a good example. The Lemon Grove Gate was the unlikely inspiration for the title of *The Lemon Grove Kids Meet the Monsters* (Morgan-Steckler Productions, 1965), a dubious tribute indeed. In the 1990s, an executive car wash was located south of the gate. In 1992, the 1,200-car Lemon Grove parking lot opened across the street.

The Lemon Grove Gate is still reported as being very lonely late at night.

19 STILL DEPARTMENT

Ernest Bachrach was Paramount's earliest designated still photographer. He started with Famous Players in New York at the Astoria Studio, and would eventually land in Hollywood, beginning next door, at RKO. Donald Biddle Keyes followed after Bachrach. It was Keyes who suggested that Paramount establish Hollywood's first designated still portrait department, in 1922, an idea which all of the other studios quickly copied. Keyes personally shot images for Lasky's big films of the era, like The Sheik (1921) and *The Ten Commandments* (1923).

Eugene Robert Richee, who had been with the studio even before Bachrach, and had previously worked for Keyes, became the studio's department head and chief glamour photographer in 1925. Richee is somewhat renowned today as the photographer who made Marlene Dietrich look like a blonde goddess in still pictures, while Joseph von Sternberg was doing the same thing in her movies. Richee also shot iconic poses of Mae West, Louise Brooks, Anna May Wong, Veronica Lake, and Gary Cooper. But at the time he was working his magic, still photography, especially still photography of movie stars, was considered even

ABOVE: Audrey Hepburn enters the still department in its original location across from the dressing room building. The Spanish crest on the wall is still visible there today, 1954. ABOVE RIGHT: A modern shot of the same building. RIGHT: The Paramount still department's job was to publicize stars as individuals, and occasionally in groups, such as here, for *Career*. Pictured, somewhat uncomfortably, are Dean Martin, Shirley MacLaine, Anthony Franciosa, Carolyn Jones and Joan Blackman, 1959.

less artistically acceptable than photographing movie stars in movies. After Richee left in 1941, A. L. "Whitey" Schafer took his job. Schafer was killed in a boating accident in 1951. Other noted Paramount still photographers included William Walling, Don English, Robert Coburn, and Otto Dyer.

For much of the studio era the still department was located in the southern part of the lot, in the still department and gallery building, which in the 1960s was known as the test stage building and Stage 3 (see #34). On June 3, 1957, the still department passed into private management and became Still Photo Lab, Inc. Its office was moved to this northeast corner of the lot so that it could accept business from outside. Bill Fraker, who had replaced Schafer, continued as manager until the 1980s, when the department was closed down.

20 STAGE 17 (1941)

WIDTH:	186 feet, 4 inches
LENGTH:	68 feet
HEIGHT:	36 feet
SQUARE FEET:	12,670

Stage 17 has been occupied over the years by dinosaurs, ghosts, aliens, and Elvis Presley.

This stage was built in 1941 at a reported cost of $115,010.49, although it seems to be basically the same building, in the same spot, as Stage 6, which stood there originally. It has an 11-foot-deep pit in the floor which measures 22 feet by 23 feet, covered with a removable hatch.

Every stage on the lot has colorful stories associated with it, although when quizzed about these happenings, many employees can never remember exactly which stages these happenings occurred in. Most old-timers seem to agree, however, that Elvis Presley drove a Cadillac through the open doors of this stage after having a few too many drinks during a nearby recording session. Whether it was Elvis himself who drove the Cadillac out again has not been recorded. All that is known for certain is that there is no Cadillac in Stage 17 today.

Another story that can be pinned to this specific stage involves comedian Redd Foxx, who, while shooting an episode of *The Royal Family* (TV, 1991–1992) here on October 11, 1991, suffered a fatal heart attack. When Foxx clutched his chest many on the stage thought he was re-creating a beloved bit from his earlier series, *Sanford and Son* (TV, 1972–1977), and so did not rush to his aid as quickly as they could have. Foxx's ghost is said to haunt the stage, although if this is true, the raucous comic's specter has been very well-behaved in recent years. Actually, Foxx died at Hollywood Presbyterian Medical Center, almost four hours after the attack, so maybe that explains his beneficence.

Shot on Stage 17:

The Lost World (First National, 1925)—shot on the original Stage 6; groundbreaking special effects were by Willis O'Brien, who later shot much of *King Kong* (RKO, 1933) on the same lot.

The Glass Key (1942)—Veronica Lake's place.

Holiday Inn (1942)—flower shop.

The Uninvited (1944)—haunted house interiors, including the nursery.

Road to Rio (1947)—assorted.

The Perils of Pauline (1947)—interiors of the costume workroom and movie theater lobby.

The Big Clock (1948)—ninth floor of office and antiques shop sets.

The Emperor Waltz (1948)—the emperor's anteroom and stable.

Song of Surrender (1949)—Deacon Parry's parlor.

Let's Dance (1950)—airline hangar office.

Ace in the Hole (1951)—newspaper office.

Houdini (1953)—the Tower of London jail cell Houdini escapes from.

The War of the Worlds (1953)—farmhouse, gully, and dirt road.

Secret of the Incas (1954)—museum and the Hotel de Turistas.

The Conquest of Space (1955)—"wheel spaceship."

Bonanza (TV, 1959–1973)—Assorted Virginia City interiors were built on this stage, until 1970, when the Cartwright family rode off to Warner Bros. Among the sets here were the interior of the evocatively named Bucket of Blood Saloon, the Silver Dollar Saloon, both floors of the Virginia City Hotel, the International House Hotel, the Virginia City Opera House, the courthouse, the church, the bank, the doctor's office, and the *Territorial Enterprise* newspaper office.

One-Eyed Jacks (1961)—assorted.

The Guns of Will Sonnett (TV, 1967–1969)—primary stage.

Mannix (TV, 1967–1975)—The exterior of Joe Mannix's office was on the European Street backlot, while the interior was here, on Stage 17.

Mommie Dearest (1981)—assorted.

Nero Wolfe (TV, 1981)—set for the short-lived, well-cast, detective series.

The Powers of Matthew Star (TV, 1982–1983)—assorted.

Clue (1985)—attic and cellar of the house.

MacGyver (TV, 1985–1992) —assorted.

Black Rain (1989)—assorted sets for this Japan-set thriller.

Dad (Universal, 1989)—assorted sets for this film, where Kevin Spacey met Jack Lemmon, who would become Spacey's mentor and friend.

Harlem Nights (1989)—Eddie Murphy shot scenes here with his idol, Redd Foxx, who would later die inside this stage.

Star Trek V: The Final Frontier (1989)—assorted.

Days of Thunder (1990)—assorted.

Bonfire of the Vanities (Warner Bros., 1990)—This is a good example of a film set in New York, which few would imagine was actually shot, in part, in Hollywood.

Ghost (1990)—see above.

Frankie and Johnny (1991)—see above; also shot at Raleigh Studios across the street.

The Addams Family (1991) —assorted.

The Royal Family (TV, 1991–1992)— primary setting.

Wayne's World (1992)—assorted.

Indecent Proposal (1993)—assorted.

Star Trek: Deep Space Nine (TV, 1993–1999)—assorted.

Angel (TV, 1999–2004)—assorted.

Everybody Hates Chris (TV, 2005– 2009)—assorted.

Star Trek (2009)—assorted.

Larry Crowne (Universal, 2011) —assorted.

The Girl with the Dragon Tattoo (Columbia/MGM, 2011)—assorted.

Happy Endings (TV, 2011–2013) —assorted.

American Horror Story (TV, 2011–)—assorted.

Veep (2012–)—assorted.

21 PROPERTY BUILDING

The so-called property building was, in fact, not a building at all, but rather one-third of the complex constructed in 1941 over an original freestanding property department, built in 1929. This "new" complex also included Stages 17 and 18 and the powerhouse. The studio hospital was also in the southwest corner, but was a separate structure with a narrow walkway between its outer wall and Stage 17.

Oliver Stratton was the department head in the 1930s and '40s when props were stored, before this building's construction, mostly to the north, in the crafts buildings. By the 1960s, the property department building and its annexes contained some 200,000 feet of floor space, which encompassed anything that could be seen and photographed

Inexplicable, and somehow familiar, property department assets, 1968.

on a set, from furniture and bric-a-brac to curtains and rugs, which had their own department.

During this era the department was managed by one Gordon Cole. Interestingly, a character named "Gordon Cole" (played by beefy character actor Bert Moorhouse) was the man in the property department in *Sunset Boulevard*, who tried to rent Norma Desmond's auto (a 1929 Isotta Fraschini touring car). Possibly not a coincidence?

Yet the story gets even stranger: Years later, in the TV series *Twin Peaks* (1990–1991), series creator David Lynch played FBI director "Gordon Cole," possibly, again, not a coincidence, as Lynch has admitted to being an admirer of Billy Wilder's film. In fact, Lynch's *Mulholland Dr.* (Universal, 2001), which included Paramount and the Bronson Gate as locations, also incorporates several echoes of *Sunset Boulevard* in its story—notably, similar themes and settings, titles taken from Los Angeles streets, and even an ingenue character named Betty. The film also included another character named "Selwyn," perhaps an echo of Goldwyn's long-forgotten partners? Sadly, no one named Gordon Cole makes an appearance in *Mulholland Dr.*

As depicted in *Sunset Boulevard*, whenever possible, the studio tried to avoid building props from scratch, and often attempted to rent items from individuals or from other studios that had made movies with similar property needs. For DeMille's *The Buccaneer* (1938), the studio rented ships which had been used by MGM for *Mutiny on the Bounty* (1935), and years later used salvaged sets and props from Twentieth Century Fox's *The Egyptian* (1954) for *The Ten Commandments* (1956). According to a studio memo, Gordon Cole, trying to find six lion skins for *The Buster Keaton Story* (1957), inquired if he could borrow them from DeMille, who presumably had a personal collection of such pelts. DeMille's response has not been preserved.

In 1968, due to the Desilu buyout, there were suddenly additional property storage buildings on the RKO side of the lot in which to store inventory. But there were also suddenly millions of new pieces to manage as well. As neither studio

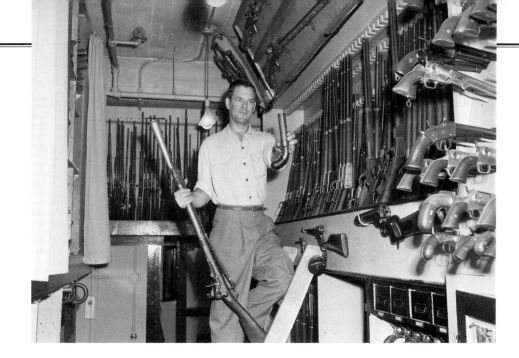

James E. Stembridge, manager of weaponry, shows off some of his lethal inventory, 1957.

had ever maintained even a partial inventory of their own department's holdings, it was impossible to even begin to inventory all of the items which the studio found itself in possession of during this era. Consequently, Paramount suddenly found itself flooded with new heavy tables and hot-dog stands and plastic fruit bowls and golden calves and fishermen's nets—all in addition to whatever they already had on hand. One solution was to temporarily close down the RKO (Gower) Mill while they tried to figure out what to do with all of the often-redundant and, truth be told, increasingly unused items. This mill was itself a redundancy, as the Paramount Mill was located just a few studio blocks away.

Ultimately, many of these props were sold off or simply thrown out or destroyed. Some of these pieces were actual antiques, and some were reconstructions, but no thought was given to an item's value or origin. At the time, few items were saved because of their association with specific movies. This unfortunate policy became even more predominant as fewer period films—for which most of the items had been collected—tended to be made on-lot in the 1970s and '80s. Even fewer are shot in California today.

In the 1970s actor Robert Reed, who was shooting both *Mannix* and *The*

Brady Bunch on the lot, often had to race back and forth between the stages to jockey from one set to another. He started using golf carts for that purpose (and later, for other purposes). Reed remembered that "the guards all knew us and were very indulgent, until one night we took the studio golf carts and raced around the lot. And I remember we drove down under one of the sets into an area that was used for prop storage. I mean, you could just drive down there and—well, I *still*, to this day, have things up in my storeroom that I stole from there. In fact, there was a memo that came out the next day about stealing on the lot. I think they knew who did it."[13]

Props were stored all over the lot, in basements and subbasements, in cellars and alcoves and catacombs, and even in the rafters above the buildings. Bill Warren, a writer and historian, remembers that just after the Desilu sale the studio was so little interested in these materials that he and Forrest J. Ackerman, editor of *Famous Monsters of Filmland* magazine, were given permission by Paramount to go into the basements and salvage anything they could find! Warren, Ackerman, and a couple of other fans eventually crawled down into a basement beneath a soundstage that Warren remembers was then being used by *Star Trek*. "It was just a big concrete-floored cellar," he recalled, "nothing unusual about it."

What was unusual was that it was filled to the dark rafters with discarded props, which, as Warren recalls, "made it fascinating and mysterious." Among the items they found that day were several priceless models from *King Kong* (1933), "including a brontosaurus, both the big one and a smaller, spring-mounted one on wheels for the water scene; there was also a big, impressive styracosaur animation model, and maybe one or two more. The rubber was crumbling; in that sense, they were fragile, but the steel armatures were sturdy and rust-free. Several went to my trunk, so for a long time after that my trunk was lined with crumbled Kong rubber."

Warren remembers that they also took several of the gas bombs used to subdue Kong in the movie, as well as a "huge, somewhat crude cutout of Mighty Joe Young, some of the Joe Young 'big money for the big monkey' coins, and the mounted human heads from *The Most Dangerous Game*. We told the gate guard what we had and he waved us through. Never heard a word from Paramount again, as far as I know."[14] Many of these now-priceless lost-and-found props were much later sold to director Peter Jackson for an "undisclosed amount."

These items seem to have come out of the RKO special effects prop department building, which now stands approximately where the Rodenberry building is now. Eugene Hilchey, a special effects prop maker, also recovered an actual Kong armature (Skelton), which later (in 2009) sold at auction for $200,000.

Astonishingly, some artifacts were still there in these dank basements even into the 1980s. Director Joe Dante remembers that "in 1985 I was doing a picture at Paramount and they were cleaning out the caverns underneath the studio. Apparently there was a lot of stuff they kept there and the dumpsters were just full of props and stuff."[15]

Exploring these basements even while those dumpsters were being filled up all around him, Dante found a true treasure: a balsa-wood "Rosebud" sled from *Citizen Kane* (RKO, 1941), which, fortunately, he rescued from destruction.

Film historian Leonard Maltin, working on the lot for *Entertainment Tonight*, shared similar memories.

[I remember] exploring these basements and dumpster-diving for old props and finding strange things like a gypsy tambourine and a medieval nose guard for a horse! Someone working for the studio tried to stop us and actually told me that "just because it's in a dumpster doesn't mean we're throwing it out!" A friend of mine working on Bob Newhart's TV show found a line-budget report for DeMille's *The Plainsman!* I also discovered some RKO blueprints, which I later donated to the Motion Picture Academy. I noticed that some of these things also were aviation-related, like safe-conduct passes dropped as leaflets over Korea! Maybe these items came out of Howard Hughes's interest in aviation. Maybe they were props as well.[16]

A dark and intriguing corner of the
Paramount property department, circa
1980.

In the late 1990s, as part of Paramount's focus on making the studio a rental lot, the company further diminished, and then phased out entirely, the property department. The RKO buildings again became the Gower Mill, and their main property building became the (Mae) West building. Maltin, whose office was in this building, recalls that he always wanted to have business cards printed with this building's name on it and the words *Come up and see me sometime.*

In 1990, historian Marc Wanamaker was brought in officially by the company to inventory and evaluate important antiques from Paramount's vast inventory for an orderly dispensation, certainly a respectful alternative to the scavenger hunts and dumpster dives of previous decades. Today the old Paramount property building, still sandwiched between two stages, is simply known as Building 213, and contains storage and offices. Props for current projects are still stored on-lot, but in no particular place. The hallways in the old building are adorned with photographs of the old, vanished, Paramount property department.

22 STAGE 18 (1941)

WIDTH: 185 feet, 5 inches

LENGTH: 99 feet

HEIGHT: 40 feet

SQUARE FEET: 18,356

What would become Stage 18 was originally a carpentry shop. For years the stage was known as the "DeMille Stage," presumably because C. B. had shot his early spectacles inside its vast expanses. Actually, the building was not even constructed until 1941, at a cost of $200,061.92, making it, along with its sisters, Stage 17 (built at the same time) and Stage 16, to the north, one of the three "newest" stages on the property. The reason the stage is associated with DeMille is probably due to Billy Wilder's *Sunset Boulevard*, which depicted DeMille directing *Samson and Delilah* (1949) on the stage. Actually, although the outside of the stage in the movie *is* Stage 18, the interiors were shot on the other side of the street, in Stage 5. When *Sunset Boulevard* wrapped, the studio did hold a clambake on Stage 18 for the cast and crew, however.

More recently the stage has been known as the "*Star Trek* Stage." Although several *Trek* projects, particularly feature films, have been shot in the space, this probably owes more to the fact that many employees have long been aware of the legend of a basement under the stage's vast Masonite floor where thousands of square feet of twenty-third-century *Trek* props are stored. The rumor, apparently, is partially true. Originally *Star Trek*, in all its big- and little-screen incarnations, stored their props in a warehouse in Burbank. But occasionally some of these items, occasionally, would be transferred here, to the basement under the stage, which had already been used for both production and production storage in past decades. In fact the basement had often been referred to by awed employees as the "gold room," because of the valuable, (and non-*Trek* related) antiques stored there.

According to a 1964 press release—always the most reliable fountain of indisputable information in Hollywood—Stage 18 has also long been known as "Old Bloody Mary," due to the countless acts of cinematic mayhem committed within its padded walls. Supposedly the first (on-screen) murder perpetuated on the site involved actor Emil Jannings, in a film whose title (if not its legacy on the stage) is now forgotten.

"Old Bloody Mary" now includes an elevated sound/control booth utilized for the taping of television shows.

Shot on Stage 18:

The Glass Key (1942)—cemetery set, and Richard Denning's apartment set.

My Favorite Blonde (1942)—For a single gag in this Bob Hope vehicle, a penguin, and his trainer, had to be hired for the day. Their big scene was shot here on Stage 18.

Star Spangled Rhythm (1942)—The Bob Hope–Jerry Colonna scene was shot here. Like many of the stars in this film, the actors donated their time for the war effort.

Double Indemnity (1944)—The Hollywood Bowl set scenes were faked here.

Going My Way (1944)—Most of the rectory interiors and the exterior garden scenes for the church were shot here.

The Lost Weekend (1945)—While the pawnshop sequence was shot on this stage, most of the film was shot in New York—very unusual for the time.

Variety Girl (1947)—assorted.

Road to Rio (1947)—assorted.

The Emperor Waltz (1948)—The ballroom and the balcony were built here.

Sorrowful Jones (1949)—police office, phone booth, stables, and tack room, etc.

Song of Surrender (1949)—assorted scenes, including the park and museum entrance sets.

September Affair (1950)—villa and concert hall sequences.

Sunset Boulevard (1950)—Exteriors only were shot here (DeMille hugs Norma in the doorway); the interior was shot on Stage 5.

My Friend Irma Goes West (1950)—TV station, and Santa Rosa Mission Hotel.

Let's Dance (1950)—Serena's (Lucille Watson) New York apartment.

My Favorite Spy (1951)—hotel lobby and Blue Aisette Hotel.

The Greatest Show on Earth (1952)—Florida circus office where Charlton Heston pleads his case for a full season.

Lucy Gallant (1953)—assorted.

Shane (1953)—assorted.

The Stars Are Singing (1953)—The dock set "yellow screen" shots were taken here. Yellow screen was a sodium vapor matte process used for opticals.

Houdini (1953)—Schultz's Dime Museum, Coney Island, and the Berlin courtroom scenes.

The War of the Worlds (1953)—"Everything was done on Stage 18," recalled Ann Robinson, the star of the movie.[17] This is almost true. Several other stages were also utilized, briefly. Second-unit photography came out of Phoenix, Arizona.

Rear Window (1954)—According to witnesses and studio documentation, the apartment set, where the whole film was shot, was created on this stage in its entirety. Assistant director Herbert Coleman, however, inexplicably maintained years later that the film was shot on Stage 17 instead. Memory can play tricks.

Everyone agrees that the set was almost too big for the stage.

In fact, the only way to get an entire three-story Greenwich Village apartment complex, with each room a separate set-within-a-set inside, was to open up the floor into the basement, so that street level on the set was actually subterranean on the stage. At one point, someone noticed that it was strange there were no cars on that street level, so cars were lowered into the basement and pushed past the camera, because there was no room for them to drive, and because of carbon monoxide issues. Construction ran from October 12, 1953, to November 13, 1953. The resultant set was 98 feet wide, 185 feet long, and 40 feet high, and included thirty-one apartments, eight of which were completely furnished. Supposedly it was, and is to date, the largest indoor set ever built at Paramount.

Lighting that set was such a colossal project that Paramount's lighting department was not up to the task; ultimately, additional lights had to be rented from both Columbia and MGM. There were four lighting setups designed for the stage, each representing different times of day, which could be dialed in, and out, as needed.

White Christmas (1954)—Columbia Inn interiors.

The Court Jester (1955)—The great hall, as seen in Danny Kaye's duel with Basil Rathbone, was (largely) shot here.

We're No Angels (1955)—The roof and bedroom window for the Ducotel home were shot here; some scenes for this sequence were shot on Stage 11, as well.

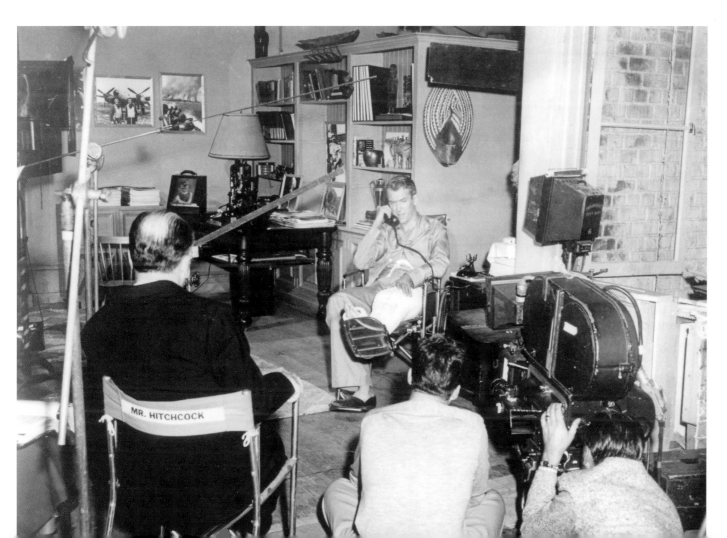

"Mr. Hitchcock" directs James Stewart on Stage 18 for *Rear Window*, 1954.

The Mountain (1956)—wrecked plane, both full-size and miniature.

The Ten Commandments(1956)—Yochabel's (Martha Scott) house, slave quarters, the palace hall, the city construction area, Jethro's tent, the city gates, the Avenue of Sphinx exteriors, the streets of Goshen, the Midian well, and Moses's house were all built and then struck here for this super epic.

Rock-a-Bye Baby (1957)—assorted.

The Sad Sack (1957)—the "Dixie Flyer."

Gunfight at the O.K. Corral (1957)—hotel room sequences and "outside the campsite" scenes.

Wild Is the Wind (1957)—Gino's (Anthony Quinn) house.

The Joker Is Wild (1957)—assorted.

Funny Face (1957)—the "Think Pink" number.

Houseboat (1958)—country club interiors, where Sophia Loren and Cary Grant danced.

Bonanza (TV, 1959–1973)—Larry Jensen remembers visiting Stage 18 in the late 1960s: "It was open because workmen were preparing for shooting to resume. The ranch house was the first set inside the door, and the saloon and sheriff's office were farther back. There was plenty of room to add other temporary sets, as needed. It was an amazing day, almost fifty years ago, that I still remember vividly."[18]

The Geisha Boy (1958)—The airplane and hotel interiors were faked here.

The Matchmaker (1958)—assorted.

But Not for Me (1959)—Ward's office, Ellie's office, and Sardi's restaurant.

Five Pennies (1959)—assorted.

Li'l Abner (1959)—Cornpone Square, Polecat Creek, etc.

Cinderfella (1960)—assorted.

The Pleasure of His Company (1961)—assorted.

One-Eyed Jacks (1961)—assorted.

The Ladies Man (1961)—Director/star Jerry Lewis constructed a three-story set with connecting bedrooms, hallways, and staircases for this movie, and used a camera crane to pan and track up and down the assorted levels. Jerry has said that *this*, not the one built for *Rear Window*, mentioned above was the largest indoor set ever built at Paramount To follow his character's antics, he installed a video camera alongside the film camera which was recording the action, thus making on-set playback of what had just been filmed (later called "video assist") a reality.

The Man Who Shot Liberty Valance (1962)—assorted.

Come Blow Your Horn (1963) —assorted.

Who's Been Sleeping in My Bed? (1963)—seen from the outside, as part of a studio lot where Dean Martin works.

Papa's Delicate Condition (1963) —assorted.

Seven Days in May (1964)—assorted.

The Patsy (1964)—assorted.

How to Murder Your Wife (UA, 1965)—According to star Jack Lemmon, some interiors were also done at MGM.

The Graduate (Embassy, 1967)—At one point in the film, when star Dustin Hoffman beats his head against the wall, the hollow sound the wall makes is an obvious (if unnoticed) tip-off that he is actually on a studio set instead of in a "real" room.

The Young Lawyers (TV, 1969–1971)—The pilot, however, was shot on Stage 15.

Darling Lili (1970)—assorted.

The Powers of Matthew Star (TV, 1982–1983)—assorted.

Clue (1985)—Based on the popular board game, the driveway, front door, and ground floor of Hill House, which was unnamed in that game, were shot here.

Marblehead Manor (TV, 1987–1988)—titular New England mansion set.

Coming to America (1988)—assorted.

Black Rain (1989)—assorted.

Harlem Nights (1989)—assorted.

Ghost (1990)—assorted.

All I Want for Christmas (1991) —assorted.

Patriot Games (1992)—Jack Ryan's (Harrison Ford) house was built on this stage.

Star Trek: Deep Space Nine (TV, 1993–1999)—assorted.

Star Trek: Insurrection (1998)—used, and expanded: a cave set built for an episode of *Star Trek: Deep Space Nine* (TV, 1993–1999).

Judging Amy (TV, 1999–2005)
—assorted.

Vanilla Sky (2000)—assorted.

Star Trek: Enterprise (TV, 2001–2005)—the bridge and other sets for *Enterprise NX-01.*

Mission Impossible III (2006)
—assorted.

Charlie Wilson's War (Universal, (2007)—also shot at LA's Downey Studios.

Spider-Man 3 (Columbia, 2007)—unknown sequences.

Disturbia (DreamWorks SKG, 2007)—This movie's plot—in which the protagonist, confined to his room, believes he has witnessed a murder—seems reminiscent of *Rear Window*'s. In fact, the heirs of the Cornell Woolrich short story upon which Hitchcock had based his film brought, and lost, a lawsuit that alleged just that. So the

coincidence of this film being shot on the *Rear Window* stage is probably unintentional.

Dinner for Schmucks (2010)
—assorted.

No Strings Attached (2011)
—assorted.

The Girl with the Dragon Tattoo (Columbia/MGM, 2011)—assorted.

American Horror Story (TV, 2011–)—assorted.

Maroon 5: One More Night (2012)—music video.

The Thundermans (TV, 2013–)—assorted.

FAR LEFT: Jerry Lewis, who is presumably somewhere in this shot, directed himself for *The Ladies Man* on Stage 18. Note the video monitor; allegedly the first time such a device was used on a feature film, 1961. LEFT: Stage 18, Empty in 2012.

ABOVE LEFT and RIGHT: The interior and exterior of the Paramount mill, where everything from tea sets to tugboats are created, 2014.

23 THE MILL

The phrase "the Mill" is a blanket term for the entire construction process at Paramount.

Director Randal Kleiser, who made the hit films *Grease* (1978) and *Big Top Pee-wee* (1988) for the studio, recalls Paramount's impressive construction capabilities: "The power of the studio system was amazing. For *Grease*, producer Allan Carr had an obligation to give Olivia Newton-John a solo song. It was hastily written during production and needed to be fit into the story. We determined it would work after the slumber party sequence. The studio built us a backyard set, in a stage, seemingly overnight, for her to sing 'Hopelessly Devoted to You.' "[19]

"We may have old-fashioned directors, money-mad financiers, and stupid front offices, but we have a tremendous 'backlot,' " Billy Wilder said about the construction departments in 1969. "All those guys, the technicians, the prop men, the special-effects men, these are the strengths of Hollywood."[20]

Executive Richard Lindheim agrees. "The shops at Paramount were just terrific. They could make anything. Often they didn't have to even do that. Especially on television, the kitchen on the set of one TV show was often the same kitchen that had been used in an earlier show, or a movie, or a hundred earlier movies, repainted or reconfigured. Everything was modular and everything was cannibalized from earlier productions—often going back decades."[21]

The Paramount Mill, built for $113,538.80 in 1935, is often now referred to as the "Marathon Mill," to avoid confusion with the RKO "Gower Mill" on the other side of the lot. A major component of any movie studio mill is the staff and plaster shop, which is "used to provide design and construction of architectural and sculptured models, [and] maintain extensive inventory of models from which molds and castings can be created." At least, that's how an unimaginative publicist for the department dryly described it in the 1960s when the studio was first reaching out to external productions. In motion picture construction, the word *staff* encompasses any architectural ornamentation used for theatrical rather than for practical effect—which isn't much better than what's spelled out above. Let's just say that the staff shop makes artificial copies of real items.

The exterior of the mill building as it looked in 1932, when visited by actress Wynne Gibson. Note the empty beer bottles, unsuccessfully hidden in back of the staircase.

In 1951 staff shop employee Albert Silva received a unique, and delayed, honor for his work on the film *Wake Island* (1942), when the Marine Corps contacted him in regard to a fake marine emblem he had designed for that picture. It seems that the US Marines had so admired his fictional version of their insignia that they now wanted to actually use it! The ersatz emblem was eventually incorporated into both the House of Representatives and Senate Armed Services committee rooms in Washington, DC.

Paramount did not have a specific catalog of their molded replicas in 1968—they were too new to the business of outside clients, and hadn't thought about such niceties—but today's version consists of ninety-five pages of wood moldings, vacuform baseboards, rails, panels, casings, walls, floors, and stairs. The department also offers a vast selection of artificial brick, walls, cobblestones, rock, tile, marble, flagstone, and metal—made to order, and more than capable of fooling both the naked eye and a high-definition camera.

The vacuform machine, which presses heated plastic into a mold to mimic that mold's texture, is today the construction department's best friend. In previous years, wood—treated and painted to resemble stone or brick, as well as plaster of Paris, rubber and later, fiberglass—were all part of the department's ample bag of tricks.

Clustered both inside and around the mill, which in 1968 was actually a whole row of buildings along the northern wall of the studio, as well as a Desilu/RKO version of many of the same departments to the west, was a carpenter shop, a prop construction shop, and separate departments for upholstery, drapery, furniture, paint, machines, welding, air-conditioning, lumber/electrical, scenic arts, and plumbing. The biggest area was devoted to set construction; in 1968, this comprised 5,300 square feet of fabricating space, in three structures. The lumber department held over 2.5 million board feet of raw lumber.

A steel-aerial tracking system above the streets and shops was used to transport sets from the mill to storage and then to the stages that needed them. In principle, this innovative way of transporting heavy equipment was borrowed from the meat-packing industry, which transported sides of beef on tracks from one department to another in a similar fashion. In reality, there was nothing else like it in the world.

Taking a page from Billy Wilder, in the late twentieth century, Paramount started calling their entire production support division, which then included thirty-three departments, backlot operations. David Mannix, a senior VP of the division, admitted in 1989 that "even though we get 95 percent of our business from in-house, we still have to fight for that business. It isn't handed to us on a silver platter."[22]

The Gower Mill, on the other side of the lot, has a more interesting pedigree than its sister. It was built in 1920 by the firm of Meyer and Holler, who also designed Sid Grauman's Egyptian and Chinese Theatres and much of the Charlie Chaplin Studios (now Jim Henson Productions), Thomas Ince Studios (now the Culver Studios), and the Goldwyn Studios (now known as The Lot). To this day there is the ghostly outline of a slot in the western wall of this building where flats representing lawyer's offices and executive dining rooms and infinite and endless hallways could be slid outside and transported to the stages.

Today, lawyers' offices and executive dining rooms and infinite and endless hallways still exist at Paramount. Except today, these things are real.

24 SPECIAL EFFECTS

In spite of what most people seem to think, the modern term *special effects* actually described, for much of the studio era, two different disciplines. There were optical effects, referred to from the silent-film era on as "trick shots," and later, as "special photographic effects," and which involved montages or opticals created in the camera or in postproduction, or matte paintings. This department was originally managed by one Paul Lerpae.

The other types of special effects were those of a mechanical nature. These sequences were staged on a set and involved invisible wires, miniatures, forced perspective, or the use of glass paintings, which were hung in front of the camera to make a set look larger than it really was. All of these disciplines were highly specialized. Miniatures, for example, were a separate department, managed by Ivyl Burks during the studio era.

Farciot Edouart and Dewey Wrigley were in charge of what we now call the special-effects department at Paramount until 1932, when Gordon Jennings reorganized and managed it with Edouart, from 1932 until Jennings's death, in 1952.

ABOVE: The epic miniseries *The Winds of War* fought part of World War II inside of B-Tank. Note the cables and pulleys the Special Effects Department is preparing with which to tow the battleships across the water, once that water is added, 1983. RIGHT: Mechanical aviation effects pieces await their next assignment, circa 1990.

Jennings was replaced by John P. Fulton, a former head of the same department at Universal. It was Fulton, with special-effects cinematographer Irmin Roberts, who figured out how to perform the complicated mechanical camera moves for Alfred Hitchcock in *Vertigo* (1958), including an innovative and disorienting effect achieved by zooming the camera in while simultaneously tracking it back, intended to simulate for the viewer the unbalanced sensation described in the film's title. Fulton also parted the Red Sea for DeMille on *The Ten Commandments* (1956), which won him the last of his three Academy Awards, two of them earned while at Paramount. Despite his success, Fulton was not as well-liked by his underlings as the less-demanding Jennings had been; nonetheless, he would stay at his desk until 1964.

In 1968 mechanical special effects were still done in-house at the big studios like Paramount, although sometimes the effects were actually worked out in the grip or property departments. A "Catalog of Services and Capabilities" from that year mentions that the special-effects department was responsible for "design and manufacture of props, action props, miniature special effects, and sheet-metal products for pictures and television. Mediums used include rubber and breakaway glass, wood, metal, and plastic." They should have found a screenwriter to punch up that copy; no wonder the department was having trouble finding clients during this difficult era.

Optical effects, which at the time primarily meant wipes and dissolves, mattes, optical fade-ins and -outs, and credit sequences were provided by the optical and title department during this period, which was managed by an independent unit, the Howard A. Anderson Company.

Founded in 1927, Anderson was one of the first outside companies in the world to create visual effects for studios on a contractual basis. The company's founder, Howard A. Anderson Jr., grew up in the special-effects industry, his father having worked in that capacity for DeMille on *The King of Kings* (Pathé, 1927).

For *Star Trek*, Anderson created that series' signature "beaming" effects, as well as many of the models of the *Enterprise* and other vessels. Anderson's office was in the Desilu photographic building, although they also had shops in the special photo stage, and off-lot, on Fairfax Avenue.

The Anderson Company was also involved in the optics for an unproduced *Trek* sequel, *Star Trek: Phase II* (1977), which eventually evolved into *Star Trek: The Motion Picture* (1979). For this very expensive and troubled production, Paramount's in-house optical unit, Magicam, (created in 1974), somewhat spitefully relegated Anderson to providing graphics for the monitors on the redesigned *Enterprise*'s bridge.

Magicam was dissolved in 1982, but the Howard A. Anderson Company happily still exists, known today as Anderson Digital. Karyn Anderson, Howard Sr.'s great-granddaughter is the current CEO.

Paramount today still has a practical effect department on-lot, which specializes in wind, rain, explosions, and breakaway props. For optical effects they use outside contractors who specialize in flying saucers, sinking ships, casts of thousands, and fighting dinosaurs—all created inside of a computer. George Lucas's Industrial Light & Magic is the best known of these effects companies, although many effects shots in today's Hollywood are now subcontracted out again to overseas markets like India.

"On the original *Star Trek* they used models," Richard Lindheim remembers. "When we did *Star Trek: The Next Generation*, it was combination of models and computer-created effects. By the time we got to *Star Trek: Voyager*, the effects were largely done behind a desk on a PC."[23]

Today's "trick shots" bear little relation to those created with models and mattes, ingenuity and imagination, by geniuses like Jennings and Fulton and Anderson and their covens of wizards.

ABOVE LEFT: The Paramount fire department in its longtime (1929–2010) location in back of Stage 10, 1997.
ABOVE RIGHT: Today the Fire Department keeps its remaining inventory in back of the security department's offices, 2016.

25 FIRE DEPARTMENT

The fire department has always been a supplement to, rather than a replacement for, the Los Angeles Fire Department, located outside the gates. One of the main functions of the Paramount fire department is to provide safety inspections in buildings and on sets to identify potential safety issues, and to monitor and control on-camera explosions and pyrotechnics.

The original fire truck on the lot was in service from 1917 to 1938, when it was replaced with a new unit designed for narrow studio streets with a 275-gallon reservoir, and a three-section ladder. The current department is equipped with a 150-gallon mini pumper and a quick-attack vehicle that can traverse rubble in an emergency.

The fire department for many years was located north of Stage 10 on the western side of a set storage building and a staff shop built in 1929. Unfortunately the building was removed with the 2010 renovation of that part of the lot. Today's department is located in the back of the old KCAL building east of Stage 19.

WIDTH: 108 feet

LENGTH: 69 feet

HEIGHT: 38 feet

SQUARE FEET: 6,929

Stage 10 was the most mysterious stage on the Paramount lot. Originally numbered Stage 4, the construction date is sometimes given as 1929, and sometimes as "prior to 1926," the latter coming from a 1990 internal building survey. But seeing that Stage 10 was attached to the music department (later known as the Crosby Building), which was obviously constructed post-sound, this is debatable.

The same document cited above intriguingly mentions that Stage 10, and the entire 300-foot-by-198-foot music department (which, again, wasn't called that at the time) was possibly moved from Selma-Vine "around 1926." Where this supposition originated is not cited in this document, or anyplace else.

Starting in 1968 the makeup department began using Stage 10 as a workshop. The large amount of floor space was ideal for the application of makeup and hairpieces and pointy ears for extras portraying aliens on assorted *Star Trek* projects. In fact, Michael Westmore, yet another talented make-up artist from that famous clan ultimately worked on many *Trek* TV projects there.

Star Trek, in its various incarnations, has actually used the stage many other times, and many other ways over its long and prosperous life. For example, *Star Trek: The Motion Picture* (1979), which launched the modern *Trek* era, used sets actually built on this stage for the aborted *Star Trek: Phase II*. Later, *Star Trek: The Next Generation* (TV, 1987–1994) used the same space for auxiliary sets, to house extras, and for one 1992 episode, "New Ground," with children working as extras. Visual effects and explosions were also occasionally generated on this stage for that series.

In 2008 Stage 10 was demolished for the construction of a new digital arts department, which is now known as the Technicolor postproduction building.

Shot on Stage 10:

The Studio Murder Mystery (1929)—An intriguing, very early talkie was set and filmed on this stage.

Make Me a Star (1932)—Another Hollywood-set project with intriguing glimpses of Stage 10, including some exteriors, was shot here.

The Cat and the Canary (1939)—dark old mansion interiors.

The Lady Eve (1941)—This matchless Preston Sturges classic was shot as *Two Bad Hats*, here and on Stage 2.

Sullivan's Travels (1941)—The morgue sets and the "colored church," where Sullivan has an epiphany while watching a Mickey Mouse cartoon, were shot here. Sturges had wanted Sullivan to be watching a Charlie Chaplin comedy. Charlie said no; Mickey said yes.

The Glass Key (1942)—Paul Madvig's (Brian Donlevy) club scenes were shot here.

Going My Way (1944)—music publisher's office.

The Blue Dahlia (1946)—Buzz's apartment and Corelli's Hotel.

The Heiress (1948)—assorted.

Let's Dance (1950)—Kitty's (Betty Hutton) apartment interiors.

My Friend Irma Goes West (1950)—the "girl's apartment."

Union Station (1950)—Donnelly kitchen.

My Favorite Spy (1951)—secret service headquarters.

Tropic Zone (1953)—assorted.

Rear Window (1954)—The sets for Gunnison's office were built on this stage for a dialogue scene later paraphrased in a telephone conversation between James Stewart and Gunnison, his editor. Gunnison was allegedly going to be played by Gig Young, although Young's name is not present in the studio records for this film. Regardless, something for this film (which was not used) was shot on this stage on Wednesday, January 13, 1954.

Secret of the Incas (1954)—assorted sets, including South American exteriors.

The Naked Jungle (1954)—Joanna's bedroom (Eleanor Parker) and Leiningen's bedroom (Charlton Heston).

The Conquest of Space (1955)—European broadcast station set.

The Seven Little Foys (1955)—assorted.

Teacher's Pet (1957)—assorted.

The Joker Is Wild (1957)—assorted.

The Space Children (1958)—the blockhouse.

King Creole (1958)—cheap apartment.

The Buccaneer (1958)—Governor Claiborne's patio.

Five Pennies (1959)—assorted.

Alias Jesse James (UA, 1959)—Titus Queasley's office set.

Breakfast at Tiffany's (1961)—assorted.

Love with the Proper Stranger (1963)—assorted.

The Patsy (1964)—assorted.

Where Love Has Gone (1964)—Hotel Hawaii.

Sylvia (1965)—assorted.

Mannix (TV, 1967–1975)—assorted.

Star Trek: The Motion Picture (1978)—assorted, including the Klingon battle cruiser destroyed by "V'ger."

Harlem Nights (1989)—assorted.

The Bradys (TV, 1990)—secondary sets for this "dramedy" reboot of the classic sitcom.

Sons & Daughters (1991)—assorted.

Indecent Proposal (1993)—assorted.

Clueless (TV, 1996–1999)—TV version of the hit film, starring Rachel Blanchard.

Sabrina, the Teenage Witch (TV 1996–2003)—assorted.

Wayne's World (1997)—assorted.

Charmed (TV, 1998–2006)—primarily used in the 2004 season.

We Were Soldiers (2002)—assorted.

Everybody Hates Chris (TV, 2005–2009)—assorted.

This building was originally constructed, or moved onto the lot as a shooting stage (Stage 10), in 1926. In 1930, as sound recording and postproduction sound recording became more sophisticated, Paramount constructed one of the first music scoring stages in the world in a walled-off section of this stage, which had just been soundproofed as part of the conversion to talking pictures.

The resultant room, 55 feet by 90 feet by 30 feet (4,500 square feet), could easily hold a sixty-five-piece orchestra, although accommodating up to ninety instruments and musicians at a time was not impossible. There was also, for several years, a Wurlitzer pipe organ permanently installed in the room. A projection booth (for running the film being scored) and an instrument council were located on the north wall. A screen for monitoring the action was on the other side.

Inside these walls, some of the greatest film music ever was created and some of the greatest songs performed. Bob Hope first recorded his signature song "Thanks for the Memories" in *The Big Broadcast of 1938* (1938), with costar Shirley Ross, in this building. Bing Crosby recorded the biggest-selling single of all time—"White Christmas"—here, for *Holiday Inn* (1942), which was much beloved by war-weary soldiers and civilians alike. Crosby recorded the same song again in this building in 1947, and a third and fourth time (it was played twice) for a later film, titled *White Christmas* (1954). That song's composer, Irving Berlin, was intermittently under contact with Paramount during this era. Henry Mancini's "Moon River" and Ray Evans and Jay Livingston's Doris Day hit, "Whatever Will Be, Will Be (Que Sera Sera)" were also first recorded here, along with hundreds of others. Elvis Presley recorded dozens of songs in the music building during his years at Paramount.

The deans of music at Paramount were Franz Waxman (*Sunset Boulevard*, 1950; *A Place in the Sun*, 1951), Victor Young (*For Whom the Bell Tolls*, 1943; *Samson and Delilah*, 1951), and Bernard Hermann (*Vertigo*, 1958; *Psycho*, 1960), but all of the great composers and performers of the twentieth century passed through those doors over the years. Occasionally the scoring stage was featured on-screen as a set as well, *The Country Girl* (1954) and *The Errand Boy* (1961) being reasonable examples.

Next door to the scoring stage was the ADR room. ADR, which stands for "automated dialogue replacement," is a way of rerecording lines which for various reasons were inaudible or unusable when recorded on the set, or, more often, on location. The original actor, or occasionally, other vocal talent, would read their lines inside this room in sync with the visuals which needed doctoring. The scoring stage was sometimes called "Stage M," while the ADR stage was "Stage L."

In 1969 an external audio company, Glen Glenn Sound, assumed management of the Paramount Music Department. They gutted the scoring stage and rebuilt it, this time with the screen on the north wall, and moved the booth onto the floor, the only apparent result being, ultimately, less room for the musicians.

In 1987 the Music Building was renamed, aptly enough, the "Crosby Building." But as with many decades-old studio departments during this era, less work was now being done under that new moniker. Producers, it seems, had discovered that eager musicians in eastern Europe would work much more cheaply than their union-paid equivalents in Los Angeles, and that they would do so in recording studios which were much less expensive than those in LA as well.

In spite of this, Paramount still shocked the Hollywood community when they closed, in 2006, and then demolished, in 2008, their legendary scoring stage. Not only was the stage leveled, but the entire music building was bulldozed at the same time.

ABOVE: Bing Crosby, seen here during the production of *Dixie* (1943) was responsible, in large part, for the continuing popularity of musicals throughout much of the 20th Century. The Paramount music building would, briefly, be named in his honor. RIGHT: The Technicolor Building, built in 2010 on the site of the long-time, long-gone Music Department, 2014.

Truthfully, the department had been neglected by this point for decades. Trash and empty liquor bottles had been hidden on the shelves in the music library because it was too much work for employees there to search out a trash can, and termites had been swarming the building for years because the studio had been unwilling to pay to have them exterminated. Yet the demolition was still a blow to many who remembered an earlier era. Ray Evans, 91 at the time, remarked that the decision was "shortsighted. They may have a good business, economic or bottom-line reason for it," he said, "but it sure takes away a little of the history, the glamour and the glitter of Hollywood. This is another nail in the coffin."[24]

In 2010 the music building was replaced by a new postproduction building. The next year, Paramount joined forces with Technicolor, the beloved creator of three-strip, and later, single-strip, color film stock. Technicolor was then trying to rebrand themselves as an overall postproduction company, and so partnered with Paramount to create a $40 million, state-of-the-art sound facility on the site of the old music building. This new, three-floor, 65,000-square-foot structure includes nine rerecording and mixing stages, three ADR stages, a Foley (sound-effects recording) stage, four DVD restoration and mastering rooms, ten "sound design" suites, sixteen editorial rooms, and even a massage room.

Despite these top-notch facilities, in the future all of the actual music will be recorded in Eastern Europe.

28 STAGE 8 (1918)

WIDTH:	113 feet, 3 inches
LENGTH:	146 feet, 7 inches
HEIGHT:	30 feet
SQUARE FEET:	16,611

29 STAGE 9 (1918)

WIDTH:	113 feet, 4 inches
LENGTH:	146 feet, 8 inches
HEIGHT:	30 feet
SQUARE FEET:	16,631

Stages 8 and 9 were built with these offices on their eastern façades, 2012.

An article referring to Stages 8 and 9 was published in *Paramount Parade* in 1937, claiming, "Here on the lot are a few buildings you pass every day, which in a mere decade have seen the rise and fall of many regimes, as many fabulous fortunes, and fabulous beauties known throughout the world, as most of history's famous ancient castles."[25]

Because this building's history—encompassing both of these stages as well as the art department and other offices on its eastern side—is so disputed and convoluted, the two stages will be discussed together here, although a separate filmography will be provided for each, as well as a separate section, below, for the art department.

An in-house newsletter from 1937, states that the building and the offices on its eastern facade were all constructed in 1918. The buildings were combined as we know them today in 1920. The same article cited above goes into some detail about the early days of the stage and the process of silent-film production in general. This article states that:

Three or four companies shot on one stage. Each set had a bell system similar to the one now used on soundstages, and whenever action started, they rang a bell so no one would wander in from an adjoining set. Floods menaced the stage. Every winter brought its rains which covered the floor of the building, especially on the cemetery side. Once the building was menaced when a careless grip let his cigar fall into a powder house nearby. No one was near, and the only damage was to a few shattered nerves and the splintered powder house, which went straight up into the air like a tin can over a firecracker. . . .

Paramount has occupied this building since 1926. When sound came, this building was used as an assembly stage, and in 1930, it was the last stage to be soundproofed and partitioned.[26]

Local birds were a major problem. The 1937 article mentions, evocatively, that "the doors were left open in those days and the building was so large that the pigeons didn't know where to fly out once they got in. They would swoop down from the rafters in the midst of a tender love scene."

Like several others on the lot, Stages 8 and 9 are sometimes referred to collectively as the "DeMille Stage," or the "Star Trek Stage" (the latter especially applied to Stage 9). Numerous *Star Trek* films, TV shows, and the 2009 feature reboot utilized this space. In 1986 more than eight hundred people celebrated *Trek*'s twenty-year anniversary on this stage, sharing an edible version of the *Enterprise* cake.

The stage could have just as easily been called the "Jerry Lewis Stage." At least six of the comic's films have shot on Stage 8 alone.

Stage 8 has two tanks in the floor. One is 30 feet by 50 feet by 10 feet deep, and the second is 16 feet by 16 feet by 12 feet deep. Stage 9 also has a tank, 18 feet by 30 feet by 8 feet deep. What these tanks were constructed for, as well as when and why, is one more mystery associated with this storied shooting space.

Shot on Stage 8:

Ashes of Vengeance (First National, 1923)—Starring Norma Talmadge, one of the largest movie sets of its time, representing eighteenth-century France, was built here.

Zander the Great (MGM, 1925)—The first time the wall was removed to make a single stage for a Mexican hacienda set was allegedly for this production, although the studio insists the stage was first divided in 1930 when it was being converted for sound production. (This begs the question: If the wall was built in 1930, how could it have been removed in 1925?)

Dr. Jekyll and Mr. Hyde (1931)—Dr. Lanyon's study.

The Jungle Princess (1936)—assorted.

The Texans (1938)—assorted.

Honeymoon in Bali (1938)—department store set.

Beau Geste (1939)—office quarters, Beau's bedroom, and assorted hallways.

Sudden Money (1939)—roadhouse set.

The Way of All Flesh (1940)—hobo camp.

Dr. Cyclops (1940)—Title character Dr. Thorkel shrinks his victim, so his lair set had to be built to normal scale, here, and oversize, elsewhere, to make those victims look smaller. The oversize sets were built on Stages 8 and 12.

Sullivan's Travels (1941)—Beverly Hills Police Department, Sullivan's pantry and living room, and mission sets.

Double Indemnity (1944)—The Dietrichson home and staircase where Barbara Stanwyck makes that long-limbed walk down the stairs was filmed right here. The exterior of the house was on New York Street's (#50) Boston district, and a real location in the Hollywood hills. Edward G. Robinson's office for that film and Fred MacMurray's apartment were also on this stage. Incidentally, the exterior for MacMurray's apartment was a real location as well: 1825 Kingsley Drive in Los Angeles.

The Great Moment (1944)—Morton dental office.

The Big Clock (1948)—Ray Milland's office.

The Emperor Waltz (1948)—forest exteriors.

Samson and Delilah (1949)—The first shots in the film, with George Sanders, were shot here. Other assorted scenes set later in the film, including those with Samson at the gristmill, were shot here as well.

Song of Surrender (1949)—Abernathy house.

Dark City (1950)—Tests of Charlton Heston (his first name spelled "Charleton") were shot on Stage 8 on March 27, 1950, his big-screen debut.

Detective Story (1951)—assorted.

When Worlds Collide (1951)—The United Nations committee room was shot here, and on Stage 14.

Road to Bali (1952)—assorted.

Houdini (1953)—Berlin hotel lobby.

Stalag 17 (1953)—Barracks #4 and Russian barracks, the tunnel, and Von Scherbach's (Otto Preminger) office; actual exteriors were in Calabasas, California.

The Country Girl (1954)—Boston and New York theater mock-ups.

The Conquest of Space (1955)—Martian desert vistas.

Strategic Air Command (1955)—General Castle's office (also shot on Stage 10).

The Rose Tattoo (1955)—Anna Magnani's home.

You're Never Too Young (1955)—Noonan's apartment.

The Desperate Hours (1955)—The interior of the Hilliard home besieged by Humphrey Bogart was constructed here. The exterior was on a backlot at Universal Studios.

Anything Goes (1956)—assorted.

The Ten Commandments (1956)—assorted.

Rock-a-Bye Baby (1957)—assorted.

The Joker Is Wild (1957)—assorted.

The Sad Sack (1957)—The barracks set, which doubled for the WAC barracks, as well, was located here.

Houseboat (1958)—A rowboat scene was shot in the tank.

The Buccaneer (1958)—This film was presented by Cecil B. DeMille, and directed by his son-in-law, actor Anthony Quinn. The trailer for this film, allegedly set in DeMille's office and hosted by the director, was shot on this stage, and Stage 16, on October 21, 1958. DeMille died on January 21, 1959, making this his last appearance on film.

The Matchmaker (1958)—assorted.

But Not for Me (1959)—McDonald's room and Kathryn's home.

The Rat Race (1960)—apartment interiors for Tony Curtis and Debbie Reynolds, and Mac's Bar.

Visit to a Small Planet (1960)—the Spelding home.

Breakfast at Tiffany's (1961)—assorted.

Blue Hawaii (1961)—beach where the "Hawaiian Sweetheart" number was shot.

The Pleasure of His Company (1961)—assorted.

The Nutty Professor (1963)—assorted.

My Favorite Martian (TV, 1963–1966)—assorted.

Seven Days in May (1964)—assorted.

The Disorderly Orderly (1964)—assorted.

The Patsy (1964)—assorted.

The Family Jewels (1965)—assorted.

Paradise, Hawaiian Style (1966)—Elvis Presley's beach house.

Mission: Impossible (TV, 1966–1973)—assorted.

Rosemary's Baby (1968)—assorted.

The Molly Maguires (1968)—Larry Jensen has definite memories about exploring the "coal mine" set for this Sean Connery–Richard Harris drama: "The company had spent the summer of 1968 in Pennsylvania, doing exteriors, and they were working on the lot, finishing interiors. The stages had been transformed into a massive set of 'underground' coal mine tunnels, with a working incline railway to the stage ceiling that took miners up in railcars pulled by cables. Between shots, we got to wander through the tunnels, which were set-decorated with tons of real coal they'd brought back from Pennsylvania. The tunnels even dripped water from cracks, courtesy of a bunch of rubber tubing, forming puddles in the coal dust. The tunnels were miserably hot and way cool at the same time!"[27]

Darling Lili (1970)—assorted.

Lady Sings the Blues (1972)—assorted.

Sextette (Crown International Pictures, 1978)—The gymnasium set for Mae West's last role was built on this stage.

Star Trek: The Motion Picture (1978)—several sets, including the *Enterprise* recreation deck and the "V'ger" probe.

48 Hrs. (1982)—assorted.

Beverly Hills Cop (1984)—assorted.

Star Trek: The Next Generation (TV, 1987–1994)—Starting in season two, assorted sets were shot here, including part of the bridge and captain's quarters. The hallways for this *Enterprise* had printed instructions and text on the walls as set dressing, presumably representing pertinent Star Fleet regulations. In actuality, these unreadable (to the audience) blocks of verbiage included the lyrics to the theme song to *Gilligan's Island* (TV, 1964–1967), among other deathless prose.

Star Trek V: The Final Frontier (1989)—assorted.

Star Trek VI: The Undiscovered Country (1991)—assorted.

Star Trek: Voyager (TV, 1995–2001)—mostly swing (temporary) sets.

Star Trek: Insurrection (1998)—assorted officers' quarters.

Star Trek: Enterprise (TV, 2001–2005)—assorted *Enterprise NX-01* crew quarters, sickbay, and dining rooms.

Mission: Impossible 3 (2006)—assorted.

Star Trek (2009)—assorted.

NCIS: Los Angeles (2009–)—occasional.

Shot on Stage 9:

Union Pacific (1939)—the big tent.

Sullivan's Travels (1941)—farmyard and bedroom where Joel McCrea fails to get a good night's sleep.

Road to Rio (1947)—assorted.

Welcome Stranger (1947)—barn, drugstore, and school.

The Emperor Waltz (1948)—the von Stolzenberg-Stolzenberg home, and town hall.

A Place in the Sun (1950)—assorted.

Sunset Boulevard (1950)—The downstairs interiors of the Desmond home and garage, with Joe's leaky room above it, were built here, as was Joe's apartment and Betty's room.

When Worlds Collide (1951)—McKenna Observatory.

Tropic Zone (1953)—assorted.

Houdini (1953)—Magician Joseph Dunninger worked as a technical consultant on this film, appearing on camera on this stage for a "prologue" on October 15, 1952. As this sequence does not appear in the film or in its shooting script, the nature of this appearance remains a mystery. Also, a montage of

Houdini doing tricks, including his vanishing elephant illusion, was shot here, on Halloween, 1952, the twenty-sixth anniversary of the magician's death.

Five Pennies (1953)—assorted.

The Seven Little Foys (1955)—assorted.

We're No Angels (1955)—store, street, house, and garden.

Strategic Air Command (1955)—stadium grandstand.

Anything Goes (1956)—assorted.

Teacher's Pet (1957)—assorted.

Gunfight at the O.K. Corral (1957)—Shanssey's Saloon and the Tombstone Social Hall.

Funny Face (1957)—Duval's Salon for the "On How to Be Lovely" number, as performed by Audrey Hepburn.

The Geisha Boy (1958)—One of the stage's underground pits was utilized here for bathhouse sequences.

The Buccaneer (1958)—The pirate market and governor's living room sets were built here.

Stage 9 in 2015.

The Matchmaker (1958)—assorted.

Five Pennies (1959)—assorted.

Li'l Abner (1959)—This stage was used for the "Put 'Em Back the Way They Wuz" number.

The Bellboy (1960)—assorted.

Visit to a Small Planet (1960)—The Mayberry living room and the "space schoolroom" were shot here. Mayberry here was the name of a character played by Ellen Corby, not *The Andy Griffith Show* location.

The Ladies Man (1961)—assorted.

Breakfast at Tiffany's (1961)—assorted New York interiors.

Hatari (1962)—the African compound.

The Man Who Shot Liberty Valance (1962)—assorted.

Donovan's Reef (1963)—the lanai and Donovan's bedroom sets.

The Nutty Professor (1963)—assorted.

Soldier in the Rain (1963)—police station and Pussycat Cafe interiors.

Love with the Proper Stranger (1963)—assorted.

The Disorderly Orderly (1964)—assorted.

Seven Days in May (1964)—assorted.

The Patsy (1964)—assorted.

Sylvia (1965)—assorted.

Star Trek (TV, 1966–1969)—unknown sequences.

The High Chaparral (TV, 1967–1971)—ranch interiors.

Rosemary's Baby (1968)—assorted.

Star Trek: The Motion Picture (1979)—assorted *Enterprise* sets.

Star Trek II: The Wrath of Khan (1982)—*Enterprise* sets, including the dilithium chamber, for Spock's famous death scene.

Star Trek III: The Search for Spock (1984)—*Enterprise* and *Enterprise-A* sets.

Star Trek IV: The Voyage Home (1986)—the hijacked *Bird-of-Prey* ship sets.

Star Trek: The Next Generation (1987–1994)—Starting in Season 2, the location for the battle bridge for the *Enterprise-D* was built here, among other sets.

Star Trek V: The Final Frontier (1989)—*Enterprise-A* sets.

Star Trek VI: The Undiscovered Country (1991)—*Enterprise-A* sets.

Star Trek: Voyager (TV 1995–2001)—Most of the *Voyager* ship sets were here.

Star Trek: First Contact (1996)—used, revamped *Star Trek: Voyager* sets.

Star Trek: Insurrection (1998)—used, revamped *Star Trek: Voyager* sets.

Star Trek: Enterprise (TV, 2001–2005)—swing (temporary) sets only.

Star Trek: Nemesis (2002)—the "mines of Remus."

Mission: Impossible 3 (2005)—assorted.

Star Trek (2009)—assorted.

NCIS: Los Angeles (TV 2009–   )—occasional.

30 ART DEPARTMENT

The longtime home of the art department was built along the walls of Stages 8 and 9 in 1918 for the Brunton Studios. Originally the art department was upstairs, and the rest of the building comprised dressing rooms and offices. Joseph Schenck, who was married to star Norma Talmadge, as well as one of the owners of Brunton Studios, had an elaborate office there, in what would later become the location of the operations desk.

The art department was responsible for the visual look and mood of Paramount's product. Sometimes called the design department, or production design department, the art director of a movie worked with the director, the construction crews, the cinematographer, and the costumers to create the overall *mise-en-scène* for a production.

In the studio era, Paramount's films visually epitomized a somewhat European sophistication and sensibility, with a witty, even continental elegance often on display, even in the very American Sturges comedies, DeMille spectacles, and *film noir*.

Director Edward Dmytryk consults with art director Walter H. Tyler regarding Tyler's saloon set sketches on Dmytryk's *The Carpetbaggers*, 1964.

The very first cinema art director was Wilfred Buckland, who worked with DeMille as far back as it was possible to go, on *The Squaw Man*, in 1913. Buckland designed and lit sets for the camera lens, not as had been done in earlier movies, as one would light a theatrical presentation. He also introduced klieg lights to motion pictures, which would remain the industry standard for decades. Lasky wrote that Buckland was "the first bona fide art director in the industry, and the first to build architectural settings for films; Buckland widened the scope of pictures tremendously by throwing off the scenic limitations of the stage."[28]

Buckland's very fruitful collaboration with what would become Paramount was influential, but not long-lasting. He left the company in 1920. In 1946, the world's first art director shot his thirty-six-year-old son, Wilfred Buckland Jr., and then turned the gun on himself. DeMille had recently had a business meeting with both Bucklands in regard to employment on his upcoming epic, *Unconquered* (1947). He received word of the tragedy while dining at the Paramount commissary.

Stephen Goosson was the first art director to work in this building, for First National Pictures. But Hans Dreier was the supervising art director at Paramount from 1923 (at Selma-Vine) and here, from 1926 through 1951. Dreier was one of the German expatriates who arrived in America between the world wars and found long careers in Hollywood. At Paramount he was nominated for Academy Awards twenty times, and ultimately awarded Oscars for *Frenchmen's Creek* (1944), *Samson and Delilah* (1949), and *Sunset Boulevard* (1950).

The outside of the building, with its staircases and bungalows, often doubled as a set. Because the streets were then dirt and lined with pine trees, it convincingly portrayed a European chateau in Mary Pickford's *Little Lord Fauntleroy* (UA, 1921), and similar films.

For *Sunset Boulevard*, someone—Dreier, perhaps—cast his own office on the lot, and the street in front of it (pine trees long since vanished), as the Paramount Writers Building, where William Holden and Nancy Olson collaborate on a doomed screenplay.

Billy Wilder, left, somewhat wryly prepares to shoot a scene in art director Hans Dreier's actual office—which probably annoyed Dreier as much as it probably amused Wilder, for *Sunset Boulevard*, 1949.

For the same film, Dreier was much praised for his *Grand-Guignol*-like funeral home interiors for Norma Desmond's Beverly Hills mansion. The exterior of the house, however, was not a set at all, but a real fourteen-bedroom mansion, located not in Beverly Hills but ten blocks south of Paramount on the northern side of Wilshire Boulevard, between Crenshaw and Irving. The home had been built in 1924 for a reported $250,000 by William O. Jenkins, a businessman and Mexican film producer, but had long been abandoned when it was sold to tycoon J. Paul Getty, who, because of building restrictions, was unable to tear it down. The "phantom house," as people in the neighborhood had taken to calling it in 1950, only lacked a swimming pool, which was crucial to the plot, and which Dreier had to build. That pool was later used in another film, *Rebel without a Cause* (Warner Bros., 1954), before it, and the house, were finally demolished in 1957.

Dreier's successor, after his retirement in 1951, was Hal Pereira. Pereira's work was less expressionistic and more naturalistic than that of his old bosses, as was his era. Pereira himself would retire in 1968.

Other notable Paramount art directors whose imaginations contributed to Paramount's visual world included, in the earliest days, Van Nest Polglase; A. Earl Hedrick, who, among many other projects, designed the Ponderosa Ranch for *Bonanza* (TV, 1959–1963); and Walter H. Tyler, who designed projects ranging from *The Blue Dahlia* (1946) to *The Odd Couple* (1968). All of this talent is gone now, as Paramount no longer has an art department.

The Dreier Building, named as a tribute to one of its longtime inhabitants, and to the studio art department, has been featured in several movies post–*Sunset Boulevard*, such as *The Buster Keaton Story* (1957), *Who's Been Sleeping in My Bed?* (1963), *Harlow* (1965), and *The Last Tycoon* (1975). In all instances, it has played the part of a studio lot.

Three rooms in this building also doubled as the studio schoolhouse. In this little complex, Paramount tutored children working on the lot as required by the state. Often the actual teaching of the children was done, rather haphazardly, between takes on the soundstages. Truthfully, Paramount was never the mecca for child stars that MGM, Twentieth Century Fox, and even hard-boiled Warner Bros., was, so there was usually little need for a dedicated "schoolhouse" such as those other studios possessed. Paramount's most promising teenage star was Dorothy Dell, who costarred in the studio's *Little Miss Marker* (1934) with Shirley Temple (on loan from Fox). Sadly, Dell died in a car accident the same year that film came out. Her room on the first floor of the dressing-room building was long thereafter considered cursed by the other actresses it was assigned to.

31 STAGE 7 (1922)

WIDTH: 166 feet, 7 inches

LENGTH: 69 feet, 4 inches

HEIGHT: 30 feet and 68 feet

SQUARE FEET: 11,549

Los Angeles contains over three hundred soundstages, more than any other city in the world. At 68 feet to the lighting grid, Paramount's Stage 7 is the tallest on the lot, and one of the tallest in Los Angeles. Only a very few stages at Sony (Columbia) and Warner Bros. tower higher. The Paramount stage, however, only

Stage 7, the tallest on the lot, is best admired from the air. Look for it just above and slightly to the right of the water tower, 1939.

rises to its full height for about a third of the stage's length, giving the building the appearance of a windowless split-level home for giants. The density of the buildings around it makes it hard to appreciate the building in any case. Stage 7, in fact, is best admired from the air. Or in a movie.

Stage 7 (or Stage 2, according to its original designation) was built in 1922, and was originally part of the same shooting space as Stage 6, with which it shares a wall. The tall section of the stage was apparently constructed in order to accommodate scenes set in theaters or on Broadway-style stages. The height allowed scenery and backdrops to be raised up and down into overhead wings while the camera recorded the action. There is some evidence that the additional height was retrofitted onto the stage, perhaps in 1929, to accommodate sound, and musicals, which briefly dominated the talking screen.

As the tallest building on the lot, Stage 7 has always attracted attention. In 1943 it had an air-raid siren attached to its tallest point, which, thankfully, was never used, except in drills.

On January 5, 1953, there was a fire on the roof of Stage 7, which fortunately firefighters were easily able to extinguish.

Shot on Stage 7:

The Vanishing Pioneer (1928)—sheriff's office and jail.

Thanks for the Memory (1937)—Bob Hope's apartment.

Sullivan's Travels (1941)—"owl wagon," cattle car, and airliner.

West Point Widow (1941)—cocktail bar.

I Married a Witch (1942)—farmhouse bedroom.

The Palm Beach Story (1942)—train interiors.

Star Spangled Rhythm (1942)—stage door, Bing Crosby's dressing room.

The Uninvited (1944)—Rick's bedroom.

The Great Moment (1944)—Preston Sturges's troubled production was shot under the titles *Great without Glory* and *Triumph over Pain*, but

nothing worked, and it was his first flop. The farmhouse scenes and the mansion of Joel McCrea's character were created here.

The Blue Dahlia (1946)—bungalow interior.

Sorrowful Jones (1949)—assorted sets: bedroom, horse's room, Sorry's (Bob Hope) old apartment, and the barbershop.

A Place in the Sun (1950)—assorted.

Dark City (1950)—Jack Webb's motel-room set.

Detective Story (1951)—assorted.

Son of Paleface (1951)—assorted.

Road to Bali (1952)—assorted.

The Greatest Show on Earth (1952)—the girls' car on the train.

Here Come the Girls (1953)—assorted.

The Caddy (1953)—assorted.

The Stars Are Singing (1953)—assorted offices and performances venues.

The Country Girl (1954)—auditorium and stage in the theater.

Secret of the Incas (1954)—used with Stage 6 as the ruined temple.

White Christmas (1954)—Florida theater, backstage sequences.

The Seven Little Foys (1955)—assorted.

You're Never Too Young (1955)—assorted.

Anything Goes (1956)—assorted.

The Mountain (1956)—rooms of Spencer Tracy and Robert Wagner, cast as brothers in this film, despite the thirty-year age difference.

Pardners (1956)—assorted.

That Certain Feeling (1956)—assorted.

The Man Who Knew Too Much (1956)—Albert Hall.

Beau James (1957)—assorted.

Gunfight at the O.K. Corral (1957)—Wyatt's office, Wiley's Hotel, and the Fly Photography Studio, the last of which is a real place in the real city of Tombstone, Arizona, during the film's 1881 setting.

The Joker Is Wild (1957) nightclub interiors for Frank Sinatra.

Rock-a-Bye Baby (1958)—assorted.

Desire Under the Elms (1958)—assorted.

Vertigo (1958)—The San Juan church, tower steeple, and bell tower were shot here, along with the shot of the girl falling from the tower and much of James Stewart's dream sequence. The "Vertigo-cam" scenes were shot here as well, over four days, January 9–10 and 13–14, 1957.

The Geisha Boy (1958)—The opening credits with the Japanese girls were shot on this stage.

But Not for Me (1959)—interior of New York theater.

The Errand Boy (1961)—assorted.

Blue Hawaii (1961)—tourist's office.

Come Blow Your Horn (1963)—assorted.

The Nutty Professor (1963)—assorted.

Papa's Delicate Condition (1963)—Based on a memoir by silent star Corinne Griffith, the interiors were shot here, while exteriors were shot at Warner Bros.

Who's Minding the Store? (1963)—assorted.

Who's Been Sleeping in My Bed? (1963)—assorted.

Seven Days in May (1964)—assorted.

Where Love Has Gone (1964)—juvenile hall.

The Patsy (1964)—assorted.

The Carpetbaggers (1964)—Nevada's (Allan Ladd) cowboy-themed living room.

Roustabout (1964)—theater interiors.

Darling Lili (1970)—Rock Hudson and Julie Andrews starred in this film, the sort of dated comedy that Peter Bart and Robert Evans felt had made Paramount out of touch with modern audiences.

Lady Sings the Blues (1972)—assorted.

Future Cop (TV, 1976–1978)—Ernest Borgnine starred in this series, later known as Cops and Robin.

The Colbys (TV, 1985–1987)—assorted.

Coming to America (1988)—assorted.

Scrooged (1988)—assorted.

Star Trek V: The Final Frontier (1989)—the "eye of God."

Brooklyn Bridge (TV, 1991–1993)—assorted.

Wayne's World (1992)—assorted.

Star Trek: Deep Space Nine (1993–1999)—assorted.

Star Trek: Generations (1994)—the Enterprise-B bridge.

Roswell (TV, 1994)—not to be confused with the 1999–2002 series.

Clueless (1995)—assorted.

JAG (TV, 1995–2005)—assorted.

Angel (TV, 1999–2004)—assorted.

Nip/Tuck (TV, 2003–2010)—assorted.

Monk (TV, 2006–2009)—Monk's apartment.

Hung (TV, 2009–2011)—assorted.

United States of Tara (TV, 2009–2011)—assorted.

American Horror Story (2011–)—assorted.

Happy Endings (TV, 2011–2013)—assorted.

The eastern entrance to Stage 6 in 2014, inside these doors scenes from *Beau Geste* and *The Brady Bunch* have been shot.

32 STAGE 6 (1922)

WIDTH: 109 feet, 3 inches

LENGTH: 69 feet, 5 inches

HEIGHT: 30 feet

SQUARE FEET: 7,584

Like many stages on the lot, Stage 6 was once a single massive building, built for $7,001.00, which was combined with Stage 7 (see above) as the original Stage 2. The internal wall was first added in 1929–1930 when the stage was converted for sound production, but the barrier has been removed several times over subsequent decades for large productions. Some of the titles listed below are identical to those listed for Stage 7. Whenever possible, it has been noted if this was a single set with no wall between 6 and 7, or two or more sets on neighboring stages.

Shot on Stage 6:

Beau Geste (1939)—barracks corridor.

Union Pacific (1939)—baggage car, telegraph offices, and railroad yard sets.

The Glass Key (1942)—DA's office.

I Married a Witch (1942)—country club.

The Palm Beach Story (1942)—Tom and Gerry's (Joel McCrea and Claudette Colbert) apartment and hall.

The Great Moment (1944)—Joel McCrea's modest house.

The Blue Dahlia (1946)—bar set.

Samson and Delilah (1949)— Delilah's chamber.

Sorrowful Jones (1949)—Steve's cafe.

Sunset Boulevard (1950)—the men's store, process shots of Joe's car and of Norma's car, and Schwab's drugstore interiors.

September Affair (1950)—living room of the Lawrence home.

Houdini (1953)—Von Schweher home in Europe, visited by Houdini.

The Stars Are Singing (1953)—Dave's flat.

War of the Worlds (1953)—the "wrecked farmhouse" set where we finally get to see the Martian creature (played by Charles Gemora).

The Country Girl (1954)—Bing Crosby's dressing room—in the film, that is.

The Seven Little Foys (1955) —assorted.

The Desperate Hours (1955)—Deputy Sheriff Jesse Bard's (Arthur Kennedy) office and police station.

Pardners (1956)—assorted.

The Mountain (1956)—the mayor's house.

The Man Who Knew Too Much (1956)—Savoy Hotel.

Anything Goes (1956)—combined with Stage 7 for some of the big musical numbers.

Vertigo (1957)—Scottie's car process shots, Judy's hotel-room set, and the graveyard sequence for Scottie's dream (which also shot on Stage 7).

Rock-a-Bye Baby (1958)—assorted.

The Space Children (1958)—Stages 6 and 7 used for process shots.

Houseboat (1958)—Caroline's (Martha Hyer) living room.

But Not for Me (1959)—assorted.

Alias Jesse James (UA, 1959)—Jesse's house and ranch.

The Jaywalkers! (1959)—school, along with Stage 7.

The Rat Race (1960)—47th Precinct police station.

Visit to a Small Planet (1960)—the Spelding kitchen and backyard.

The Ladies Man (1961)—assorted.

Soldier in the Rain (1963)—Assorted sets were shot here, including Slaughter's office. Slaughter was played by the gregarious Jackie Gleason. Perhaps this is why the production paperwork tells us that "This is NOT a closed set."

Good Times (Columbia, 1967)— Sonny and Cher make their starring debuts.

The Molly Maguires (1968)—used along with Stage 7.

The Brady Bunch (TV, 1969–1974)— unknown usage, probably for occasional swing (temporary) sets.

The Day of the Locust (1975)—As the characters exit the stage door, one can see the Hollywood sign in the background, although during the period the film is set, and in other scenes in the film, that sign actually said "Hollywoodland."

The Last Tycoon (1975)—assorted.

Marathon Man (1976)—The elaborate water-processing plant set for the film's climax was located here. Star Laurence Olivier was so physically infirm at the time that an elevator had to be constructed in the set to transport the actor into the upper levels and platforms for his scenes in the climax.

Star Trek: The Motion Picture (1978) —the "airlock" set.

Star Trek IV: The Voyage Home (1986)—parts of the Klingon *Bird-of-Prey*.

Star Trek: The Next Generation (TV, 1987–1994)—*Enterprise* sets for the first season, later moved to Stages 8 and 9.

The Bradys (TV, 1990)—assorted.

The Hunt for Red October (1990)
—assorted.

Ferris Bueller (TV, 1990–1991)
—assorted.

Brooklyn Bridge (TV,
1991–1993)—assorted.

JAG (TV 1995–1996)—assorted.

Primal Fear (1996)—assorted.

The Out-of-Towners (1999)
—assorted.

Angel (TV, 1999–2004)—assorted.

Monk (TV, 2002–2009)—assorted.

United States of Tara (TV,
2009–2011)—assorted.

American Horror Story (TV,
2011–   )—assorted.

Happy Endings (TV,
2011–2013)—assorted.

33 STAGE 5 (1922)

WIDTH:	247 feet, 4 inches
LENGTH:	76 feet, 4 inches
HEIGHT:	34 feet
SQUARE FEET:	18,879

Barry Williams reflected on his career with *The Brady Bunch* (TV, 1969–1974): "For me, there was always an air of excitement about going to the studio. Despite the long hours and hard work, I looked forward to each day on the Paramount Stage 5 with a real sense of anticipation. To me, it was even more amazing than Disneyland. Who needs Frontierland or Adventureland when you can have the *Star Trek, Mission: Impossible, Odd Couple, Love, American Style,* and *Happy Days* sets to play on?"[29]

Stage 5, the largest undivided soundstage on the lot in terms of square feet, was initially built as "Stage 1," at a reported cost of $177,414.37. Again, the construction date has been disputed, although curiously, not those suspiciously precise construction costs. The studio insists it was built in 1922, so in light of other convincing evidence, this is what we will go with here. We do know that the stage was enlarged somewhat in 1946. During World War II the studio used to have regular blood drives on Stage 5. All employees, from the front office to the backlot, were encouraged to give blood for the cause.

Like several other stages at Paramount, Stage 5 has a basement level

underneath for storage. For a recent episode of the TV show *Monk* (2002–2009), this basement was undoubtedly well-cast as a dusty cellar.

The divided-off area on the western wall of the stage, now known as the vent room, was the original matte studio for special-effects artist Jan Domela, who is also, you might recall, sometimes credited with designing the Paramount logo.

Shot on Stage 5:

Wings (1927)—Years after the fact, star Richard Arlen told the *Los Angeles Times* that his screen test for this historic picture was shot on this stage.

Dr. Jekyll and Mr. Hyde (1931)—Carew "dream room" set.

Beau Geste (1939)—Sets built to represent crest of hill, Central Park, a casino, and a speakeasy were shot here.

The Way of All Flesh (1940)—hotel lobby.

My Favorite Blonde (1942)—theater set.

Wake Island (1942)—the "Jap transport" set, as the production records insensitively phrased it, was here.

The Palm Beach Story (1942)—the Everglades Club.

Star Spangled Rhythm (1942)—Frisbee's office and other studio offices.

The Uninvited (1944)—Mary Meredith's retreat.

Smiling starlet Ellen Drew enters Stage 5. Note the bowling trophies in the Studio Club display case, 1938.

The Great Moment (1944)—Harvard Medical School.

Road to Rio (1947)—assorted.

The Heiress (1948)—assorted.

The Emperor Waltz (1948)—the dressing room, the Golden Fiddle Inn, and the hunting lodge.

A Foreign Affair (1948)—Marlene Dietrich's apartment and other interiors.

Samson and Delilah (1949)—Samson's chariot.

Sunset Boulevard (1950)—The upstairs of Norma's monstrous house was built here, along with the offices of Sheldrake and Gordon Cole. The interior of the set where DeMille was seen directing *Samson and Delilah* was here too. Those famous scenes, where at least two generations of Hollywood collided, were shot over two days, May 23 and 24, 1949.

My Friend Irma Goes West (1950)—process shots of the Pullman and club cars on train.

Union Station (1950)—suburban train interiors and Bill's sedan.

Ace in the Hole (1951)—trading post and bedrooms.

Road to Bali (1952)—assorted.

Shane (1953)—assorted.

The Country Girl (1954)—police station.

The Conquest of Space (1955)—The scenes of men floating in space were shot here in 1953, two years before the film came out, and twelve years before the first actual spacewalk.

You're Never Too Young (1955)—apartment set, Union Station, and campus exteriors.

The Court Jester (1955)—the "road near the ocean."

Strategic Air Command (1955)—miniature aircraft and sets.

That Certain Feeling (1956)—Larkin apartment and pet shop.

The Man Who Knew Too Much (1956)—police station waiting room, and interior of Ambrose Chapel.

The Vagabond King (1956)—tavern set.

The Joker Is Wild (1957)—assorted.

Funny Face (1957)—living room set.

The Sad Sack (1957)—the "Pink Camel."

King Creole (1958)—the King Creole Club.

Vertigo (1958)—This stage housed Madeleine Elster's office, Scottie's apartment, the interior of the bell tower, Ernie's restaurant, and the flower shop sets. Additionally, the livery stable sequence was shot here, utilizing some sort of treadmill apparatus.

Li'l Abner (1959)—General Bullmoose's bullroom.

Blue Hawaii (1961)—The Coco Palms Hotel in Hawaii was re-created here.

Donovan's Reef (1963)—Dedham's and Donovan's (Jack Warden's and John Wayne's) places.

The Nutty Professor (1963)—assorted.

Who's Been Sleeping in My Bed? (1963)—assorted.

The Disorderly Orderly (1964) —assorted.

Law of the Lawless (1964)—saloon.

Where Love Has Gone (1964)—the Miller (Susan Hayward) home.

Roustabout (1964)—"Mother's tea room."

Harlow (1965)—assorted.

Young Fury (1965)—the McCoy homestead, as well as the saloon and hotel sets.

The Night of the Grizzly (1966)—This stage housed the Wyoming ranch of Jim Cole (Clint Walker), where a fight with a grizzly bear was staged. The bear, "Satan," was in part played by Mickey Simson, who was best known as the diner owner Rock Hudson brawls with in *Giant* (Warner Bros., 1956).

Paradise, Hawaiian Style (1966)— lobby of the Maui Sheridan, office of Danny (James Shigeta), and a steak house too.

Star Trek (TV, 1966–1969)—Scenes for the 1968 episode "Assignment Earth" were shot here.

The Graduate (Embassy Pictures, 1967)—assorted.

Rosemary's Baby (1968)—assorted.

Yours, Mine and Ours (UA, 1968)— Lucille Ball and Henry Fonda starred as two single parents with large families who marry. The concept was reworked into *The Brady Bunch*, which very soon would shoot on the same stage.

The Sterile Cuckoo (1969)—assorted.

The Brady Bunch (TV, 1969–1974)— Producer Lloyd Schwartz remembers working on Stage 5: "One time the kids were running around like lunatics, as kids do, and I was ordered to put a stop to it. I was ordered to keep 'em off the overhead catwalks and off the backyard swing on the set and basically to put 'em in glass cages and pull 'em out for their close-ups. So I said I'm not going to do that, because what's coming across on-screen is that these are real kids, and the minute we start imposing these restrictions on them, we remove them from being real kids. And on-screen they won't react as real kids. I hope it never happens, but every one of those kids needs a chance to break an arm. And they said Okay."[30]

Darling Lili (1970)—assorted.

Heaven Can Wait (1978)—assorted.

The Bad News Bears (TV, 1979–1980)—Corey Feldman, one of the young stars of this TV version of the popular theatrical hit, once recalled that at the time there was still graffiti on the stage and dressing-room walls scribbled there by the long-departed Brady Bunch kids.

The Brady Brides (TV, 1981)—*The Brady Bunch* cast returns to Stage 5!

Mommie Dearest (1981)—assorted.

Star Trek II: The Wrath of Khan (1982)—*Enterprise* and Genesis chamber sets.

A Very Brady Christmas (1988) —assorted.

Bonfire of the Vanities (1990) —assorted.

The Two Jakes (1990)—assorted scenes for this well-intentioned *Chinatown* sequel.

Star Trek VI: The Undiscovered Country (1991)—assorted starship and alien craft interiors.

Patriot Games (1992)—CIA headquarters were on this stage.

That Thing Called Love (1993)—A cast on the cusp of stardom, Sandra Bullock, River Phoenix, Dermot Mulroney, Zoe Cassavetes, and

Samantha Mathis, shot the Bluebird Café interiors here.

Viper (TV, 1994–1999)—assorted.

The Brady Bunch Movie (1995)— different Bradys, same stage.

Vampire in Brooklyn (1995) —assorted.

Primal Fear (1996)—assorted.

The Relic (1997)—assorted.

Star Trek: Insurrection (1998)— *Enterprise-E* bridge.

The General's Daughter (1999) —assorted.

Angel (TV, 1999–2004)—assorted.

Mulholland Dr. (Universal, 2001)—assorted.

Monk (TV, 2002–2009)—assorted.

Medical Investigation (TV, 2004–2005)—assorted.

Threshold (TV, 2005–2006) —assorted.

Hung (TV, 2009–2011)—assorted.

United States of Tara (TV, 2009–2011)—assorted.

American Horror Story (TV, 2011–)—assorted.

Veep (TV, 2012–2015)—the Oval Office sets.

34 TEST STAGE AND STAGE 3 (c. 1926)

WIDTH: 59 feet, 4 inches

LENGTH: 94 feet, 2 inches

HEIGHT: 37 feet

SQUARE FEET: 5,587

Until 1957, the still department occupied this $35,000 building, but by the late 1960s the offices where Paramount's photographers had worked their magic had long ago moved to another building (check #20 on your map). Yet this stage where the still photo department had long popped their flashbulbs was built not for them at all but primarily as a special-effects lab, probably for screen-testing performers, as well, and only later on, as the still department asserted itself, as a photographer's studio. This would explain why, on its website, the company lists precisely one (probably erroneous) title for this so-called soundstage: *Living It Up* (1954), a Dean Martin / Jerry Lewis vehicle.

The confusion seems to have arisen when Paramount leased their actual Stage 3 (see #10 on your map) to the Howard A. Anderson Company, an independent visual-effects firm, in 1968, while they were renumbering their stages to include RKO's. In order to keep the numbering more or less intact, they moved the Stage 3 sign across the lot to this little building. That sign is still there today. The building it hangs in front of today contains both Stage 3 and the very glamorous-sounding film shipping department.

The truth is that the building all of this confusion has swirled around for so long was actually built as Stage 5, sometime prior to 1926, and was occasionally referred to as the "Pomeroy Stage." Roy Pomeroy won the first Oscar for special effects, when that category was called "Mechanical Effects," for *Wings* (1927). He pioneered the idea of rear screen projection for Paramount, before becoming head of the sound department, being dismissed, and then dying, an apparent suicide, in 1947.

It is sad, and very Hollywood-ironic, that this building lost its name (Pomeroy's) and then its identity and its true place in history, just as Pomeroy himself did. This was all inadvertent, of course. In Hollywood, it always is.

35 SCREENING ROOM (5)

The largest theater on the lot in the 1960s was called the studio theater, part of the postproduction complex behind the administration building. The theater at the time seated 291 people and could accommodate both 16mm and 35mm film. The building had originally been built in 1928 and was then called Screening Room 5. It was highly desired by the studio's biggest directors because its large screen and auditorium were comparable to that found in a commercial theater, so was good for gauging how that movie would look and sound in the real world.

LEFT: The Sherry Lansing theatre, center, named after the successful and long-lasting (1992–2004) executive, has been the preferred venue for film screenings on the lot for nearly ninety years, 2016. ABOVE: The outside of the Gower, or RKO screening room, as it looked in 2015.

In the 1940s Hal Wallis and Cecil B. DeMille used to compete with each other about who would get to use Screening Room 5. Music executive Bill Stinson remarked that "everybody thought that DeMille would, because of his longevity, but Wallis always got it. He was powerful."[31]

With the acquisition of RKO, their screening room—next to their commissary, and almost as large as Paramount's Screening Room 5—became available. Old habits die hard, however, and later executives continued to prefer the familiar Paramount room instead. The RKO theater was condescendingly christened the "Little Theater" to avoid confusion, and finally torn down when the commissary was expanded.

Screening Room 5 was luckier. It was remodeled in 1992 and eventually renamed the "Studio Theater," to reflect its favored status. In 2012 it was rechristened again as the Sherry Lansing Theater, after the retiring CEO, who, like Wallis and DeMille, reportedly enjoyed watching dailies there.

Today, Paramount boasts seven screening rooms, including the 516-seat Paramount Theater and the Gower Screening Room, which they refer to in their promotional materials as "the longest-operating studio theater in Hollywood." What this means is that this site was originally Projection Building 3 at RKO, as early as 1929, and it's still in operation today. The seating capacity of the Gower Screening Room is 119. Even today, it's the third-largest on the lot. The smallest theater is the very exclusive Screening Room 8, located beneath the Lansing Theater (capacity, 6). It is also doubles as a sound-mixing stage.

36 BARBERSHOP

One of the social centers of the studio, where gossip was exchanged and hair was cut and faces were shaved, the studio barbershop has been shifted about the lot more times than perhaps any other department. The following locations have all been reported by patrons looking for a shave at Paramount over the years.

In its earliest days the barbershop was located outside of Stage 2. After that it

The Paramount barber shop, wherever its current location, has been a constant on the lot for generations. Here Kirk Douglas, then appearing in *Gunfight at the OK Corral*, gets a trim, and a bonus manicure, for an apparently very news-hungry studio photographer, 1957.

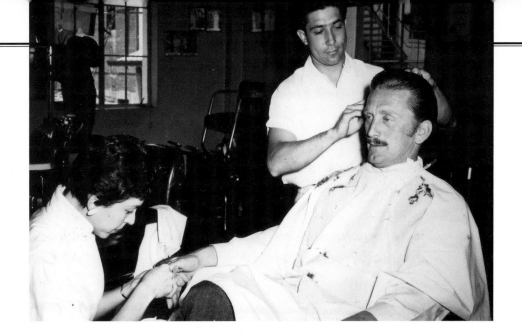

was long reported to be in a corner of the camera vault (Sturges Building), built in 1931.

The Paramount barbershop was originally operated by one Victor Hoenig, and later, for forty years, by Victor Bates. It had a single chair, open from Tuesday through Friday. Bates himself could be seen for years by passersby on Avenue E, seated in that chair himself between customers. In 1940, a haircut was fifty cents. A manicurist and bootblack were also available, although a separate shoeshine shop was once on the south side of Stage 4, and in the 1990s, in the Cooper Building.

These decades of relative tranquility in the haircutting trade came to an end in the late 1990s when the barbershop was inexplicably shuffled over to a corner of the Head Building. It was next reported adjacent to the commissary. After that, there were sightings by shaggy employees on the southern side of Stage 25, near Lucy Park. This didn't last either, however.

Today, the surviving and well-traveled department consists of the studio salon, which as of this writing is located in a corner of the old Gower Mill building. There is also a traditional barbershop, complete with a barber pole, just north of the Bronson Gate. If you find yourself on the lot, you had better get over there quick, as odds are neither one of them will be there for long.

A DeMille monogram as taken from C.G.'s personal stationary. (Image courtesy of Hollywood Heritage)

37 DEMILLE OFFICES AND GATE

Cecil B. DeMille had several offices on the Paramount lot, including one he occupied from 1932 to 1934 on the site of an old Gloria Swanson dressing room after his return to the studio in 1932. But it wasn't until after World War II that Paramount built the DeMille Unit Building on Marathon Street, along with the director's own DeMille Gate. In 1951 Paramount, or DeMille, had a $51,000 second floor added to the complex. Unlike every other building named on the lot after a person, DeMille actually occupied the building with his name already above it.

"The office was not at all the glamorous Hollywood sort of place you might imagine it to be," remembers Cecilia de Mille Presley. "His office was full of books and artwork, preproduction art for whatever project he was working on. There was an outer office as well, with some secretaries, a waiting room, some inner offices where Grandfather kept his writers, whom he liked to keep close, and an office for Henry Wilcoxon."[32] Wilcoxon was DeMille's one-time leading man, and later, his trusted associate producer.

In front of the building was a rose garden. When DeMille died in 1959, a humble grip, still wearing his work clothes from the studio, picked some of these flowers, held them together with a rubber band, and brought the makeshift bouquet to DeMille's wake. A. C. Lyles, in a biography of DeMille, remembered that "there were a lot of people at the service. Hundreds of people. We had big, big bouquets of flowers that people all over the world had sent—kings, queens, presidents . . . I thought that [this] represented more than anything the feeling that all of us at Paramount, the employees of Paramount, our family, the Paramount family, had about Cecil B. DeMille—that grip's little bouquet of flowers."[33]

The office is still there. "I went inside once a few years ago just to see what it looked like after all of these years," remembers Presley. "I told the woman at the reception desk that my grandfather had once been in that office. She looked surprised. 'Is your name . . . DeMille?' she asked me."[34]

Executive Y. Frank Freeman used to keep boxer dogs, four of them, near

the DeMille Gate next to the office. According to actress Carolyn Jones, "at night, around seven o'clock, when practically everyone was gone, they'd close the gates and let those dogs loose. They played with film cans like they were Frisbees. Guys would sail the cans in the air and those dogs would run and catch them. I remember seeing them chomp on them and the film cans would just crumple in their mouths. They were patrol dogs."[35]

The DeMille Gate, located alongside the office, was sometimes also referred to as the Irving Avenue Gate. The entrance was ornate, with intricate wrought-iron patterns and a pedestrian entrance inside of the larger one. But because it

ABOVE LEFT: The DeMille Gate off of Marathon Street as it looked in 1959 at the time of the director's death. Note the adjacent RKO Marathon gate, far left. ABOVE RIGHT: The entrance to Cecil B. DeMille's office as it looked in 1956. Note, again, the monogram.

DeMille in his lair, pretending to be at work for a publicity camera, 1942.

was not as memorable as the Bronson Gate, it often played an entrance to a studio which no one wanted to identify specifically as Paramount. This was the gate seen in *Make Me a Star* (1932), shot under the appropriate title *Gates of Hollywood*, *Sitting Pretty* (1933), and *The Carpetbaggers* (1964). The gate was manned by security guard Victor Moore in *Star Spangled Rhythm* (1942).

In the 1990s the DeMille office was occupied by superstar Eddie Murphy and producers Don Simpson and Jerry Bruckheimer.

38 FILM VAULTS

If the film vault building here seems insufficient, size-wise, to the task of maintaining the Paramount library, the truth is that film elements were (and to a lesser degree, still are) stored all over the lot, even under soundstages, and all over the world. It should also be noted that, in the 1960s, over thirty years' worth of the company's historic features were made the responsibility of Universal, still the case today.

Thirty-five-millimeter film was, and is, both fragile and heavy; we won't even discuss VistaVision and other formats. A "reel" of film, historically, is 1,000 feet, but film was usually projected, confusingly, on 2,000-foot reels, which lasted about 17 minutes. So a 100-minute feature, referred to as a twelve-reeler, would ship to theaters on six 2,000-foot reels. Most film was stored and shipped in heavy cans which contained three or four reels each.

Film needs to be refrigerated for long-term storage. Experts recommend a vault temperature of about 40 degrees Fahrenheit, at 25 percent relative humidity. Nitrate stock, which was the norm until the early 1950s, was highly flammable, and so needed to be stored in partitioned brick bunkers, an entire building of which still exists on the lot, if only because it is too solidly built to be easily torn down.

Today, more than half of all films are shot digitally, and nearly all films are projected that way. Because no one knows how long images will last stored inside a hard drive, the preferred method of vault storage is still on film. For Paramount product, a duplicate inventory of materials is stored in a mine in Pennsylvania. On the lot, in 1990, for the purpose of storing media of all formats, Paramount constructed the massive archive building behind the B-Tank Sky (see #52). Today, this building is the primary depository of the studio's estimated $3 *billion*, 8,800-film library.

ABOVE LEFT: Steve McQueen drives to work in front of the Paramount film vaults, and behind the wheel of his famous 1956 Jaguar XKSS, circa 1966.
ABOVE RIGHT: The same building as it looked in 2016.

A busy Paramount cutting room in 1937.

Originally film editors were called "cutters." As director Edward Dmytryk put it, "a cutter who called himself a film editor would have been considered a snob."36 It was only after the Wagner Labor Relations Act in 1935 and unionization that the latter term became official in Hollywood, and "cutters" discovered that they had actually been "editors" all along.

Originally, perhaps because of the cutting and pasting involved, the job, whatever its title, was considered woman's work. Editing was one of the few craft positions that women were considered qualified for. It was only with the advent of sound and the subsequent additional technical burdens associated with it that men forced their way into the editing room.

For generations editing was usually accomplished on a machine called a Moviola, named after a similarly named company founded in 1924. On a Moviola, or like machine, uncut film was monitored through a small viewing screen while separate, magnetic audio track, hand-synchronized with the picture, was threaded concurrently through a second gate on the same unit. The editor controlled both sound and picture using pedals located at the bottom of the machine. Once editorial choices were made, the film was physically cut and spliced on a nearby table.

At Paramount, the editing department itself was located in a squat collection of buildings south of the commissary, surrounded by film-storage vaults and scene docks. The sound of clattering Moviolas chewing through film was common in this part of the lot for decades.

Today, all "film" cutting is accomplished digitally. Steven Spielberg was reportedly the last major filmmaker to use a Moviola. At Paramount, happily, some editing is still done at the original (expanded and rebuilt) location, but the whir of those noisy original editing machines has been silenced forever.

The harried staff of the Paramount commissary take a moment to pose for a group shot. Pauline Kessinger, the boss, is in the center, 1953.

The original commissary, which opened in September 1927, was called the Paramount Studio Restaurant. From approximately 1933 to 1936, it was the classier-sounding Paramount Café. In 1937 it was rechristened, for no apparent reason, the Paramount Studio Café. In 1939 it was remodeled and renamed yet again, as the Continental Café. Whatever its name, the building was then located on the edge of the backlot north of some editorial buildings.

Paramount was much more democratic than other studios in that although there was a second dining area for executives, it was only used for special parties and for entertaining outsiders. Some stars and producers had tables set aside in the main dining hall for their exclusive usage, but this was more of a working necessity than a sign of any sort of entitlement. Think about it: If stars tended to eat with other stars, it was because stars had more in common, and probably more to talk about, with other stars than with the gardeners or the grips.

The commissary did have a long table just for DeMille. In fact, a Norman Rockwell portrait of Victor Mature as Samson hung on the north wall under that table for years. Someone was once heard to quip "Here comes Jesus Christ and the disciples!" when DeMille and his entourage entered. "He used to sit at the middle of a long table, dining with the most interesting people, not just entertainment people, but famous scientists and religious figures and philosophers," DeMille's granddaughter Cecilia remembers. "Except when he was shooting—then it had to be all business. Making a movie is like fighting a war!"[37]

Jane Russell, Bob Hope, Trigger, and Roy Rogers, on the lot shooting *Son of Paleface*, enjoy a quiet lunch in the Paramount commissary, although Trigger's name card has been placed in front of Bob, 1952.

Actor George Takei, shooting *Star Trek* (TV, 1966–1969) on the lot, also remembers that in 1968, Adolph Zukor was still regularly dining at the commissary as well. "Thin, bald, and frail, he still turned heads and his name was still spoken with whispers when he entered the room. The founder of old Hollywood was still watching over his factory and his flock," Takei has wryly recalled.[38]

In 1976, Ronald L. Davis interviewed Pauline Kessinger, who, for almost thirty-five years, was the Paramount commissary head. The legend on the lot was that Zukor had found Kessinger standing on the lot one day and had built a commissary around her! A story which Kessinger never exactly denied.

Her job duties included managing a staff of almost eighty, supervising the executive dining room, a coffee shop, and a backlot cafe. She also had to prepare box lunches for crews shooting on location. "We would sometimes have as many as a thousand or fifteen hundred lunches to prepare, and we'd have a crew come in at four in the morning to put up the box lunches. Sometimes there'd be four or five locations filming at once, and we had to keep all of those lunches separated for the drivers to pick them up."[39]

The commissary itself, like much of the rest of the studio was an odd mix of glamour and industry. The atmosphere inside was usually congenial and relaxed,

with writers playing word games, technicians talking shop, and comedians like Martin and Lewis repeatedly disrupting everyone's lunch by jerking tablecloths from under the food and "dropping" their trays on the floor. Trigger, Roy Rogers's horse, was slightly better behaved, although he once came inside and kicked a hole in the wall. Yet for all of the perceived anarchy, the waitresses changed the color of their uniforms, which looked like modified French maid outfits, regularly, and for years there were elaborate chandeliers above the tables, which were actually remnants from a movie which had used the commissary as a location. "The set dresser just forgot to take them down," said Kessinger.[40]

In 1933 a 6.4 magnitude earthquake centered in nearby Long Beach rattled Los Angeles. Newsreels of the day featured W. C. Fields, shooting *International House* (1933) on the lot at the time, leading his cast mates to safety even while the quake was happening. Much later, however, it was discovered that the footage was actually faked by Fields and his director, A. Edward Sutherland. Over in the commissary Kessinger was having coffee with Gary Cooper when the big one struck. "He grabbed me by the hand, and we went through the kitchen, with him

ABOVE LEFT and MIDDLE: A real collector's item, the cover and interior of two different Cafe Continental menus, signed by several dozen Paramount stars. The "Paramount Specials," in the right column, are almost more interesting than the autographs, circa 1959. **ABOVE RIGHT:** The commissary in 1966. Note the elaborate, if inappropriate, chandeliers, left over from some long-forgotten movie which had once filmed in the dining room.

pulling me behind those long legs of his. We went out under the water tank."[41]

In 1938 the commissary was expanded and air-conditioning and two new private dining rooms were added. Seating capacity was increased by a hundred seats, allowing for a capacity of five hundred employees at one time.

Kessinger and her staff tried hard to accommodate the tastes of all of their clientele. Consequently, the Paramount commissary had a much better reputation than the RKO version next door. William Demarest, filming *My Three Sons* (TV, 1960–1972) at Desilu, used to go over to Paramount for lunch, preferring their deli menu to that of his own studio's. Lorne Greene, while shooting *Bonanza* (TV, 1959–1973), enjoyed Russian Jewish beet soup with sour cream for lunch, which costar Michael Landon used to jokingly call "ham cream" because of the dish's pink complexion. So Kessinger's staff dutifully added borscht to the menu.

The commissary expanded into an even larger footprint in the mid-1950s, but with the acquisition of Desilu in 1967, Paramount suddenly had two commissaries. They continued to operate them both concurrently and alternately until 1970, when both were closed. Kessinger was sent home, where she died in 1995.

In 1979 Paramount officially reopened the old RKO Café, which had been built in 1929, as the Paramount Café, after expanding the original building into an old RKO rehearsal hall and screening room. The "new" commissary continued to be the social center of the lot. In the 1990s, as Richard Lindheim was dining there, A. C. Lyles came up to his table and informed him that Bob Hope had passed away. Lindheim was properly sympathetic, but a few minutes later Lyles returned and said, "I called Bob's wife Dolores and she said 'You want to talk to Bob?' So I was mistaken." In fact, Hope would not die until 2003, at the ripe old age of one hundred.[42]

In 1987, what was still left of the original Paramount cafeteria on the other side of the lot was demolished and the five-story Adolph Zukor Building was constructed on the site, as a home for the marketing, distribution, licensing, and advertising departments. The studio called the construction "the first new office building on the lot in forty years."[43]

The current Paramount restaurant, now named The Café–Paramount Commissary, has a segregated dining room and a second cafe for working stiffs. Nearby is a third restaurant called The Watertower Café, which features casual fare for employees on the go.

41 LASKY-DEMILLE BARN

The story of the little barn where Paramount began did not end with *The Squaw Man*, or even at Selma-Vine. According to a 1936 company newsletter, DeMille himself shot parts of *The Call of the North* (1914), *The Virginian* (1914), *The Only Son* (1914), and *Joan the Woman* (1916) on the site. When the company moved to their permanent home in 1926, the barn came along. DeMille himself has often been given the credit for rescuing the structure from the fate that befell almost all of the rest of that lot. (This, apparently, is not true, as DeMille was on his unhappy hiatus from the company at the time.)

Someone at Paramount, however, made the decision to have the structure towed the 1.3 miles between Paramount's past and its future. That someone was Jesse Lasky, who was in fact the subject of a 1926 *Los Angeles Times* article about the salvation of the barn. The article also went on to report that "the very window frame of the window from which Mr. Lasky used to gaze when he was dreaming of the great things that might be accomplished by his company is to be removed and placed in his new private office."[44]

Ultimately, and in spite of this article's assertion that the barn was saved as a "pet superstition," whether the building was rescued out of sentimentality or practicality is subject to speculation. It should be noted, however, that except for an iron incinerator, which survived at the new lot until 1940, apparently no other buildings from the old plant were similarly salvaged.

For whatever reason, the barn was towed through the gates and dropped

A somewhat idealized drawing of the Lasky-DeMille barn, 1939

Yul Brynner, rehearsing his role as the dashing (and for him, very hirsute), pirate Jean Lafitte, with his fencing instructor, inside the barn for *The Buccaneer*, 1958.

behind the Gloria Swanson dressing room, near what would eventually become DeMille's office—once he returned home to the studio in 1932.

If the building was kept intact for reasons of sentiment, then the studio did little else to distinguish it from its newer sisters rising up around its walls. The barn was first used for storage, dressing rooms, the shipping department, and then, briefly, as the home of the research library. In 1929 Jim Davies, the studio masseur and boxing instructor, convinced his boss, Richard Kline, Paramount's "physical instructor," that the barn would be the perfect location for a gymnasium. Davies was correct. It would serve mainly as the studio gym for the next fifty years.

In 1935 Paramount threw a slightly tardy twentieth-anniversary party for the surviving members of *The Squaw Man*'s crew at the barn. DeMille and his old director, Oscar Apfel, were the hosts. Together they posed for publicity photos with the camera used to shoot the film. Even then, it must have seemed like it had all happened a hundred years earlier.

In 1937, additional locker rooms and showers were added to the interior of the barn. The exterior look of the structure was not altered.

After Kline's departure in the early 1950s, the department was managed by Davies until his death in 1957, and still later by Orlando Perry, a former bartender. Steve McQueen, Elvis Presley, Marlon Brando, and even Sophia Loren were clients. Roman Polanski used to take martial arts lessons from Bruce Lee there. During this era the barn itself was apparently moved two more times. The first shuffle was in 1955 when it was rolled north to the edge of Western Street, and again, slightly, in 1956, to make room for an expansion of the commissary.

During all of these years the barn continued to be used as a set. *The Man I Love* (1929), *The Search for Beauty* (1934), *Dr. Broadway* (1942), *The Devil's Hairpin* (1957), the TV movie *Flesh and Blood* (1968), and the feature film *The One and Only* (1978) all cast its interior, rather unimaginatively, as a gymnasium. The exterior, parked on the edge of Western Street as it was, was also used as a set. Frequently it inadvertently echoed its own roots by portraying a barn or a stable. Eventually rails were laid in front of its porch and it became a train station, most often the Virginia City train station, for the long-running TV series *Bonanza* (1959–1973).

In 1956, the barn was designated a historic landmark by the state of California. Bunting was strung across its porch and a podium was set up in front of the railroad tracks for the occasion. Lasky and Goldwyn returned to the lot, probably for the last time, and joined DeMille on the stage for the presentation. A commemorative plaque was placed next to the door.

By 1979, the barn had outlived all of the studio's founders; DeMille, Lasky, Goldwyn—all were gone. The barn had outlasted Western Street, onto which it

ABOVE LEFT: The 1956 dedication of the barn as a state historical landmark brought the founders of the studio together for the last time. Seated on the left are DeMille, Goldwyn and Lasky, and at the podium, Y. Frank Freeman. Note the prop railroad tracks in the foreground. ABOVE RIGHT: The plaque placed on the barn that day.

had been annexed, and even lasted longer than Zukor, who had died three years earlier, at the age of 103. But that year Paramount decided they needed to build a (second) powerhouse and a telephone routing station on the site. The historical designation of the structure would have made this agenda problematic, so Jack Foreman, head of the Hollywood Chamber of Commerce at the time, received a phone call from the studio, offering to donate the barn "to the community."

Like it had been fifty years earlier, that October the barn was once again picked up, loaded onto a flatbed truck, and driven out the gates. It was deposited very near its original location, in an open lot on Vine Street, across from the famous Capitol Records building. It would ultimately stand there for three years, rotting outside on jacks, while the owners of the land, the Palace Disco Theater, tried to get someone to come and take it away. Universal Studios, three and a half miles up the road, and trying to be helpful, offered to take the barn as an attraction in their popular theme park, but were vilified by local activists for trying to hijack Hollywood's history. Herb Steinberg, a VP at Universal, shot back that "the alternative presented to me was that it was going to be knocked down and made into so much lumber."[45]

A solution agreeable to everyone was finally hammered out at nearly the last minute. Hollywood Heritage, a preservation organization founded in 1980, accepted a donation of the barn jointly from Paramount Pictures and the Hollywood Chamber of Commerce, and then proceeded to move the building once more, this time to a parking lot across the street from the Hollywood Bowl. The property had been earmarked almost twenty years earlier as a site for an unrelated Hollywood museum that had never been built, so the location seemed apt.

This last journey, on February 15, 1983, another 1.3-miles trip for the well-traveled artifact, was accompanied by a marching band, classic cars, klieg lights, and speeches by all the interested parties aboard a double-decker bus, which followed behind during the trip. Happily, the barn still stands on the site with the plaque on the door.

Back on the lot, Orlando Perry, then in charge of the gym, relocated his department to the other side of the lot inside a former dance rehearsal stage near Van Ness. His department is still on the lot today, although the original building has been moved slightly north, and combined with a nearby annex. In 1995 the department was renamed Vita Nuova ("new life" in Italian), although this classy moniker did not last long. Today it's known only as the "fitness center."

42 MAILROOM / MESSENGER DEPARTMENT

At its peak, responsible for some eight thousand pieces of mail a day, the mailroom was the nerve center of the lot.

During the dark days of World War II when there was a shortage of male messengers, Paramount, like other studios, enlisted women to deliver their mail. Sadly, unlike with their male counterparts, no one ever assumed that this position was a shortcut to an office on the lot or a job as a producer. After V-J Day, those women were sent back to their prior lives.

In the Jerry Lewis vehicle, *The Errand Boy* (1961), Lewis was a studio mailroom employee whose antics did little to enhance the reputation of actual mailroom staffers on the lot. In the film, the mailroom office building, like many actual Paramount buildings, portrayed itself.

In the 1960s the mailroom, managed by one H. Sanford, was open from 8:30 a.m. to 6:30 p.m., offered inter-office mail pickup/delivery six times a day, and had a fancy self-sealing postage and folding machine on-site.

Today the mailroom, at least as of 1990, is located in Bungalow 12, on the eastern side of the plant, near the Van Ness Gate. The old mailroom building, now a sliver of real estate which is part of production support services, has been (as of 1988) renamed the A. C. Lyles Building. Lyles himself was not happy with this honor. "They named a bathroom after me," he complained quietly.

43 STAGES 14, 44 12, 45 13, AND 46 11

STAGE 14 (1929)
STAGE 12 (Now Includes Stages 12 and 14) (1929)
Measurements of both stages combined are as follows:

WIDTH:	216 feet, 7 inches
LENGTH:	95 feet
HEIGHT:	38 feet
SQUARE FEET:	13,378

STAGE 13 (Now Stage 12) (1929)

WIDTH:	94 feet, 9 inches
LENGTH:	64 feet, 6 inches
HEIGHT:	38 feet
SQUARE FEET:	6,083

STAGE 11 (1929)

WIDTH:	94 feet, 8 inches
LENGTH:	64 feet, 3 inches
HEIGHT:	38 feet
SQUARE FEET:	6,083

ABOVE: In 1988 producer A.C. Lyles received the dubious honor of having this decidedly unimpressive-looking old mailroom building named after him. RIGHT: The building containing Stages 11, 12, 13, and 14 is on the right. New York Street stands to the left and the cemetery is in the background, 1935.

Stages 11, 12, 13, and 14 were combined into one building for the purpose of sound production, burned in early 1929, and were rebuilt the same year. Although a separate filmography is provided for each stage, note that many of the titles overlap and that the stages have occasionally been renumbered over the years.

STAGE
14

Old and new numbers are included, but titles listed under those numbers indicate that a production was shot on a spot rather than under a stage-number sign. The actual stage number for the spot where these projects originated is included whenever possible. Note that vertical lift doors were always a fixture in the internal walls of the stages, so many pictures had sets which spilled over onto neighboring stages.

In spite of the perceived show-business proclivity toward superstition, Stage 13 would be part of the initial construction and would remain a part of the complex until the mid-1990s, at which time the wall between 12 and 14 would be opened up and 13 would be renamed Stage 12, which it remains today. (Yes, it is very confusing.)

Originally Stages 12 and 14—which, remember, is the current Stage 14—contained monitoring rooms for the recording of sound on the set. These booths, which were similar to Studios H and K in the same building, were removed in 1942 to make Stages 12 and 14 larger.

The histories of the other parts of this 173-foot-by-190-foot building are included in the Sound Department (#48) section.

Shot on Stages 12 and 14:

Hollywood on Parade, No. A4 (Criterion, 1933)—Bing Crosby comes out the stage door; Mary Pickford tells him she heard him singing inside. "Way out here?" he exclaims. "I thought these stages were soundproofed."

Beau Geste (1939)—barracks at Fort Zinderneuf.

Sullivan's Travels (1941)—the Kansas City hotel.

The Glass Key (1942)—Madvig's (Brian Donlevy) office scenes were shot here (Stage 12).

Star Spangled Rhythm (1942)—captain's cabin (Stage 12).

Going My Way (1944)—corridor and dressing rooms (Stage 12).

The Great Moment (1944)—Dr. Jackson's laboratory (Stage 14).

The Blue Dahlia (1946)—farmhouse.

The Perils of Pauline (1947)—Grand Hotel (Stage 14).

Samson and Delilah (1949)—temple of Dagon upper boxes and floor (Stage 14).

Song of Surrender (1949)—hotel balcony on Stage 14.

Sorrowful Jones (1949)—ambulance entranceway and hospital (Stages 12 and 14).

September Affair (1950)—plane and jeep process shots.

Detective Story (1951)—assorted.

Son of Paleface (1951)—assorted.

Road to Bali (1952)—assorted.

The Greatest Show on Earth (1952)—Brad's wagon (used both stages).

Lucy Gallant (1953)—assorted.

Tropic Zone (1953)—assorted.

Yul Brynner on a break from filming *The Ten Commandments* makes a phone call outside Stage 12, 1956.

BUSINESS ONLY

White Christmas (1954)—assorted.

That Certain Feeling (1954)—gallery (Stage 14).

The Court Jester (1955)—The king's chamber and parapets, as well as Danny Kaye's room, were here, constructed on both Stages 12 and 14.

Strategic Air Command (1955)—sets on Stages 12 and 14.

The Ten Commandments (1956)—Stages 12 and 14 were opened up again for this one. Sets using either, or both, of these stages included Rameses' council chamber, the palace corridor and stairway, the exteriors of the royal barge, the prison cell, the bulrushes, the palace garden, the Egyptian border, the "shrine of the river god," the secluded palm grove, a "jutting crag," the top of the city

gates, the "furthermost Sphinx," and lastly, a treadmill sequence involving horses and chariots.

The Man Who Knew Too Much (1956)—embassy set.

The Mountain (1956)—the snowbank (Stage 12).

Gunfight at the O.K. Corral (1957)—Tombstone barbershop.

Wild Is the Wind (1957)—Gino's (Anthony Quinn) house; upper floor was on Stage 12, and airport waiting room, on Stage 14.

Funny Face (1957)—The Quality magazine offices were on Stage 14.

The Buccaneer (1958)—Lafitte's living room and the swamp sets were here.

The Jaywalkers! (1959)—saloon.

Alias Jesse James (UA, 1959)—the Dirty Dog Saloon.

Cinderfella (1960)—assorted.

The Ladies Man (1961)—assorted.

The Pleasure of His Company (1961)—assorted.

The Man Who Shot Liberty Valance (1962)—assorted.

Hatari (1962)—Arusha Hotel and Sean's bedroom.

McLintock! (1963)—Birnbaum's store (Stage 14) and the saloon/hotel lobby (Stage 12).

Who's Minding the Store? (1963) —assorted.

The Carpetbaggers (1964)—The Cord offices and family home, the aircraft factory, and Rina's (Carroll Baker) fall from the chandelier were shot on both Stages 12 and 14. This later scene was very controversial in 1964 because Carroll was naked at the time, although only European audiences got to see the uncut sequence; it remains, arguably, one of the first intentional nude scenes shot on a Hollywood soundstage.

The Family Jewels (1965)—assorted.

El Dorado (1966)—the Twin Spurs Saloon was on Stage 12, the church and bell tower, on Stage 14.

Rosemary's Baby (1968)—assorted.

The Molly Maguires (1968) —assorted.

Paint Your Wagon (1969)—assorted.

On a Clear Day You Can See Forever (1970)—assorted.

The Day of the Locust (1975)—outside of the stage, looking into the backlot.

Saturday Night Fever (1977)—unknown sequences.

Airplane II: The Sequel (1982)—used both Stages 12 and 14.

Top Gun (1986)—assorted.

The Hunt for Red October (1990) —assorted.

Soapdish (1991)—The TV studio soap opera set was here.

Regarding Henry (1991)—assorted.

Dangerous Minds (1995)—assorted.

Losing Isaiah (1995)—assorted.

Eye for an Eye (1996)—assorted.

Star Trek: First Contact (1996)—Stage 14 as engineering room set.

Face/Off (1997)—assorted.

The Relic (1997)—assorted.

Sabrina, the Teenage Witch (TV, 2000–2003)—assorted.

Lemony Snicket's A Series of Unfortunate Events (2004)—assorted.

Charmed (TV, 2004–2006) —assorted.

Star Trek (2009)—assorted.

Glee (TV, 2009–2015)—high school cafeteria set.

Shot on Stage 13:

Dr. Jekyll and Mr. Hyde (1931)—Ivy's second apartment.

Thanks for the Memory (1937)—Gil's (Otto Kruger) apartment.

Beau Geste (1939)—the barracks at Fort Saida.

The Cat and the Canary (1939)—the "smokehouse."

Sullivan's Travels (1941) —courthouse.

West Point Widow (1941)—hospital sets built on Stages 13 and 14, as well as assorted other sets.

The Palm Beach Story (1942)—small restaurant.

The Blue Dahlia (1946)—Golden Lion club and police homicide office.

Road to Rio (1947)—assorted.

The Heiress (1948)—assorted.

Road to Bali (1952)—assorted.

Shane (1953)—exteriors shot in Jackson Hole, Wyoming.

The Caddy (1953)—assorted.

Tropic Zone (1953)—Ronald Reagan on the island of "Puerto Barrancas."

Secret of the Incas (1954)—assorted jungle tomb sets.

Strategic Air Command (1955)—General Espy's office.

The Trouble with Harry (1955)—Vermont locations.

You're Never Too Young (1955)—Nancy's (Diana Lynn) drawing room.

The Court Jester (1955)—the Basil Rathbone–Danny Kaye duel was shot here and on Stage 18.

Pardners (1956)—assorted.

The Ten Commandments (1956)— Seti I's robing room and bedchamber; also Nefretiri's bedchamber, Bithiah's apartment, the tent and slave camp, Mount Sinai exteriors (Stages 13 and 14), Dathan's tent, and some (cut) frog effects for the plague sequences were all shot on this stage. Also, at the very end of this very long production, on August 21, 1956, DeMille's little-seen filmed introduction to the movie was recorded here as well.

The Tin Star (1957)—assorted.

Gunfight at the O.K. Corral (1957)— Long Branch Saloon set.

Houseboat (1958)—Tom's (Cary Grant) apartment.

One-Eyed Jacks (1959)—as northern California.

The Ladies Man (1961)—assorted.

The Pleasure of His Company (1961)—assorted.

Hatari (1962)—the Safari Bar.

Papa's Delicate Condition (1963) —assorted.

The Nutty Professor (1963) —assorted.

Who's Minding the Store? (1963) —assorted.

The Patsy (1964)—assorted, Jerry Lewis comedy, with Peter Lorre contributing his last performance.

The Carpetbaggers (1964)—The studio commissary for Norman Pictures was created here, as was a "cheap apartment" set.

Roustabout (1964)—office set.

Where Love Has Gone (1964)—art museum.

Nevada Smith (1966)—Karl Malden's ranch house.

Rosemary's Baby (1968)—assorted.

The Molly Maguires (1968) —assorted.

Yours, Mine and Ours (UA, 1968)— Lucille Ball returned to the lot for this one.

Paint Your Wagon (1969)—assorted.

On a Clear Day You Can See Forever (1970)—assorted.

Once Is Not Enough (1975) —assorted.

Staying Alive (1983)—assorted.

The Hunt for Red October (1990) —assorted.

Flight of the Intruder (1991) —assorted.

The Butcher's Wife (1991)—assorted.

Soapdish (1991)—assorted scenes for this Sally Field comedy.

All I Want for Christmas (1991)—assorted.

Regarding Henry (1991)—assorted.

Dead Again (1991)—assorted.

Brooklyn Bridge (TV, 1991–1993)—assorted.

Eye for an Eye (1996)—Sally Field suspense drama.

Sabrina, the Teenage Witch (TV, 1996–2003)—assorted.

Charmed (TV, 2004–2006) —assorted.

Everybody Hates Chris (TV, 2005–2009)—assorted.

Star Trek (2009)—assorted.

Glee (TV, 2009–2015)—the auditorium scenes.

Shot on Stage 11:

Sudden Money (1939)—cigar store.

The Way of All Flesh (1940) —speakeasy.

The Glass Key (1942)—Jeff's (William Bendix) apartment.

Holiday Inn (1942)—The upper hallway and Linda's room were shot here. The beloved "White Christmas" number was shot here on December 22, 1941, almost on Christmas! Retakes, however, dragged on until January 17, 1942, perhaps because the studio and star Bing Crosby were a bit worried about the sentimental song's commercial prospects. The music itself, of course, would have been prerecorded.

The Palm Beach Story (1942)—ladies' washroom.

Stage 11 looking north. The Sound Building, or as it is now known, the Balaban Building, is in the background, 2013.

Going My Way (1944)—Carol's apartment.

Double Indemnity (1944)—The supermarket interiors were on this stage. The exteriors were at Jerry's Market at 5330 Melrose Avenue, very close to the studio.

The Big Clock (1948)—Van Barth's bar, where "The Big Clock" number is performed.

A Foreign Affair (1948)—the "denazification office" set and Jean Arthur's office.

Let's Dance (1950)—the judge's chamber.

The File on Thelma Jordan (1950) —courtroom.

Union Station (1950)—parlor hideaway.

Son of Paleface (1951)—assorted.

Road to Bali (1952)—assorted; the only color "Road" movie, and the last one produced by Paramount.

Tropic Zone (1953)—assorted.

Lucy Gallant (1955)—assorted; Edith Head plays herself!

The Ten Commandments (1956)—The "Sinai slope" effect sequence was created here, using models and black velvet, along with a retake of a "Streets of Goshen" sequence.

Pardners (1956)—assorted.

Teacher's Pet (1957)—assorted.

Vertigo (1958)—Midge's (Barbara Bel Geddes) apartment.

The Colossus of New York (1958)—the laboratory.

Houseboat (1958)—Houseboat interiors which would not fit on Stage 16 ended up over here.

But Not for Me (1959)—Boston hotel.

Breakfast at Tiffany's (1961) —assorted.

The Errand Boy (1961)—assorted studio interiors.

Donovan's Reef (1963)—assorted.

Papa's Delicate Condition (1963) —assorted.

Who's Minding the Store? (1963) —assorted.

The Disorderly Orderly (1964) —assorted.

Seconds (1965)—assorted.

Ship of Fools (Columbia, 1965)—1933 set, ship interiors.

The Day of the Locust (1975)—The apocalyptic destruction of the Waterloo set was shot here.

47 STAGE 15 (1938)

WIDTH: 163 feet, 11 inches

LENGTH: 110 feet

HEIGHT: 56 feet

SQUARE FEET: 18,040

History indicates that Stage 15 was built, in 1938, for *Spawn of the North* (1938), on the site of the studio's original B-Tank (#52). Sadly, history usually plays little part in either Hollywood's movies or Hollywood's movie studios, so all of this is speculative—although to this day the stage has a 138-foot-by-92-foot tank in the floor which is 6 feet deep and includes an extendable hydraulic wall. It had to be built for something. Construction costs for the stage have been reported as $90,986.35.

Oddly, this massive mini ocean is oft-credited by the studio as having been used in Hitchcock's *Lifeboat* (Twentieth Century Fox, 1944), although all production records and oral histories regarding the production of that film indicate that it was made in a similar tank on Stage 6 at Fox. So this story appears to be an urban legend created by someone who must have seen a similar film shooting at Paramount during this era. Even conventional wisdom doesn't seem to work in this instance, yet the story endures.

A motor-driven gimbal was installed in 1989 for *The Hunt for Red October* (1990). Sets built on top of this platform could be rocked and tilted for special effects. The contraption remained in the stage after that movie for usage by future productions for several years.

The stage was damaged in the famous 1983 fire, which started while *Star Trek 3: The Search for Spock* (1984) was in production inside. The damage to the stage was minimal and the film went back into production almost immediately.

Stage 15's southern wall has an internal door connecting it to Stage 14 (or rather Stage 12 in the 1960s), allowing production, when necessary, to spill out into the adjacent stage. The western wall outside of Stage 15 is covered with elaborate New York Street backlot facades. During the reconstruction of the backlot after the fire one of the first sets erected was the high school facade for *The Bronx Zoo* (TV, 1987–1988). The *Rizzoli & Isles* (TV, 2010–2016) Boston Police Department "building" currently stands nearby.

Shot on Stage 15:

Holiday Inn (1942)—The "Easy to Dance With" and "I'll Capture Her Heart" musical numbers were shot here.

I Married a Witch (1942)—The special-effects department here staged a stunt involving a taxi crashing into an oak tree. The budget for the effect was $395.00.

The Palm Beach Story (1942)—Pennsylvania Station; also J. D. Hackensacker's (Rudy Vallee) home.

Star Spangled Rhythm (1942)—the "Old Glory" number.

Two Years Before the Mast (1946)—Aquatic scenes were shot in the tank.

The Blue Dahlia (1946)—Sunset Strip scenes.

Road to Rio (1947)—assorted.

The Perils of Pauline (1947)—balloon miniatures, scenes with "rain and lightning," and Artcraft Studio scenes.

Samson and Delilah (1949)—The very spectacular Temple of Dagon set was here.

Dark City (1950)—Swede's place.

September Affair (1950)—the flower stand.

My Friend Irma Goes West (1950)—the Quicksand Club.

Let's Dance (1950)—the porch at the mountain lodge.

Union Station (1950)—tunnel.

A Place in the Sun (1951)—The famous rowboat scene with Montgomery Clift contemplating the murder of Shelley Winters was shot in the big tank.

Son of Paleface (1951)—assorted.

When Worlds Collide (1951)—The rocket-ship platform and gangplank for the loading of passengers were built here and on Stage 13. The exteriors of that rocket were taken in Topanga Canyon, California.

The Greatest Show on Earth (1952)—circus tent interiors and yellow-screen shots of the actors, to which parade backgrounds would be added later.

Botany Bay (1952)—aquatic scenes shot in tank.

Shane (1953)—assorted.

The Caddy (1953)—assorted.

Elephant Walk (1954)—assorted.

White Christmas (1954)—This partial remake of *Holiday Inn* (1942) saw the return of both Bing Crosby and Stage 15.

Lucy Gallant (1955)—assorted.

The Court Jester (1955)—The courtyard and the forest, as well as some tournament scenes, were shot here. Future Oscar winner George Chakiris, for *West Side Story* (UA, 1961), was an uncredited dancer here.

To Catch a Thief (1955)—assorted.

Strategic Air Command (1955)—Thule Air Force Base, as well as an arctic landscape and a B-47 cockpit.

The Ten Commandments (1956)—the golden calf, Nefretiri's room and balcony, the brick pits, Rameses' palace balcony, and Mount Nebo exteriors.

Hollywood or Bust (1956)—assorted.

The Mountain (1956)—campsite exteriors on the trail (also Stage 14).

Desire Under the Elms (1957)—assorted.

The Buccaneer (1958)—The battle of New Orleans was shot largely on this stage.

But Not for Me (1959)—Atwood's office; also Central Park.

Alias Jesse James (UA, 1959)—ranch house and "fork in road."

Li'l Abner (1959)—"Dogpatch."

Cinderfella (1960)—assorted.

LEFT: In 1938, where Stage 15 would soon rise stood the studio's original B-Tank, visible here, top left, sporting a black, tarped roof. Stages 11-14 are beneath, parallel to the original Paramount water tower. The RKO lot and water tower are on the right. ABOVE: The same approximate view in 1960. Stage 15, with twin ventilation shafts running across the roof is top left.

The Errand Boy (1961)—assorted.

The Ladies Man (1961)—assorted.

McLintock! (1963)—the McLintock (John Wayne) home.

Who's Been Sleeping in My Bed? (1963)—assorted.

Soldier in the Rain (1963)—carnival scenes; Adam West had a small part in this scene.

Roustabout (1964)—the midway.

Family Jewels (1965)—assorted.

El Dorado (1966)—The sheriff's office, inside and out, where much of the action happens; John Wayne, of course, was that sheriff.

Chuka (1967)—assorted.

True Grit (1969)—assorted scenes; John Wayne again.

Darling Lili (1970)—assorted.

Saturday Night Fever (1977) —unknown.

Black Sunday (1977)—assorted.

Heaven Can Wait (1978)—assorted.

Star Trek III: The Search for Spock (1984)—the Genesis planet.

Star Trek IV: The Voyage Home (1986) —assorted.

The Hunt for Red October (1990) —assorted.

Flight of the Intruder (1991) —assorted.

Soapdish (1991)—assorted.

The Addams Family (1991) —assorted.

Regarding Henry (1991)—assorted New York interiors.

Death Becomes Her (Universal 1992) —assorted.

Jennifer Eight (1992)—assorted.

Sliver (1993)—Sharon Stone and William Baldwin monitor room set.

Drop Zone (1994)—assorted Florida interiors.

Star Trek: First Contact (1996) —"deflector array."

The Birdcage (UA, 1996)—Miami, Florida.

The Relic (1997)—museum interiors.

Deep Impact (1998)—assorted.

Star Trek: Insurrection (1998)— Ru'afo's flagship.

The Truman Show (1998)—assorted.

Charmed (TV, 1998–2006)—assorted.

The General's Daughter (1999)—assorted.

Sabrina, the Teenage Witch (TV, 2000–2003)—assorted.

Star Trek: Nemesis (2002)—bridge of the *Enterprise-E*.

Andy Richter Controls the Universe (TV, 2002–2003)—one 2002 episode, "Twins," shot here.

Lemony Snicket's A Series of Unfortunate Events (2004)—assorted.

Charmed (TV, 2004–2006) —assorted.

Star Trek (2009)—transporter room.

Glee (TV, 2009–2015)—assorted William McKinley High School interiors; the same fictional high school, or at least a high school with the same name, also appeared in the TV shows *The Wonder Years* (1988–1993) and *Freaks and Geeks* (1999–2001).

48 SOUND DEPARTMENT

The original four soundstages constructed for recording dialogue on-set mostly burned down before they were even completed. They were quickly rebuilt in 1929 with the technology for recording this sound in the same general area. These facilities were enormous and cumbersome, but they were at the cutting edge of the technological frontier at the time.

In the late 1920s, when this complex was created, sound was recorded on

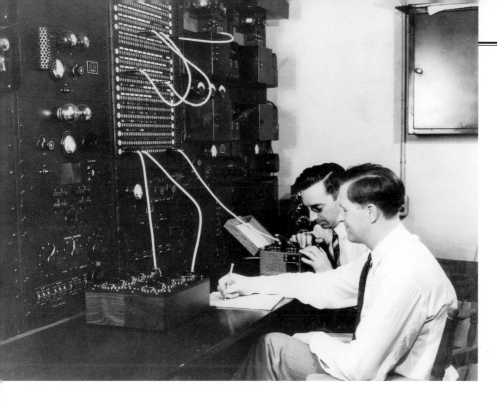

An early sound mixing room. The technicians somehow are managing to look confident, 1929.

the set and into a mixing board, which originally had three channels where sound from up to three microphones could be recorded. The three channels were for music, dialogue, and sound effects, although that would not always be the case. The mixer would have to decide, on-set and spontaneously, what, and how much, to channel through his board and into the absurdly heavy cables which ran throughout the building (all four stages were constructed in the same building for a reason) and into an amplifier in the adjacent "Sound Building," where the sound was recorded onto discs or optically onto magnetic tape.

Today the sound is recorded on the set, or on location using relatively light-weight equipment, but when this complex was constructed, and earlier, when those first talking pictures were made at night while these stages were being rebuilt, the process of capturing and recording sound was almost impossibly difficult. And that sound, once captured, was hard to edit, synchronize, and later, to project.

Original sound cameras were not sound cameras at all, but rather massively blimped silent cameras, modified with motors to keep the speed at a consistent and standardized twenty-four frames per second, and wrapped in blankets and boxes to keep those motors, or rather the sound of those motors, off that all-important soundtrack.

As if creating sound movies were not hard enough, in the late 1920s there were also two competing systems for Paramount to choose from for exhibiting sound pictures. Warner Bros.' Vitaphone had been first, but the Vitaphone soundtrack was shipped to theaters on discs, and was maddeningly difficult to synchronize, and to keep synchronized with the projected image. Fortunately Paramount chose the Fox Movietone system instead, which utilized an optical soundtrack attached to the edge of the film itself, and which quickly became the industry's dominant format.

In 1928 sound department head Roy Pomeroy, previously a special-effects technician had to invent a way to string together sound and image. The first film he was handed was the already-shot silent baseball drama *Warming Up* (1928). As historian Ron Haver put it, "The studio had no sound-editing equipment yet; Pomeroy worked with two projectors running in synchronization—one for picture, one for sound. The actual cutting and matching of picture and sound was done with a stopwatch, a metronome, and the mathematical certainty that the Movietone sound image was twenty frames ahead of the picture."[46]

Eventually the warrens of vacuum tubes, wire and electrical signal amplifiers, electro-acoustic transducers (loudspeakers), multichannel electronic amplifiers, compressors, filters, and sound mixers occupying the walls separating the stages and the offices between the stages, and ultimately the adjacent sound building itself, were thinned out, torn down, and reduced as the problems associated with early motion picture sound recording were solved, marginalized, or worked around. The offices carved out of these stages were converted into dubbing and ADR rooms where audio problems were solved in postproduction rather than while these problems were happening live on the adjacent soundstage.

The sound building itself on the northern side of the complex was managed in 1969 by Glen Glenn Sound. As part of the push to turn the floundering department into a lucrative rental service, Paramount, or rather Glen Glenn, offered Nagras (portable sound-recording machines) for $5.00 a day. Walkie-talkies, PA systems, and megaphones were available on a per-day basis as well. Glen Glenn also managed the recording booths "H" and "K," originally where the sound was piped into, but in the 1960s were ADR stages. Today "H" is a meeting room and "K," a Foley stage.

Rothacker Aller Laboratories, located on 5515 Melrose Avenue, shortly before it was destroyed by a fire in 1929.

The "Sound Recording Building" maintained that name until 1987, when as part of the renaming-buildings era, it became, for one reason or another, the "Balaban Building." There are still postproduction offices inside, although not exclusively so.

An equivalent building was constructed across the fence at RKO about the same time, and with similar technical considerations. It included a sound department, and echoing its sister, the attached Stages 4, 5, and 6.

Paramount never had a dedicated film-processing lab on the lot, although Rothacker Aller Laboratories—on Melrose in front of the studio, and destroyed in a fire in 1929—probably processed some of the studio's early product. Paramount's contracted lab, Harris Ensign Labs, was at one time located on the old Selma-Vine lot, and they continued to use it for many years. The operation eventually became part of Deluxe Laboratories.

49 STAGE 16 (1938)

WIDTH: 170 feet, 5 inches

LENGTH: 104 feet, 9 inches

HEIGHT: 40 feet

SQUARE FEET: 17,851

Stages 15 and 16, looking west. Note the plaque on the wall of 16 designating the titles of a handful of the hundreds of films shot inside, 2013.

Again, dating the construction of such a notable building as Stage 16 has proven to be both daunting and difficult. The plaque on the stage wall says that it was built in 1938. The internal building survey estimates 1941. But as the Planning and Development Department has blueprints on file which also say 1938, in this case we will use the earlier number. Everyone seems to agree that the construction costs were $161,972.11.

Stage 16 includes another pit for aquatic scenes or for building sets below floor level. In this case, the pit, some 50 feet by 80 feet across, starts shallowly and then veers downward as it works its way west, eventually reaching a maximum depth of 12 feet. When the tank is not being used (which is most of the time), it is covered, like most stage floors, with a wood panel floor and a Masonite cover to dampen sound levels.

There is some evidence that, as for the B-Tank beneath Stage 15, the Stage 16 tank, in form or inspiration, predated the stage itself. In any case the tank survives today, although again, no one can even remember the last time it was actually filled with water.

Shot on Stage 16:

The Glass Key (1942)—Bonita Granville's bedroom.

Wake Island (1942)—assorted.

Holiday Inn (1942)—The title inn, including the showroom and stage for musical numbers, was built here.

Star Spangled Rhythm (1942)—assorted scenes and numbers.

The Perils of Pauline (1947)—the Danbury Theater, the Barnside Theater, and the classy-sounding Casino De Paree.

Samson and Delilah (1949)—The very troublesome lion fight with Victor Mature and an allegedly placid big cat was shot here over six days, from November 8–13, 1948. Additional scenes would also be shot in the B-Tank (between September 7 and 16), on Stage 4, and by a second, and even a third

unit, in Lone Pine, California. When Mature refused to tussle with a live lion, DeMille accused the actor of cowardice. Mature could not be persuaded, however. The scene never was completed to the director's complete satisfaction.

Song of Surrender (1949)—church and terrace scenes.

Let's Dance (1950)—The "Tunnel of Love" number with Fred Astaire

and Betty Hutton was shot here, and on Stages 6–7 and 12 (but mostly here).

My Favorite Spy (1951)—Lily's (Hedy Lamarr) limousine, a hotel corridor, and Peanut's (Bob Hope) hotel suite.

The Greatest Show on Earth (1952)—During the film's spectacular train wreck sequence, this stage was filled with circus animals which escape in the melee. The greatest

FAR LEFT: The aftermath for *The Greatest Show on Earth*'s colossal train wreck sequence as created on Stage 16, 1952. LEFT: Alfred Hitchcock, top center, and his crew meticulously lining up the nail-biting opening sequence for *Vertigo* on Stage 16, 1958.

problem occurred when a large cage of monkeys was opened. The simians were so frightened of the lions and tigers that they panicked and fled the building. Some of them were finally recaptured running loose amid the graves at the cemetery.

Stalag 17 (1953)—A miniature POW set was built here for optical effects.

White Christmas (1954)—The title song was (re)recorded in Scoring Room 1 on September 19, 1953, for playback on this stage.

That Certain Feeling (1954) —merry-go-round.

The Conquest of Space (1955)—The Earth rocket model was filmed here.

You're Never Too Young (1955)— hotel set.

That Certain Feeling (1955) —assorted.

The Ten Commandments (1956)—The construction pavilion interiors, the Seti I throne room, the "defile rocks" and "throne of defile," the destruction of the golden calf, the burning bush, the summit of Sinai, and "rocky crevice" were all shot, or partially shot, on this stage. The dramatic cloudscapes during the assorted biblical miracles, and the corridor through which the children of Israel pass through the Red Sea were also largely composed here. The last sequence alone took John P. Fulton and his crew twenty days' (and twenty nights') toil to work out the technical details.

The Vagabond King (1956)—The rose garden, council chamber, and palace ballroom sets were built and filmed here.

The Joker Is Wild (1957)—assorted.

Gunfight at the O.K. Corral (1957)—exteriors of the road from Tombstone.

The Buccaneer (1958)—bayou scenes.

Rock-a-Bye Baby (1958)—assorted.

Desire Under the Elms (1958) —assorted.

Houseboat (1958)—The interior and exterior houseboat scenes were filmed utilizing the tanks.

Vertigo (1958)—Argosy Bookstore, Midge's car, mission exteriors and cloisters, Ransohoff's suit department, art gallery, and rooftop sets.

The Five Pennies (1959)—assorted.

Bonanza (TV, 1959–1973)—assorted exteriors.

Visit to a Small Planet (1960)— assorted, including spaceship exteriors.

The Errand Boy (1961)—assorted.

The Night of the Grizzly (1966)— campsite exteriors.

Looking for Mr. Goodbar (1977) —assorted.

Foul Play (1978)—as with *Vertigo*, assorted San Francisco scenes were faked on this stage.

Star Trek III: The Search for Spock (1984)—assorted.

Clue (1985)—assorted mansion set interiors.

Pretty in Pink (1986)—Assorted scenes for this 1980s classic were recorded here.

Star Trek: The Next Generation (TV, 1987–1994)—assorted swing (temporary) sets, including part of the pilot, "Encounter at Farpoint" (1987).

She's Having a Baby (1988) —assorted.

Star Trek IV: The Undiscovered Country (1991)—the frozen penal colony set.

Star Trek: Voyager (TV, 1995–2001)— assorted swing (temporary) sets.

Star Trek: Insurrection (1998)— Ba'ku caves.

Elizabethtown (2005)—the film for which critic Nathan Rabin coined the phrase "Manic Pixie Dream Girl" to describe Kirstin Dunst's character in this film, an archetype going back to *Bringing Up Baby* (RKO, 1938), shot just a few soundstages to the west, come to think of it.

Mission: Impossible 3 (2006) —assorted.

MTV Video Awards (TV, 2008) —unknown.

Glee (TV, 2009–2015)—assorted.

Larry Crowne (Universal, 2010) —assorted.

Dinner for Schmucks (2010) —assorted.

New York Street, 1931.

50 NEW YORK STREET

Unlike other studios which built permanent sets as anticipated for general production use, Paramount was so haphazardly managed as far as their physical plant that "permanent" backlot sets seemed to appear only when no one bothered to tear them down and another project appropriated the remains. For example, in 1936, for *Champagne Waltz* (1937), a 200-foot exterior set was built in the area where New York Street would later rise—and then be completely removed. But the more impressive of these one-picture sets, or parts of them, were sometimes, luckily, shoved aside for convenience, rather than destroyed. Eventually these pieces of sets would be adapted into pieces of other sets, which in turn would again be adapted into pieces of other sets. Eventually, a backlot would be born.

The date usually given for New York Street's construction, with no justification or documentation I've been able to uncover, is 1927. But those sets which eventually became "New York" did so almost more through a will of their own than through any sort of intentional design. In that sense, Paramount's New York Street set goes back to before Paramount was even on the lot. So it is hard to draw with any authority any sort of straight line from the Brunton Studio sets, which already stood on the lot in 1927, to the 1983 fire. But intuition and imagination, and a good eye for detail, could well lead to the discovery of architectural features from Paramount films in the 1930s that were still very recognizable in films made in the same place in the 1970s, and even beyond.

Are these, in fact, the same sets then? That depends on your definition of "same." They may look alike. They may be in the same place. But at Paramount, and at other studios, sets were destroyed, or wore out, and then would be replaced by later "copies." Can you even call something a copy which was based on something not real in the first place? Remember that these second-, third-, or fourth-generation sets mimicked the look of the originals, but only because they were created from the same blueprints or elevations, which were copied only because it took too much time for the Paramount art department to draw up new ones. So then, rhetorically speaking, is this copy, or copy of a copy, of the original set to be considered the same thing because it is located in the same place? Or are these second-, third-, or fiftieth-generation sets, in fact, a newer, Frankenstein-like creation, with their own history and filmography?

The original set had three districts, New York Street, Boston Street, and McFadden Street, and covered 96,000 square feet—about two and a half acres. An incinerator tower, near Stage 16, was unfortunately often visible on-camera near the back of this set. So the 160-ton eyesore was laboriously moved to the northeast corner of the lot in 1942. A Brownstone Street, and, in the 1960s, a Modern Street was added, which was just that—a strip of garish, era-specific suburbs.

ABOVE: The "original" New York Street, if such a word is possible for such a ghostlike location, ran from the top of the lot nearly to the DeMille's Office and Gate, both of which are visible center, near the bottom of this equally haunting 1938 study. RIGHT: Paramount's Sprawling, maze-like New York Street as seen from the northwest, 1933.

186

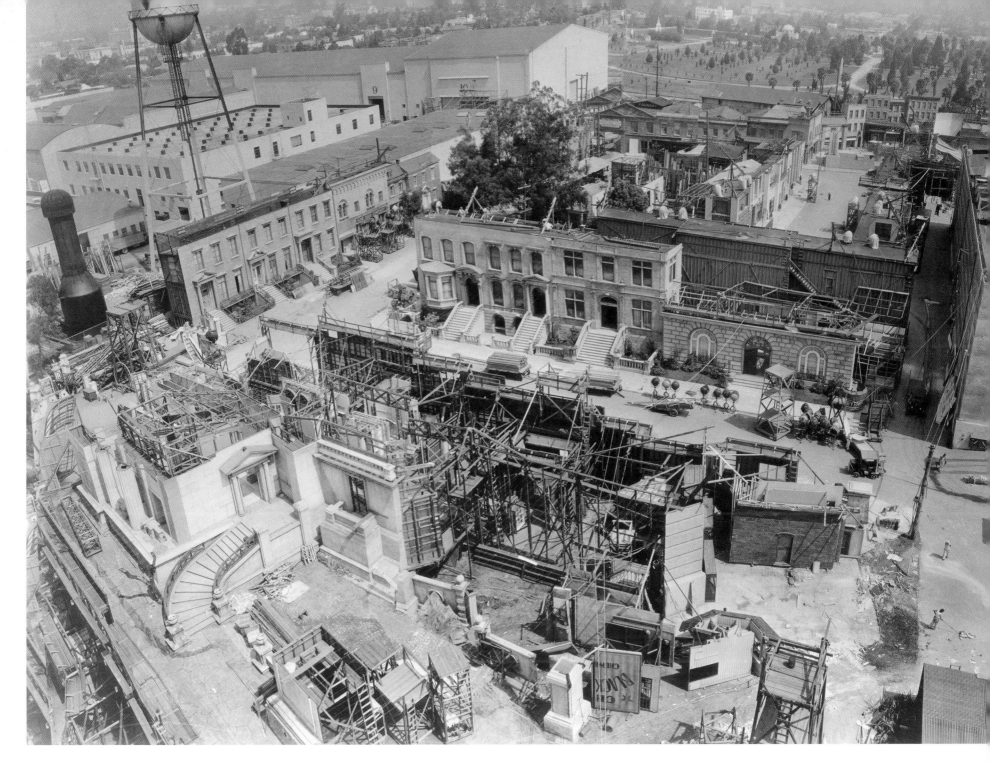

Modern Street was just that, a strip of ugly, 1960s specific storefronts, which perfectly captured their era, 1969.

Surprisingly, this haphazard, trial-and-error set eventually became one of the best standing sets in the industry. "This was a really beautifully designed backlot, which was completely enclosed, so you couldn't shoot off it by accident. It was a little square within another square. It was really nicely designed and it worked really well," director Joe Dante once recalled.[47]

Yet like ancient Egypt and modern Las Vegas, it didn't last. On August 25, 1983, a fire started on a New York Street backlot tattoo parlor set. Two hundred firefighters from nearly forty-one companies fought the spectacular blaze. Security guard Fritz Hawkes reportedly cried when he saw the set in flames. Those flames also damaged the nearby Stage 15, where *Star Trek 3: The Search for Spock* (1984) was then filming. That film's star, William Shatner, posed for publicity photos of himself pitching in to help the firefighters put out the blaze.

Ultimately, 350,000 square feet—New York Street itself, and the surrounding real estate—was completely destroyed. Only a single New York–styled wall, built in front of Stage 16, survived the inferno. That wall exists to this day and is the only part of today's New York Street, built on top of telephone poles, as was the original set, instead of steel girders like the remake.

The value of the destroyed property was set at $3 million, although Shatner's costar, George Takei, the only *Trek* star from Los Angeles, correctly pointed out that the loss was much greater than that. Takei noted correctly that the set "had been a wonderful part of our movie heritage. So much history took place on these streets; so much of our collective memories were recalled in these plaster stoops and painted canvas brick walls." Takei also noted that "the studio backlot was as important a part of our Hollywood heritage as covered bridges were to New England or boat landings were to the communities along the Mississippi River."[48]

Arson was suspected to be the cause of the blaze, although a subsequent investigation never gained any traction. Gossip in Hollywood circles mentioned

a disgruntled employee or even fingered a studio executive interested in the insurance payout. Neither theory ever led to a specific suspect or arrest.

The loss of New York Street deprived Paramount of its last backlot. Although the insurance company paid to replace the sets Paramount seemed to be in no hurry. Instead, an unsightly grouping of trailers and sheds were constructed in the ashes. Occasionally this area was cleared and temporary sets were built in the space, for projects like *Soapdish* (1991), *Dear John* (TV, 1998–1992), and *The Bronx Zoo* (TV, 1987–1988).

Not until 1991, almost a decade after the fire, was a new set constructed on the footprint of the old. The new five-acre, 67,013-square-foot New York Street consists of forty-six different facades. A press release at the time mentioned that the "entire complex is rigged for environmental effects; they include steam rising from manhole covers and grates, adjustable rain conditions, throughout, and exploding fire hydrants." Districts included on the set: Greenwich Village, SoHo, the Upper East Side, the Lower East Side, the Financial District, Washington Square, and Brooklyn.

FAR LEFT: The New York Street Fire reduced the physical remnants of more than fifty years of production to ash in 1983. ABOVE: The new, New York Street rises, very belatedly, from that ash, 1991.

New York Street framed by Stage 15 (covered with brown facades) to the left, and the water tower on the right, as it looked in 2006.

The creator of the new five-acre set was Albert Brenner, a production designer for films like *Bullitt* (Warner Bros., 1967), *Pretty Woman* (Disney, 1990), and *Frankie and Johnny* (1991). He brought years of on-set experience and went about the task with a production person's interest in detail, variety, and sightlines, something which had rarely been done in the hasty and truncated construction of Paramount backlots in the past.

For example, Brenner put steam vents under manhole covers and overhead pipe fittings for simulating rain. He also inlaid basins along and under the sidewalks for temporary placement of trees or signage. And he prewired the set, which meant that lights only had to be plugged in. Brenner also laid out one continuous unbroken route that could, if necessary, run from the Gower Gate down Paramount's Twelfth Street and then all the way through New York

Street to Stage 15, so that with additional set dressing the camera could look across six blocks of real estate. He told the employee newsletter at the time of construction, "Manhattan is a long flat island, and if you look down some streets you can see forever."[49]

Brenner made sure to build the inside of the set out of metal, with places to add "wild" interior sets, as opposed to the cramped, dirt-floored spaces in the old set and those wooden telephone poles holding up earlier structures. Lastly, to rule out the possibility of another fire, he interlaced the entire set with plenty of sprinklers and then coated the whole thing in fire-retardant paint.

The project was almost entirely created in-house, with all the materials coming from various on-lot departments. It was completed in two phases. Bob Hope and Dorothy Lamour were the guests at the August 3, 1992, dedication of phase one, which coincided, somewhat, with the company's eightieth anniversary.

Another permanent set would be built on the backlot in 2005. "Chicago Street" was actually a little annex to the older street built on the back of that set's Brooklyn facade. It was instigated, at the cost of about half a million dollars, for the Showtime series *Barbershop* (TV, 2005). Art director Donald Lee Harris echoed other designers when he told the *Los Angeles Times* that "it's all in the detail . . . we're trying to make it look like we didn't build it this morning."[50]

This Chicago Street was a new invention; it rose, more or less, where a train shed stood originally. But the rest of the new backlot was built, again, more or less, on the site of the original, and in some cases, copied that original's architecture and iconography—although by that time, this was more tribute than convenience, and a very nice tribute it was. For this reason we are not breaking the following list of titles into "before the fire" and "post-blaze" categories. It's all New York Street.

LEFT: Inside New York Street, steel girders and sprinkler heads, 2012.
ABOVE: The August 3rd, 1992, dedication of the rebuilt New York Street. Bob Hope, Dorothy Lamour, and Brandon Tartikoff officiate. Among the spectators are Los Angeles Mayor Tom Bradley and actors Brent Spiner and Donald O'Connor.

The question is academic, of course, but as we haunt the boulevards and brownstones of Paramount's longest-lasting set, it might be worthwhile to ponder the permanence of memory and of architecture, and to wonder, which lasts the longest?

Shot on New York Street:

Special Delivery (1927)—The earliest designated usage by Paramount of a "New York Street" at this studio was for this Eddie Cantor comedy, directed by a pseudonymous Roscoe "Fatty" Arbuckle.

Consolation Marriage (RKO, 1931)—The studio next door rented Paramount's New York Street to play contemporary (1930s) Manhattan.

The Great Victor Herbert (1939)—as early-twentieth-century New York.

Sudden Money (1939)—furniture store.

Beau Geste (1939)—The French Foreign Legion classic, surprisingly, used New York Street area, if not New York Street itself, to shoot "Ext: Zinderneuf and sand dunes" scenes.

Dr. Cyclops (1940)—Treadmill-based effects scenes were shot here.

The Way of All Flesh (1940)—Europa Café, the radio store, and a park bench on Brownstone Street.

West Point Widow (1941)—Nancy's (Anne Shirley) home.

Sullivan's Travels (1941)—"hobo jungle."

Holiday Inn (1942)—McFadden Street appeared in a few road scenes.

I Married a Witch (1942)—Wooley (Frederic March) house exteriors; also the 1861-set Pilgrim Hotel scenes.

The Palm Beach Story (1942)—Tom and Gerry's (Joel McCrea and Claudette Colbert) apartment exteriors; also Brownstone Street played the West Palm Beach Station.

The Glass Key (1942)—Madvig's club exteriors for special effects.

Star Spangled Rhythm (1942)—"Sharp as a Tack" number.

Going My Way (1944)—Street scenes with the juvenile delinquents on the backlot's McFadden and Boston Streets.

The Great Moment (1944)—General Hospital.

Double Indemnity (1944)—the La Golondrina Café set exterior.

The Uninvited (1944)—"Cliff Head" exteriors.

The Bells of St. Mary's (RKO, 1945)—church and street.

The Blue Dahlia (1946)—"cheap hotel" set on McFadden Street.

The Perils of Pauline (1947)—New York Street as New York.

Welcome Stranger (1947)—McFadden Street locations.

The Big Clock (1948)—The Patterson house was on Brownstone Street.

A Foreign Affair (1948)—Erika Von Schluetow (Marlene Dietrich, of course) had an apartment on Boston Street in this film.

The Heiress (1949)—McFadden Street as 1880s New York.

Sorrowful Jones (1949)—Bob Hope visits Broadway, a Chinese laundry, and a mortuary on New York Street.

Dark City (1950)—McFadden Street as a "Southside Street," and "Sammy's Café." Also Brownstone Street was cast as the location of Lizabeth Scott's apartment.

Let's Dance (1950)—jewelry store, the supper club, and Kitty's apartment (Brownstone Street).

September Affair (1950)—Lawrence home exteriors.

My Friend Irma Goes West (1950)—Opening scenes, which were set in New York, before Irma went west, were shot on Boston Street.

Union Station (1950)—as a "street near station."

My Favorite Spy (1951)—theater alley.

Carrie (1952)—Jennifer Jones and Laurence Olivier in 1890s Chicago, shot on something known as "Chicago Street," which, from visual evidence, was probably the backlot's Boston Street.

Limelight (UA, 1952)—Charlie Chaplin rented a McFadden Street tenement building for this bittersweet recollection of the music halls of his youth.

The Greatest Show on Earth (1952)—Used as various towns; Boston Street, for example, was used as the city the circus limps into after the train wreck.

The War of the Worlds (1953)—The evacuation and looting of Los Angeles scenes were shot on New York Street. McFarland Street hosted a movie theater set.

The Stars Are Singing (1953)—the Cosmopolitan opera house.

Houdini (1953)—Scenes set at Times Square in 1913, a Berlin house in 1910, and at Houdini's brownstone, among other places, were shot here. On October 9, 1952, star Tony Curtis was injured stepping off of a New York Street curb into some cables. He was treated by the first-aid department and returned to work.

The Naked Jungle (1954)—Sometimes New York Street was used for locations which had nothing to do with an urban setting at all. For this George Pal–produced adventure about ants attacking a South American plantation, fire pots were ignited on New York Street and the flames in the sky were matted into the film's jungle setting.

Secret of the Incas (1954)—dark alley (also built on Stage 8).

That Certain Feeling (1954)—police station.

The Country Girl (1954)—The stage alley set and Boston theater facade were located here.

Anything Goes (1956)—pier and boat alley.

The Man Who Knew Too Much (1956)—McFadden Street played the rear of Ambrose Chapel. Also a Mosque set was built for the film at the end of New York Street.

The Vagabond King (1956)—side door of church.

The Delicate Delinquent (1957)—Jerry Lewis plays the title role, on New York Street.

The Sad Sack (1957)—Jerry Lewis again plays the title role, again on New York Street.

Funny Face (1957)—A bookshop exterior was shot here; the exterior was built on Stage 12.

Beau James (1957)—as Mulberry Street, Forty-Fifth Street, and Times Square.

The Buccaneer (1958)—McFadden Street was used for a few shots.

The Colossus of New York (1958)—Boston Street as the title character—New York, not the colossus.

King Creole (1958)—drugstore and alley exteriors.

But Not for Me (1959)—McFadden Street played the outside of Ellie's New York apartment; also used for theater exteriors.

The Rat Race (1960)—McFadden Street, for the exterior of Mac's Bar.

Visit to a Small Planet (1960)—street and intersection.

Breakfast at Tiffany's (1961)—Assorted New York scenes were shot here.

The Carpetbaggers (1964)—theater, Cord Plastic factory, the LA hotel exterior, and the wedding chapel scenes were shot here.

Roustabout (1964)—Used for theater exteriors only; most of the film was shot at the Albertson Ranch in Hidden Valley, California.

Harlow (1965)—The New York Street theater was used for a Jean Harlow movie premiere.

Star Trek (TV, 1966–1969)—New York Street was used for the 1968 episode, "A Piece of the Action."

That Girl (TV, 1966–1971)—The credit sequence for this popular series was shot in the actual city of New York, and in New Jersey, the rest of the show was Hollywood-based.

Mannix (TV, 1967–1975)—numerous; Modern Street was oft-used.

Mod Squad (TV, 1968–1973)—numerous; again, Modern Street was oft-used.

The Young Lawyers (TV, 1969–1971)—Boston Street, mostly.

Barefoot in the Park (TV, 1970–1971)—Short-lived TV spin-off from the successful feature film, with New York Street playing New York, and Scoey Mitchell and Tracy Reed playing the roles made famous by Robert Redford and Jane Fonda.

The Odd Couple (TV, 1970–1975)—New York was usually played by stock shots and location footage of the cast, but on occasion, such as the fourth-season episode "The New Car" (1973), New York Street filled in as well.

The Godfather (1972)—as the backlot of Woltz International Pictures, for a single shot.

Happy Days (TV, 1974–1984)—The legendary sitcom only used New York Street regularly for the first two seasons, which were filmed movie-like, with a single camera, after which three cameras and a studio audience kept the show largely stage-bound.

The Last Tycoon (1976)—New York Street played itself, somewhat.

Laverne & Shirley (TV, 1978–1983)—The famous opening credits with the title characters singing was shot on McFadden Street.

Rescue from Gilligan's Island (TV movie, 1978)—The ticker-tape parade after the castaways were rescued, which supposedly took place in Honolulu, was staged here.

Grease (1978)—The "Frosty Palace" diner exterior was created here, although the exterior is barely seen in the finished film.

Taxi (TV, 1978–1983)—The well-regarded sitcom used mostly stock shots for its seedy New York milieu. A couple of episodes, such as 1979's "Elaine's Secret Admirer," used New York Street as well.

Police Squad (TV, 1982)—Joe Dante directed the episode "Ring of Fear (A Dangerous Assignment)," shot in front of the backlot church.

MacGyver (TV, 1985–1992)—The first phase of the reconstruction project was used in the 1991 episode "Good Knight MacGyver." Probably used in later episodes as well.

The Bronx Zoo (TV, 1987–1988)—The Benjamin Harrison High School set was constructed here, post-fire.

Star Trek: The Next Generation (TV, 1987–1994)—The 1988 episode "The Big Goodbye," the 1992 episode, "Time's Arrow," and the 1994 episode "Emergence" were shot here.

Allstate Insurance commercial (TV, 1991)—unknown scenes.

Brooklyn Bridge (TV, 1991–1993)—The new Brooklyn Street was used, along with the rest of the set, as well.

The Untouchables (TV, 1993–1994)—used occasionally as Chicago.

Star Trek: Deep Space Nine (TV, 1993–1999)—Two-part 1995 episode "Past Tense," 1996 episode "Home-front," 1998 episode "Far Beyond the Stars," and the 1998 episode "Shadows and Symbols."

NYPD Blue (TV, 1993–2005)—occasional.

Friends (TV, 1994–2004)—used in 1995 episode "The One with the Baby on the Bus."

Star Trek: Voyager (TV, 1995–2001)—1995 episode "Non Sequitur," 2000 episode "11:59."

JAG (TV, 1995–2005)—numerous sequences in numerous episodes.

Austin Powers: International Man of Mystery (New Line, 1997)—The nightclub exteriors were shot here.

Absolute Power (Columbia, 1997)—Clint Eastwood used this set as a Georgetown assassination site.

Volcano (Twentieth Century Fox, 1997)—New York Street played a soot-covered Los Angeles street.

Ally McBeal (TV, 1997–2002)—used, on occasion, for this Boston-set series.

Man on the Moon (Universal, 1999)—Andy Kaufman (Jim Carrey) is ejected from Paramount . . . and New York Street.

Star Trek: Enterprise (TV, 2001–2005)—2002 episode "Fusion," 2002 episode "Carbon Creek," 2003 episode, "The Expance," 2003 episode

"Carpenter Street," and "Storm Front," a 2002 two-part episode.

NCIS (TV, 2003–   )—occasional.

CSI: NY (TV, 2004–2013)—occasional.

Barbershop (TV, 2005)—see above.

Everybody Hates Chris (TV, 2005–2009)—regularly used as Tattaglia High School neighborhood.

Spider Man 3 (Columbia, 2007)—Jazz nightclub sequences were shot here.

Indiana Jones and the Kingdom of the Crystal Skull (2008)—Part of the

car chase and the diner scene were shot on New York Street.

Cloverfield (2008)—A monster rampages through Manhattan, played by New York Street, as extended by a large process screen.

Fame (2009)—Naturi Naughton music video.

Surrogates (Disney, 2009)—as someplace, sometime in the future.

Do You Remember (2009)—Jay Sean music video.

Rizzoli & Isles (TV, 2010–2016)—Boston Police Department building is wall in front of Stage 15 on Brooklyn Street.

Rock That Body (2010)—Black Eyed Peas music video.

The Artist (Weinstein Company, 2011)—several scenes, including Bérénice Bejo on Brooklyn Street.

51 SCENIC ARTS

Approaching south through New York Street, then as now, a visitor would be struck by the magnitude of a large wall towering over that entire backlot district. Sets covered part of the wall, as they do now. On the other side, then as now, is the B-Tank (#52). In the 1960s, the area included another partial train shed, sometimes used for special effects, and a Brownstone District. Today it is called Washington Square, although aesthetically, it has the same general look. The wall has changed as well. Today it houses the studio's archive building. In 1968 it was the home of the scenic arts department.

Scenic arts was responsible for creating painted backdrops of cityscapes and jungle vistas and western towns, which stood in the back of sets, or even on the other side of the B-Tank. The work these artisans did could be surreal, and even abstract in its execution, for fantasies like *Alice in Wonderland* (1933) and science fiction films like *When Worlds Collide* (1951). But typically the results were required to be convincingly photo-realistic.

Paramount's scenic arts department was, rather ingeniously, located inside the B-Tank backdrop, seen here during pre-production on *Whispering Smith*, 1947.

Originally these large backdrops, made of canvas, had to be painted on scaffolding attached to the side of a stage wall, or elsewhere. But when the B-Tank was constructed in 1946, provisions were made to use the wall, which itself held up an enormous backdrop in front of a massive lake, as headquarters for the scenic artisans. So the building, ironically, was there to support the work of the scenic artists, and was in fact a large example of that craft itself.

Inside this remarkable structure, accessible through New York Street, were the offices, locker rooms, and stockrooms for scenic arts, storing scenic

backings as well as providing general storage for other studio departments.

It's all gone now. Paramount no longer has a scenic arts department. Backdrops are created from photographs, using large-scale printers, or inside of a computer. A whispered memory of the old Scenic Arts did surface in the late 1980s, however, when the sky backdrop was being rebuilt and a room full of rolled canvas backdrops depicting those city streets and cityscapes was inadvertently unearthed. No one had been aware of this room for decades. Unusually, in a business where below-the-line people consider what they do only a craft—like bricklaying and chimney-sweeping— it was discovered that some of these beautiful cycloramas were actually signed, by one "M. F. Paul." A search of payroll records yielded contact information, which astonishingly yielded Mr. Paul himself, still very much alive. The probably bemused Paul was brought back to the studio with great fanfare and was reunited with his original artwork at a party held in his honor.

52 B-TANK

One of the most iconic places at Paramount first appeared in 1942 for DeMille's *Reap the Wild Wind*. It was originally just a vast tank, 175 feet by 195 feet, with a capacity of 91,423 gallons when it was being used. As there was no filtration system, the water in the tank tended to stagnate quickly, even before the last miniature ship had sailed into the painted sunset. The basin was only about 4 feet deep, although a rocker pit in the center, 8 feet by 8 feet by 14 feet deep, could allow for additional depth as needed. The project cost a reported $50,000 to build. When not being used, the tank is a parking lot.

One of DeMille's famous casts of thousands enjoy their lunch behind the scenes on *The Sign of the Cross*. The large, oddly lettered wall on the left was a prop ship hull, often used as part of what would become the A-Tank, 1932.

In January 1946, at an additional cost of $105,231.85, a large wall at the northern end of the tank was added, 175 feet wide by 61 feet high, with (usually) a blue sky backdrop painted across it. It was utilized by productions in need of an unobstructed or consistent background that would not change as a real sky would, with actual clouds moving across it during the day.

The enormous prop, both the tank and its new backdrop, was referred to on the lot as the "B" (or second) tank, presumably because it was the second one of its kind on the lot—which is actually a fallacy. You see, there have actually been *two* B-Tanks, and an A-Tank as well, at Paramount over the decades.

A-Tank, the first of its kind, was located slightly south above the DeMille office and between Irving and Windsor Streets. This particular location, sometimes called "Arena Tank," had been built in the mid-1930s, perhaps for DeMille's *The Crusades* (1935). The A-Tank never had the massive backing which B-Tank became famous for, although temporary back-drops were put up around it. Likewise, black Duvetyne was often used to tent the basin to keep the world at bay.

Other ways were often found to keep the rest of the studio out of the sightlines as well. For example, for *The Lady Eve* (1941), the wall of an ocean liner was built at the top of the tank and the full-size boats were navigated in front of it, with the hull camouflaging the not-so-nautical backdrops. Sometimes A-Tank was used just to build temporary sets in as well, such as the bungalow set seen in *The Blue Dahlia* (1946), and part of the compound in *Stalag* 17 (1953).

The next tank, the original B-tank, was where Stage 15 is now. In fact, Stage 15 was

Paramount's original A-Tank as seen in *The Lady Eve* (1941).

built *over* this pit in 1938. That tank still exists, but somehow the name "B-Tank" moved outdoors and the Stage 15 tank is now known, very imaginatively, as the "Stage 15 Tank." The current B-Tank, the one still used and still called B-Tank, is now the only "Blue," or "Blue-Sky Tank." So does the "B" stand for "blue" tank, or for "big" tank?

Films shot in this second B-Tank, meaning in the tank itself, or against its backdrop, are legion, and a complete accounting is probably impossible, as the studio never bothered to keep records. Early titles included *Torpedo Boat* (1942), *The Fleet's In* (1942), *Wake Island* (1942), *Road to Morocco* (1942), *The Story of Dr. Wassell* (1944), and *Whispering Smith* (1947), which, except for the last, all used water in the tank.

Samson and Delilah (1949), staged part of its troublesome lion fight here. *Captain China* (1949) flooded the basin with water again. *My Friend Irma Goes West* (1950) used the tank as a mine tunnel. *When Worlds Collide* (1951) used it as a Red

Cross camp, while *The Greatest Show on Earth* (1952) shot some train miniatures in front of the sky. *Houdini* (1953) filmed the 1920 Bell Island Bridge scenes in the water. The basin was again filled with water for *The Court Jester* (1955), *The Birds and the Bees* (1956), and *The Buccaneer* (1958). For *We're No Angels* (1955), the studio built a dock and a street at the edge of this water. *Houseboat* (1958) and *The Geisha Boy* (also 1956) used water as well.

Famously, the legendary parting of the Red Sea sequence in DeMille's remake of *The Ten Commandments* (1956), which involved dumping millions of gallons of water into the tank and then reversing the image, was partially shot here—in part on stage, in part in the arena, and in part on the actual Red Sea. Less well known is the fact that the basin of the B-Tank also housed that film's temple granary set and parts of the obelisk and city that Moses built for the Egyptians.

Director Randal Kleiser, like many of us, grew up watching Moses, or rather DeMille, part the Red Sea. When he went to Paramount to film the blockbuster *Grease* (1978), it was like a holy pilgrimage. "I was obsessed by the Red Sea Tank," he explains. "This was where it had happened. I was honored to be working at the same place, in the same studio, on the same stages where that, and so much else, had happened."[51]

Another landmark sequence, perhaps not on par with the parting of the Red Sea, but still weirdly important in popular culture, was also achieved in the tank. *Rescue from Gilligan's Island* (TV, 1978) shot the scenes where the hapless castaways from the 1964–1967 TV series are rescued in the big tank. Series creator Sherwood Schwartz broke his knee while climbing on the tank wall while scouting the location with his cinematographer, Bob Primes.

In *The Winds of War* (TV, 1983) miniseries, many of the colossal World War II sea battle sequences were achieved in the big tank using elaborate miniatures and shooting with high-speed cameras. Because of the increased frame rate of these cameras, it slowed the resultant picture down and made the projected tiny battleships look large enough to conquer the Japanese Navy.

The B-Tank Sky has a special relationship with the *Star Trek* franchise. At

ABOVE: Leonard Nimoy inadvertently recalls Cecil B. DeMille, as he directs *Star Trek IV: The Voyage Home* using a megaphone in front of B-Tank, 1986.

ABOVE RIGHT: Boats in bathtubs on a colossal scale for the short-lived (1975–1976) TV series *Barbary Coast*.

least two original series projects, "A Private Little War" (1968) and "The Omega Glory" (also 1968), used the backdrop, if not the tank. In the big-budget, big-screen feature film *Star Trek: The Motion Picture* (1979), the scenes set on the planet Vulcan were created here. In a later sequel, *Star Trek IV: The Voyage Home* (1986), the tank was again filled with water to represent San Francisco Bay for the film's climax. William Shatner, Captain Kirk in the series and the films (and apparently for all eternity), has long told the apocryphal story that at the time of filming, no one at the studio remembered that the tank was there because of the cars parked on its bottom. This statement is particularly risible because Shatner had already been involved in the earlier *Trek* projects using the set, as well as a previous series featuring the B-Tank Sky he himself had starred in, *Barbary Coast* (TV, 1975–1976).

In 1990, the B-Tank Sky backdrop / scenic arts department was removed and rebuilt with a new building, originally to be named the Howard W. Koch building, but instead, mysteriously anointed only as "The Archive" behind its northern wall. When the massive screen was taken down, both employees and locals who could see it from the street panicked. Publicists at the studio assured them that the sky would rise again. And it did.

The latest, and probably last, incarnation of the B-Tank includes the studio archive behind the "sky." Also note the cars parked inside that "Ocean."

The B-Tank Sky backdrop, and occasionally even the lake under it, are still used today, even in the twenty-first century, and even at $30,000 per fill. These more-recent tenants who filled the tank with water or dirt are as follows: *Mannix* (TV, 1967–1975, dirt), *The Day of the Locust* (1975, dirt—specifically the exteriors of the courtyard apartments), *The Last Tycoon* (1975, water), *Escape From Alcatraz* (1979, water), *Happy Days* (TV, 1984 episode, water), *The Golden Child* (1986, dirt), *Critical Condition* (1987, water), *The Hunt for Red October* (1990, water), *Patriot Games* (1992, water), *Congo* (1995, dirt), *Waterworld* (Universal, 1995, water), *Snake Eyes* (1998, dirt), *The Truman Show* (1998, dirt), *Stuart Little* (1999, water), *The General's Daughter* (1999, water), *Orange County* (2002, water), and *The Curious Case of Benjamin Button* (2008, water). "The Proposal" episode of the long-running series *Cheers* (TV, 1982–1993) used the lake as the setting for a romantic, if less-than-successful, sailboat wedding proposal. Kanye West has even performed in front of the backdrop, on the 2008 *MTV Video Music Awards*.

As guest parking is in the lot under the big screen, for decades visitors to Paramount have been directed to the B-Tank by security upon entering. In a *Los Angeles Times* letter in 1989 William Thut wrote: "I was new to Los Angeles when my agent set up my first meeting on the Paramount lot. I tried to dismiss images of Gloria Swanson on her way to meet DeMille as I approached the gate. But I was finally sure I was in Hollywood when I received directions from the guard: 'Drive straight down this road and park under the Sky.' "[52]

53 WESTERN STREET

Like RKO, Paramount has always suffered somewhat in that their location, right in the center of Hollywood, became valuable quicker than the outlying suburbs of Culver City and Burbank. With the "movie boom" of the 1910s and '20s came escalating real estate prices, so relatively early in the game, the studios with the most desirable and centralized locations, and who had been responsible for the sudden local growth to begin with, found themselves with no place to expand beyond their current locations. Paramount's lot was big enough for this to not be as much of a problem as it was for RKO and for Columbia, but they never had the space for the sprawling back-lots that could be found at some of the other, outlying studios.

To alleviate this problem, just south of B-Tank for many years there stood an open area upon which sets could be constructed on a temporary basis and then dismantled after the project had wrapped. This same system of a "backlot" consisting only of a blank canvas is still in effect in many European studios, where "standing sets" only stand until the current project finishes principal photography.

Before the construction of Western Street, the empty area was used for large-scale sets. *The Story of Dr. Wassell* (1944), for example, cast the real estate as an Asian port. Director Cecil B. DeMille is on the camera crane. (Photo courtesy of Larry Jensen)

This open area was the home of many large-scale projects, including DeMille's *The Story of Dr. Wassell* (1944), for which the entire area was dressed as a southeastern Asian port warehouse district, complete with two full-size Virginia & Truckee Railroad locomotives.

When B-Tank was constructed in 1942, some of this six-acre area was swallowed up by the vast basin under the backdrop, although some of the "Upper Western Street" facades were built on or above this basin between 1968 and 1970. In later years the area became a parking lot, as the basin itself already was, although it was still used as a set. For example, in *On a Clear Day You Can See Forever* (1970), parts of the film's elaborate fox-hunting sequence was staged in this area.

The Paramount Western Street, which of course was actually several streets, owes its origins to *Whispering Smith* (1948), for which the town of "Whispering Bend" was constructed, in 1947, in that area south of the B-Tank. Two thousand feet of railroad track were laid, and a hardscrabble city built around it.

However, this time many of these sets were saved. In fact, the street was expanded upon after the film wrapped. As in other Paramount backlots, this happened almost more by accident than by any sort of design or intent on the part of the studio. The street was not removed, so the next Western that came along built its sets around and exploited the already-standing ones. Even after the *Whispering Smith* sets (which truthfully were not that impressive) had been replaced, or had mutated into something else, "Western Street" continued to thrive, giving producers—particularly low-budget ones like A. C. Lyles—a template on which to base their productions.

As the set expanded weed-like across the open area and north toward the B-Tank, the studio gymnasium (aka, the Lasky-DeMille Barn), an authentic Western locale if there ever was one, was conscripted into service. As noted above, Upper Western Street buildings were sometimes constructed inside the tank as well—when empty, of course—allowing them to utilize the sky backdrop. (Otherwise, Hollywood, and even the "Hollywood" sign, would have been visible in the background.)

Likewise, the Western town expanded west as well. But on this side was the wall leading into RKO. Consequently, camera angles were limited by the fact that the RKO scene docks and property storage facility, as well as a 30-foot-high sawdust silo, would have made for strange backdrops for projects set in Dodge City, Kansas, and Tombstone, Arizona. As a solution, in 1955 Paramount craftsmen built a "mountain" on this outer flank of the Western Street, actually constructed of chicken wire and plaster. A painted backdrop was erected directly behind it of a cloudy blue sky, similar to the B-Tank backdrop, but this proved to be unnecessary, as California usually provided something similar anyway. As long as that wood silo was covered up, it didn't seem to matter.

LEFT: Western Street, seen complete with its chicken wire and plaster mountain range behind the facades, 1969. BOTTOM LEFT: The same view of Western Street during its 1979 demolition. The mountain range is still there, but just barely.

By Hollywood standards, and especially by Paramount's, the Western Street had a long and photogenic life. Although unlike other Western Streets at other studios, the Paramount version had little lasting identity of its own. Walls and buildings were moved in and out, film by film, and the street mutated according to the needs of whatever was there at the moment. Western fans who obsessively track the appearances, however fleeting, of every hitching post and swinging saloon door on other Western sets are often unable to do so in Paramount Westerns. This is because, except for the Lasky-DeMille Barn, most of the structures there were short-lived or easily adapted to other needs. The only connection between *Whispering Smith*, for example, and TV's *Bonanza*, is in the physical location of the ground the sets for each were built upon. Western Street, if one is to assume that a shared space for different sets is to be called a "street" at all, stood for thirty years, yet, there was no quintessential film, or era, or scene, or building which gave the place its identity.

Even the very impressive *Whispering Smith* rolling stock did not survive the film's release, and was in fact moved immediately up to the ranch. The studio did not return this rail equipment to the set until 1958, for *Last Train from Gun Hill*. Perhaps because the track had to be laid through an existing village rather than a set more or less built from scratch around that track, there was now only room for 700 feet of rail. According to historian Larry Jensen, that track curved behind buildings on one side of the street, just far enough for the train to get out of sight, and extended in the other direction just far enough for the train to be able to clear the depot platform. Sadly, this was the last time a real locomotive train would be brought onto the lot, although passenger cars would be used as props on occasion. In fact, at least two "train storage scene docks" existed for these cars, and for effects sequences, at the top and bottom of New York Street for many years.

In spite of the set's mirage-like ability to blend in rather than stand out, or perhaps because of it, a lot of film was exposed on Western Street. The following is only a sample.

Shot on Western Street:

Sun of Paleface (1951)—Roy Rogers and Trigger, who would later appear with the comedian in *Alias Jesse James* (UA, 1959), have cameos in this Bob Hope Western.

Warpath (1951)—set in South Dakota, mostly shot on location in Montana.

Aaron Slick From Punkin Crick (1952)—as Punkin Crick, presumably.

The Life and Legend of Wyatt Earp (TV, 1955–1961)—occasional.

Pardners (1956)—Dean Martin and Jerry Lewis out west.

The Rainmaker (1956)—The Lasky-DeMille Barn was being used as a railroad station on Western Street, and in fact had a few feet of track laid out in front of it for this adaptation of the N. Richard Nash play, when it was designated a landmark by the State of California in 1956.

Gunfight at the O.K. Corral (1957)—Many Paramount Westerns were shot at the studio ranch, or at other studio ranches, or on distant locations, with only the interiors done on soundstages on the lot. This big-budget version of the oft-filmed tale of the West's most famous shootout was shot in various locations in California and Arizona. In fact, Old Tucson, in Arizona was the primary location, with only incidental footage shot on the studio backlot.

DeForest Kelley played Morgan Earp in this picture, and went on to portray *Star Trek*'s venerable Dr. McCoy. He later shot a *Trek* episode, "Spectre of the Gun" (1968), which found the crew of the *Enterprise* wandering amid an O.K. Corral created by an alien race, not portrayed by Western Street, as one might imagine, but built on a soundstage out of obvious false fronts and studio flats. This suggests that the alien architects had watched their share of Westerns, but, like most of us, and on the Paramount Western Street in particular, couldn't quite reconstruct all of the details.

The Tin Star (1957)—Like *Gunfight at the O.K. Corral*, this film was also an A-list picture, with a good cast and intelligent script, but it was shot almost entirely on the lot and on the backlot. The premise of the film—a young deputy and a seasoned sheriff clean up a town—was later adapted into a TV series (*The Deputy*, 1959–1961) also with this film's star, Henry Fonda, but with less success.

Have Gun—Will Travel (TV, 1957–1963)—occasional.

Houseboat (1958)—The village grocery store in this Cary Grant charmer was on Western Street.

U.S. Marshal (TV, 1958–1960, occasional)—set in contemporary Arizona.

The Trap (1959)—Western Street played Tula, a desert community someplace in California, although the film itself was not a Western.

Alias Jesse James (UA, 1959)—Bob Hope comedy which included cameos by Gene Autry and Roy Rogers and Trigger, as well as James Arness, Ward Bond, Gary Cooper, Fess Parker, Jay Silverheels, Hugh O'Brian, Ward Bond, Gail Davis, and, of course, Bing Crosby, who says of Hope: "This fellow needs all the help he can get."

The Jayhawkers! (1959)—This was a vehicle for Fess Parker, who had just cameoed in the same year's *Alias Jesse James*. Here Western Street played the towns of "Harper" and "Abilene."

Bonanza (TV, 1959–1973)—Here Western Street was Virginia City, Nevada—at least until the 1970 season, when the series moved to Warner Bros. The change in the look of Virginia City was explained as being caused by a fire in the episode "The Night Virginia City Died," which aired on September 13 of that year.

Walk Like a Dragon (1960)—a rare Western which addressed the issue of racism and slavery perpetuated in California against the Chinese.

The Errand Boy (1961)—Western Street appears briefly as itself. Jerry Lewis appears more prominently as the title role.

One-Eyed Jacks (1961)—This was one of the most expensive films in Paramount's history, due to director-star Marlon Brando's penchant for retakes and retakes of retakes. Western Street was rebuilt, to no particular effect, as Monterey, California, for the film, an expensive, interesting flop.

Bonanza (TV 1959–1973), shown here shooting a 1962 episode, was a long-lasting tenant on Western Street. That same year John Ford would use the same set for *The Man Who Shot Liberty Valance* and (as a Hawaiian Village) in *Donovan's Reef* (1963).

The Man Who Shot Liberty Valance (1962)—Several latter-day historians have mentioned that none of this mournful Western classic was shot on Western Street, and that the exteriors were instead lensed on leased sets at MGM's Lot Three. This is untrue. While MGM's Western Street is indeed utilized, and many supposed exteriors were shot inside soundstages, Paramount's Western Street is featured prominently as the town of Shinbone in James Stewart's prolonged flashbacks.

Donovan's Reef (1963)—Like the later *Paradise Hawaiian Style* (1966), this John Wayne vehicle cast Lower Western Street as a South Pacific Island village.

Soldier in the Rain (1963)—Lower Western Street hosted the "Pussycat Café."

McLintock! (1963)—Upper Western Street hosted John Wayne and an-all-star cast.

Stage to Thunder Rock (1964)—Filmed in 1963, this was the first of producer A. C. Lyles's series of low-budget Westerns shot on the set. Lyles's films all utilized once-popular actors and directors who, by the 1960s, were probably just happy to have a job at Paramount.

Lyles would go on in his later years to be credited as a "consulting producer" on the TV series *Deadwood* (TV, 2004–2006), which was partially shot, like many of his features, north of Hollywood, in the San Fernando Valley.

Law of the Lawless (1964)—A. C. Lyles again; Iverson Ranch, another popular Western location in the San Fernando Valley, is intercut with Western Street, as "Stone Junction, Kansas."

The Carpetbaggers (1964)—George Peppard, driving across the lot of Norman Studios, passes Western Street.

The Hallelujah Trail (UA, 1965)—This big-budget Western comedy was mostly shot in Arizona.

Apache Uprising (1965)—A. C. Lyles Western, with the set playing the town of "Apache Wells."

Town Tamer (1965)—A. C. Lyles Western, with the set now playing the town of "White Plains."

Black Spurs (1965)—another A. C. Lyles Western, with the set playing the town of "Lark."

Young Fury (1965)—yet another A. C. Lyles Western, with Upper and Lower Western Street this time playing the town of "Dawson."

Branded (TV, 1965–1966)—occasional.

Waco (1966)—A. C. Lyles again; this time Western Street is playing "Emporia, Wyoming."

Nevada Smith (1966)—as a "small Western town."

The Night of the Grizzly (1966)—Upper Western Street as a Wyoming burg.

Paradise, Hawaiian Style (1966)—This Elvis Presley vehicle cast Western Street as a Polynesian village. Interesting what a lot of palm fronds can do.

Johnny Reno (1966)—A. C. Lyles is back, with the set again playing the town of "Stone Junction, Kansas."

Mission: Impossible (TV, 1966–1973)—used in a 1971 episode, "Encore."

Fort Utah (1967)—A. C. Lyles Western; the title fort was in Santa Clarita, California, but Western Street appeared as well.

Hostile Guns (1967)—A. C. Lyles Western, with the set playing the town of "Huntsville."

Red Tomahawk (1967)—A. C. Lyles here tried to reteam Betty Hutton with Howard Keel; the two had displayed some chemistry in *Annie Get*

Your Gun (MGM, 1950), but Hutton dropped out. Joan Caulfield played her role in the finished film.

The Guns of Will Sonnett (TV, 1967–1969)—occasional.

The High Chaparral (TV, 1967–1971)—occasional.

Buckskin (1968)—Yes, this is another A. C. Lyles Western, with the set playing the town of "Glory Hole." Really.

Arizona Bushwhackers (1968)—This was the last of A. C. Lyles's all-star Westerns. This one is narrated by an (uncredited) James Cagney, who owed Lyles a favor. Western Street plays "Colton, Arizona."

The Brady Bunch (TV, 1969–1974)—In the 1971 episode, "Ghost Town U.S.A.," the Brady family visits Western Street. Series star Robert Reed once recalled upending a stolen golf cart on this set, resulting in the injury of an extra.

Little House on the Prairie (TV, 1974–1983)—Western Street was apparently only used once, in the 1975 episode "To See the World," although interiors were shot on Paramount stages.

The Last Tycoon (1975)—Robert De Niro crosses the lot, including, naturally, Western Street.

Western Street in 1979 just after the final fadeout. Today most of this real estate is a parking lot. Note the Lasky-DeMille Barn to the right.

Western Street was removed in 1979, along with almost all of the standing sets south of New York Street, to make way for a parking lot. An interesting, long-standing rumor holds that the studio had been afraid to remove the facades while John Wayne was still alive. Rumors they might have been, but the facts are that the set was not demolished until after the legendary cowboy passed away on June 11 of that year.

Since then, many studio employees have agreed that the lot has never felt quite the same to them again. Larry Jensen, who remembered Western Street, and came back for an aborted Harrison Ford project in 1991, has said that "standing in the parking lot where the Western town had been, remembering what used to be there, was particularly depressing. Paramount seemed more like a factory than the friendly and magical place I'd visited in the 1960s. After that, most days I parked in the big structure on the east side of the lot, walked to the trailer, put in my time, and went home."[53]

European Street, top, was a tiny strip of Tudor-paneled buildings and alleys with an adjacent park area. Nickodell Restaurant is tantalizingly just on the other side of the studio wall, 1976.

European Street seems to have been made up of facades and flats which existed on the lot from the late 1950s as part of the upper New York District's McFadden Street, which was seen in, among other films, Jerry Lewis's *The Errand Boy* (1961). In the mid-1960s these sets were moved or replicated to create a small European Street with vaguely Teutonic facades and a tiny park to the west, with some equally tiny trees at the bottom of the lot, beneath Marathon Street.

Incidentally, on the *other* side of European Street, just outside the gate, was the popular employee watering hole, Nickodell Restaurant, which for years, until 1993, would be like a second commissary for many employees.

European Street was, as mentioned, supposed to represent Europe, or at least some place with European influences in evidence. Tudor-style paneling was on some of the walls, and cement spread over plywood to impersonate stucco was the order of the day. And yet the craftsmanship on the set—even an impromptu, cannibalized set like this one—was so good that the result tended to be both convincing and versatile, almost in spite of itself.

From the mid-1960s on, European Street played the office exterior, supposedly "17 Paseo Verde Street" in Los Angeles, of Detective Joe Mannix, the cool but often beat-up or shot-at PI from *Mannix* (TV, 1967–1975). *Mod Squad* (TV, 1968–1973), also set in LA, used the same architecture, at the same time, at the same place.

Actually, during this era, this supposedly European set played a wide variety of American and even extraterrestrial locations, usually for television. *I Spy* (1965–1968), *Get Smart* (1965–1970), and *Mission: Impossible* (1966–1973) all found the Iron Curtain–era look of the set a convincing, and, more importantly, economical stand-in for actual Cold War locations.

Hogan's Heroes (TV, 1965–1971) was shot on a former Desilu property in Culver City. In fact, the POW camp, Stalag 13 (called Camp 13 in the pilot), was built on the site of "Tara," the plantation from *Gone with the Wind* (MGM, 1939). Yet perhaps because Paramount was eager to attract rentals from other studios, European Street shows up as a German city several times, most notably in the season three episode, "Is General Hammerschlag Burning?" In 1970 Paramount was charging the *Hogan's Heroes* production office $750 a day for the use of this set, a savings of $100 over what other external productions were then being charged.

Most creatively, European Street appeared in at least three *Star Trek* (TV, 1966–1969) episodes: "Patterns of Force," "All our Yesterdays," and "Assignment Earth." It should probably be noted that the set always played Earth (or an Earth-like place).

The street was removed in 1979 as part of the same renovation push that also deprived the studio of its Western Street. The property was turned into a parking lot, on the southern side of which a few European-style buildings survived as storage warehouses until recently.

55 SCENE DOCKS

Scene docks are large areas, either enclosed or open to the elements, where sets and scenic pieces and even large property items are stored when not in use.

"The one sector of the lot where time stands still is the scene dock, way in the northwest corner. There the only sounds are the canvas flapping over the N.Y. Street," a 1937 employee newspaper reflected. "Jack Burke and Mike Powell have had a little office there for well-nigh ten years. Its walls are lined with faded publicity stills and movie ads. 'We used to have a lot more,' Mike remarked wistfully, 'but somebody stole 'em.' "[54]

In the 1960s Paramount was awash with old sets for a few reasons: Production was down; items formally stored at the ranch had been moved onto the lot; and the vast graveyards of scenic pieces previously controlled by RKO

were now the responsibility of Paramount as well. The company listed 66,000 square feet of available scene-dock space in 1968, but the total was probably much more than that, seeing that scenery was being stored everywhere, and much less than that, because all of the bays were filled far past their intended capacity.

Scenery was stored north of the mill, along Van Ness Avenue, in the RKO transportation building, behind the RKO commissary, and in lofts behind the B-Tank sky backdrop and backlot mountain range. It was also standing, wrapped in canvas sheeting for protection, all over the backlot and on the crowded studio streets. During the entire studio era, the trend had been to save everything for future reuse. But in the mercenary 1960s, when that future was very much in doubt, and when there was no fiscal reason for making the next project's bottom line lower, the studio started junking the spoils of an empire it had taken decades to amass. Pieces were broken up, hauled off, or carted away, to the astonishment of longtime employees who had been told to save, and catalog, everything which might someday be usable. Thousands of sets from hundreds of movies slowly just disappeared.

Eventually it was decreed by the college-educated businessmen who ended up presiding over new Hollywood that a movie studio should resemble a campus rather than a movie studio, and so a push was made to banish unsightly sets, and even scaffolding and lights, from studio streets. To make this happen, eventually millions of dollars of valuable equipment followed those sets out the back gate and into oblivion.

Today's scene docks are enclosed, small, and only house flats for projects still in production, and which will, with utter certainty, be used again (and hopefully not have to be viewed by executives walking from their BMWs into their office suites).

LEFT: Scene docks are designated areas used to store sets. But at Paramount those sets have always been stacked or dumped wherever there was open space at the moment. Here dozens of flats, props, and even manufactured trees and rocks await their next assignment adjacent to Western Street and the Lasky-DeMille Barn, 1952. ABOVE: Paramount scene docks hidden by their own mountain range. Note the miniature oil wells and the RKO tower in the background, 1955.

RIGHT: The original Paramount water tower in 1950 far left. . . and at the time of its demolition in 1951.
BELOW: The current Paramount water tower, courtesy of RKO, 2016.

RIGHT: The original Paramount water tower in 1950 far left. . . and at the time of its demolition in 1951.
BELOW: The current Paramount water tower, courtesy of RKO, 2016.

56 THE WATER TOWER

The current studio water tower, and the one visible in 1968, was actually not the historic Paramount water tower at all. The 138-foot-tall tank, which people today photograph and remark about, is actually the original RKO water tower, erected in 1929. The tank has a capacity of 950,000 gallons, although there has not been so much as a pint of water stored inside that tank for many years. The water tower is maintained as a talisman only, a tribute to the cliché of Hollywood as an industrial site where dreams are created on an assembly line.

The RKO water tower has occasionally been seen on camera, often on television, for episodes of *Mannix*, *Mod Squad*, and *Mission: Impossible*. In the feature *The Last Tycoon* (1975), it springs a leak as the result of an earthquake.

The original Paramount water tower, which was located adjacent to the B-Tank and roughly parallel to the commissary, was torn down in 1951, allegedly because it cast a shadow across parts of the backlot which were being used for filming. The old tank was 150 feet high, with foundations which extended 24 feet below grade. It had a capacity of 100,000 gallons.

With the Paramount water tower gone, the RKO tank was, for many years, the tallest structure in Hollywood. The studio once had a red light on the top to warn low-flying planes of its presence.

Desilu put their name on the side of the tank in 1958. Paramount didn't get around to painting their own logo on it until 1983.

57 STAGE 29 (1929)

WIDTH: 145 feet, 4 inches
LENGTH: 107 feet, 9 inches
HEIGHT: 35 feet
SQUARE FEET: 15,659

58 STAGE 30 (1929)

WIDTH: 107 feet, 4 inches
LENGTH: 90 feet
HEIGHT: 35 feet
SQUARE FEET: 9,660

59 STAGE 31 (1929)

WIDTH: 145 feet, 1 inch
LENGTH: 106 feet, 9 inches
HEIGHT: 35 feet
SQUARE FEET: 15,488

60 STAGE 32 (1929)

WIDTH: 143 feet, 10 inches
LENGTH: 109 feet
HEIGHT: 46 feet
SQUARE FEET: 15,678

These four stages just north of the Gower Gate house were built by RKO in 1929. Again, although a separate filmography is provided for each, they were built at the same time as a single construction project, and have often been

An aerial view of the RKO and Paramount lots in 1930. RKO stages 7–10,
inside one colossal building, are top
left. In 1968 the same stages would be
renumbered 29–32 by Paramount.

used with the walls between them removed, or partially removed, creating a truly awe-inspiring shooting space. In fact, Stages 30 and 31 have a removable partition between them to this day. So we will deal with the stages as a single entity, with the specific solo characteristics and achievements of each stage listed when possible.

In *The Last Tycoon* (1976), John Carradine brings guests into the opened ele-phant doors of this complex, and they are almost rendered speechless. "It's so big!" they whisper, to which Carradine assures them that "It's big all right. They don't have anything bigger in the whole world." The words are apt because the whole world—many worlds, in fact—have been created in this mysterious, haunted space.

Haunted is quite literally a word which has often been applied to these buildings. Perhaps this has something to do with the fact that these four stages are the ones farthest north on the lot, and therefore closest to the cemetery. Stages 31 and 32, in particular, seem to be home to psychic phenomena, or over-active imaginations, depending on one's opinion on the subject.

For example, an oft-told tale about Stage 32 involves a security guard secur-ing the stage for the night and then shutting off the lights, only to hear heavy footsteps clomping across the darkened floor. This was surprising, since the guard was certain he'd been alone in the building, and because an elaborate set was standing on the stage, which would have made crossing through it in the blackness next to impossible. Startled, the guard flipped on his flashlight and arched it across the myriad darkened flats and shadowy shapes, trying to find the source of the sound, even as the phantom footsteps echoed in the darkness. Yet, he was alone. There was no one else in the building.

These are the stages where the beloved Fred Astaire and Ginger Rogers musicals were primarily made. The series of films, which ran from 1933 to 1939, are renowned today for their impossibly polished Art Deco sets, designed under the supervision of Van Nest Polglase, and the impossibly polished dancing of the two stars. Of Rogers, Astaire once remarked, "She may have faked a little, but we knew we had a good thing going."

Inexplicably, Stage 29 includes a mural of gamboling whales on its western wall, 2016.

Stage 29 was the original RKO Stage 7. Stage 30 was Stage 8, 31 was Stage 9, and 32 was RKO's Stage 10. In 1968 the stages had just been renumbered. For a few awkward months after the Desilu merger, Paramount continued to use the old RKO numbers, but finally adapted the system they use today. For these stages and other former RKO buildings, the Paramount names and numbers will be used, with the RKO equivalents also included.

When looking at the stages on the map, they appear to be identical boxes, but each has its own idiosyncrasies. In fact, Stage 30 is considerably smaller than its sisters because of the built-in support areas, added in 1983–1984, which include two stories of dressing rooms and control rooms along the north wall, constructed for *Solid Gold* (TV, 1980–1988). Awkwardly, these cubicles do not open into the stage, meaning that crew members using these rooms have to exit to get back in. Stages 29 through 31 have full basements, long used for storage. Stage 32 has a tank, 60 feet by 60 feet, which has recently been used as a basement, as well. All four now have built-in bleachers for live-audience shows.

The outside of the buildings are equally confounding. Stages 31 and 32 had a permanent New York exterior built on them during the Desilu era, as close as they possessed to a backlot anywhere in the Gower plant. To this day the southern wall of Stage 29 has a life-size mural of some frolicking blue whales painted on it. The big mammals are 180 feet long by 85 feet high, and were painted in 1994 by noted environmental artist Robert Wyland. Whatever merits this admittedly unique contribution to the studio may possess as art, or as an environmental message, the "whaling wall" (as it is called) makes no sense aesthetically at a movie studio, and looks as ridiculous and awkward and out-of-place as an eight-story portrait of Marilyn Monroe would be on a wall at SeaWorld.

Shot on Stage 29:

Young Bride (RKO, 1932)—The library set was shot here; this film also shot on Stage 9 at the RKO Pathé lot.

What Price Hollywood? (RKO, 1932)—This early attempt to mythologize Hollywood was shot under the working titles *The Truth about Hollywood* and *Hollywood Merry-Go-Round*. It has been partially remade three times, so far, using the title *A Star Is Born*. The movie cabaret set and Mary's (Constance Bennett) bungalow and bedroom were constructed here.

Flying Down to Rio (RKO, 1933) —assorted.

Flying Devils (RKO, 1933)—"Fairview Field."

Of Human Bondage (RKO, 1934)—Victoria Station, as well as the hospital and Philip's (Leslie Howard) apartment.

Strictly Dynamite (RKO, 1934)—Nick's (Norman Foster) office and assorted other settings.

The Nitwits (RKO, 1935)—George Stevens directed this Wheeler and Woolsey comedy filmed under the title *Murder in Tin Pan Alley*. Street and jail scenes were shot here.

Hooray for Love (RKO, 1935)—a "Harlem street."

The Informer (RKO, 1935)—Most of this foggy, Irish-set John Ford Oscar winner was shot on this stage.

The Arizonan (RKO, 1935)—The interiors and exteriors of the Silver City, Arizona, jail were shot here.

Break of Hearts (RKO, 1935)—cafe scenes.

Quick Money (RKO, 1937)—garbage dump scenes.

Russian Dressing (RKO, 1938)—This short subject shot its "Russian Café" scenes here.

Having Wonderful Time (RKO, 1938)—process shots involving a subway kiosk.

Bringing Up Baby (RKO, 1938)—Butcher shop scenes were lensed on this stage. The famous screwball comedy also shot elsewhere on the lot, as well as at RKO Pathé Studio in Culver City; at Twentieth Century Fox, where the town of "Westlake" was played by Fox's New England set (rented for $312.50 a day); at the Columbia Ranch's "Deeds home set" (at

$500 per day); and at the Bel Air-Country Club. For some reason the film's memorable climax, where the brontosaurus skeleton becomes suddenly extinct, was staged across the street on Stage 4 at Prudential Studios, as it was called at the time.

Gunga Din (RKO, 1939)—Temple sequences were shot here and next door on Stage 30.

You'll Find Out (RKO, 1940)—The creepy manor house where Kay Kyser is menaced by Boris Karloff, Bela Lugosi, and Peter Lorre.

Citizen Kane (RKO, 1941)—process shots of Kane's unhappy car ride into the Everglades.

Dear! Deer! (RKO, 1942)—This Leon Errol short subject shot taxi process shots here.

Pretty Dolly (RKO, 1942)—Another Leon Errol short subject; the "Errol Building" interiors were shot here this time.

The Magnificent Ambersons (RKO, 1942)—The Amberson veranda process shots were composed here for this Orson Welles's near-masterpiece. Sequences were also

shot in other RKO stages here and in Culver City.

Cat People (RKO, 1942)—the zoo, New York Street, and museum sets.

Bombardier (RKO, 1943)—corner office with snow and wind effects.

The Falcon and the Co-eds (RKO, 1943)—Miss Keyes's office.

Hitler's Children (RKO, 1943)—orphanage and the American-German school sets.

Curse of the Cat People (RKO, 1944)—Amy's bedroom, the Reed family backyard, and the "bridge and meadow."

West of the Pecos (RKO, 1945)—Process shots involving the stagecoach and watering hole scenes were filmed here. Robert Mitchum was the star.

Man Alive (RKO, 1945)—showboat settings.

Pan-Americana (RKO, 1945)—club car and corridor; also Dan's Cuban suite.

Betrayal from the East (RKO, 1945)—Beauty parlor sets were shot here; the title "betrayal" does not happen here.

The Spanish Main (RKO, 1945)—*Barracuda* cabin.

The Body Snatcher (RKO, 1945)—assorted sets, including the graveyard.

Riff-Raff (RKO, 1947)—Gredson's apartment and hall sets.

I Remember Mama (RKO, 1948)—The Fairmont Hotel was shot here. James Arness had a supporting role in this film. He would be back in 1951.

Guns of Hate (RKO, 1948)—Morgan's office.

The Miracle of the Bells (RKO, 1948)—courtroom.

The Thing from Another World (RKO, 1951)—The radio room with block of ice was shot here, along with the famous scene of the thing (James Arness again) on fire. "No visitors, please," the call sheets warned lookie-loos.

She Couldn't Say No (RKO, 1954)—Seller's (Robert Mitchum) room.

Lassie (TV, 1957–1964)—The famous collie was an occasional tenant.

Mission: Impossible (TV, 1966–1973)—assorted.

Mannix (TV, 1967–1975)—assorted.

The Bold Ones: The Lawyers (TV, 1969–1972)—three and a half shooting days in November, 1968.

The Godfather: Part II (1974)—assorted.

Solid Gold (TV, 1980–1988)—primary sets.

Scrooged (1988)—assorted.

Arsenio Hall Show (TV, 1989–1994)—This popular alternative to Johnny Carson's *Tonight Show* opened each episode with the words "From Stage 29 at Paramount Studios on Melrose Avenue . . ."

Star Trek: First Contact (1996)—*Enterprise-E* sets.

The Beautician and the Beast (1997)—assorted.

All That (TV, 1997 episodes, 1994–2005)—assorted.

Moral Court (TV, 2000–2001)—primary set.

15 Minutes (2001)—Robert De Niro returns to one of *The Godfather: Part II* stages

Star Trek: Nemesis (2002)—the spaceship *Scimitar.*

Dr. Phil (TV 2002–)—The popular TV psychologist shoots his syndicated series here.

Shot on Stage 30:

Ghost Valley (RKO, 1932)—Living room and hallway sets were here; the film also shot next door on Stage 31. Some of the exteriors were at Universal Studios.

Is My Face Red? (RKO, 1932)—Tony Mugatti's room and Bee's bedroom. Tony and Bee were played by, respectively, Sidney Toler and Arline Judge.

Symphony of Six Million (RKO, 1932)—outer office sets.

Hold 'Em Jail (RKO, 1932)—Inserts for this Wheeler and Woolsey comedy were shot here. The film also shot on other stages here and at Pathé, and football scenes were shot at MGM's Lot 2.

Flying Down to Rio (RKO, 1933)—assorted.

The Gay Divorcee (RKO, 1934)—assorted.

Where Sinners Meet (RKO, 1934)—Latimer (Clive Brook) living room.

Top Hat (RKO, 1935)—theater club and theater boxes.

Break of Hearts (RKO, 1935)—"Ritz Bar" and "music hall stage."

Bringing Up Baby (RKO, 1938)—the Vance home.

Swing Vacation (RKO, 1939)—short subject which shot office scenes here.

Gunga Din (RKO, 1939)—the tower of the Thuggee temple.

You'll Find Out (RKO, 1940)—the ballroom and garden.

The Magnificent Ambersons (RKO, 1942)—garden and kitchen sets.

Fight for Freedom (RKO, 1943)—This stage was used, along with Stage 9, for numerous sequences for this very much fictionalized Amelia Earhart biography. Rosalind Russell played the aviatrix.

This Land Is Mine (RKO, 1943)—factory.

Rookies in Burma (RKO, 1943)—Various Burmese locations are violated by Carney and Brown, RKO's Abbott and Costello.

Ladies' Day (RKO, 1943)—baseball home plate process shots.

The Falcon in San Francisco (RKO, 1945)—park, boiler room, and taxi (process) shots.

ABOVE LEFT: An unidentified employee slogs up the (current) Avenue C in 1968. Stages 30 and 31 are ahead. **ABOVE RIGHT:** The same Avenue C as seen in 1991.

First Yank Into Tokyo (RKO, 1945)—The Yank is played by Tom Neal; Tokyo is played by Stage 30.

The Locket (RKO, 1946)—Italian restaurant.

Don't Fool Your Wife (RKO, 1948)—Leon Errol short subject; Leon's home.

The Window (RKO, 1949)—Woodry apartment sets; child actor Bobby Driscoll starred.

The Thing from Another World (RKO, 1951)—plane (process shot); also greenhouse set.

Blackbeard, the Pirate (RKO, 1952)—The "great cabin set" was here. Bobby Driscoll (see above) would later costar with Robert Newton in *Treasure Island* (Disney, 1950). Another of Robert Newton's stereotype-creating pirate portrayals was delivered on this stage, with the actor over-emoting right into the catwalks. The always-unpredictable Newton was actually pretty well-behaved during this production. Assistant director Jim Casey only reported Newton missing for a day and three-quarters' work, "due to Mr. Newton's difficulty in remembering lines—did not appear after lunch." Sadly,

the flamboyant actor would die from the effects of alcohol only four years later.

Mannix (TV, 1967–1975)—assorted.

Little House on the Prairie (TV, 1974–1983)—assorted.

The Day of the Locust (1975)—Although the climax of this one takes place at Grauman's Chinese Theatre, the logistics of filming at the actual landmark would have been difficult, so the forecourt of the theater, complete with its famous handprint squares, was re-created on this stage and on

the adjacent Stages 31 and 32. Hollywood Boulevard was also constructed in such detail that even the magazines in a boulevard newsstand were purchased or re-created to reflect the late 1930s period of the film.

Charles Ziarko, a second assistant director, remembers even today how vintage cars were driven in a loop outside the stage doors and around again in order to achieve the proper speed for the background. A group of 750 extras, costumed and made up to reflect the period, portrayed the crowd gathered for a premiere, including "stars" Tyrone Power Jr. and Dick Powell Jr., who played their own parents. Mae West and Gloria Swanson both visited the stage and probably felt like they had truly stepped back into another era. When director John Schlesinger shot the scenes where the mob outside the theater turns violent and attempts to burn the city, Ziarko had to stop the extras from throwing those expensive vintage magazines into the bonfires.

King Kong (1976)—Inexplicably, the studio likes to claim that their remake of the 1933 RKO picture was shot on their lot. This is untrue. According to all surviving accounts, the picture was shot on stages and on the backlot at MGM, and at Culver Studios. Some pre-production tests might have been shot at Paramount, although even that is debatable. What did happen on this stage in association with that movie is the press conference to announce its production, and to introduce Jessica Lange, who sat in a Styrofoam Kong paw for the occasion. The stage was dressed with appropriate jungle foliage at the time, so it is possible that someone may have thought the film was being made there.

Busting Loose (TV, 1977–1978)— Adam Arkin busts loose.

Joanie Loves Chachi (TV, 1982– 1983)—The *Happy Days* magic failed to spill over to this sitcom spin-off.

Under the Boardwalk (1988) —assorted.

Scrooged (1988)—assorted.

Soul Train (TV, 1991–2006) —assorted.

Addams Family Values (1993)—assorted.

The Beautician and the Beast (1997)—assorted.

The *Doctors* (TV, 2008–   )—This talk show is also shot on Stages 31 and 32.

Shot on Stage 31:

Ghost Valley (RKO, 1932)—See the note for Stage 30.

Hold 'Em Jail (RKO, 1932)—short subject; Edgar Kennedy's living room set. Kennedy, the always exasperated character actor, famous for his "slow burn" in which he tried, for a time, to hide his frustration with his family or his job, or with a better-billed or better paid, fellow comedian. RKO

cast Kennedy to type, in this long running (17 years) series, starting in 1930.

King Kong (RKO, 1933)—backstage at the theater scenes.

Emergency Call (RKO, 1933)—country hospital exteriors.

Top Hat (RKO, 1935)—This stage was used, along with Stage 30. Sequences shot here include the carnival and hotel scenes, and the main titles for foreign versions.

Follow the Fleet (RKO, 1936) —assorted.

Shall We Dance? (RKO, 1937) —assorted.

Carefree (RKO, 1938) —assorted.

Having Wonderful Time (RKO, 1938)—dining room scenes.

The Hunchback of Notre Dame (RKO, 1939)—Many scenes for this ambitious production were shot on this stage, including the bell tower and window sequences, the print shop, the court of justice, the beggars' headquarters, and the bridal suite for the poet (Edmond O'Brien) and the gypsy (Maureen O'Hara).

Citizen Kane (RKO, 1941)—The great hall of Xanadu was shot here and next door on Stage 32. It is possible

that this was, in fact, a single set, using both shooting stages, although it's more likely there were different Xanadu sets on both stages.

The Great Gildersleeve (RKO, 1942)— Gildersleeve's basement was on this stage; most of the rest of his house was on Stage 26, however.

Pretty Dolly (RKO, 1942)—Leon Errol short subject; office sets.

The Magnificent Ambersons (RKO, 1942)—exteriors of street with sky backing.

Cat People (RKO, 1942)—Producer Val Lewton invented a new sort of horror film on these stages. *Cat People* and its follow-ups relied more upon the power of suggestion than on overt thrills. An example: One of the scenes shot here, involving Jane Randolph alone in a pool locker room, induced shudders using only silhouettes and sound effects. The result was chillingly effective, and the studio liked that the shadows were more economical than actual "monsters." But one of the preview cards filled out by a test audience member noted that the "best performance was by the leopard."

```
FIFTH DAY-SIXTH DAY, WEDNESDAY, 7-31-68                    Page 4.
LOCATION:  PARAMOUNT MARATHON, STAGE 1
INT. VIANS' LAB-ACT IV        12-4/8   41   1-Kirk    uniform w/o phaser (15)
                                            2-Spock      "
Scs. 111 thru 149: Long talk re:            3-McCoy   torn shirt uniform
McCoy.                                      8-Gem
                                            9-Lal     Robe
                                            10-Thann  Robe

                                            EXTRAS:  5 SI
- - - - - - - - - - - - - - - - - - - - - - - - - - - - - - - - - -
                    (COMPANY MOVE TO STAGE 9)
INT. HUT - TEASER              6/8      1   11-Dr. Linke   jumpsuit  (3)
                                            12-Dr. Ozaba   jumpsuit
Sc. 9: Shoot scene as per script-           EXTRAS:  SI
to BURN IN on Viewing Screen.

NOTE: TIEDOWN CAMERA.              EFX: Earthquake.

INT. BRIDGE-ACT IV-NEW TAG     1-7/8    4   1-Kirk    uniforms w/o phasers (17)
                                            2-Spock
Scs. 151-153-154-155:  Tag.                 3-McCoy
                                            4-Scott

                                            EXTRAS:  5 SI
                                                     4 Atmos.
            (END FIFTH & SIXTH DAYS - TOTAL PAGES:  15-1/8)
                    (END OF PRINCIPAL PHOTOGRAPHY)
MAIN VIEWING SCREEN-STOCK        4/8    4

Sc. 152:          PLANET BELOW GLEAMS AMONG THE STARS        1/8
Scs. 155-156-157:                                            3/8
EXT. SPACE-ENTERPRISE-STOCK      3/8    3

Scs. 1-150-157:
VIEWING SCREEN-VIDEO-TAPE RECORDER      1

Sc. 9:
VOICE OVER

Scs. 1-2:              KIRK
- - - - - - - - - - - - - - - - - - - - - - - - - - - - - - - - -
EFX & OPTICALS                         28

Scs. 2-9-12-13-36-39-41-42-43-70-
    73-74(?)-76-78-78B-79-82-100-
    108-109-118-120-127-131-134-138-140-141.
                    (END OF POST PRODUCTION)
                    **              **
```

A very rare original *Star Trek* call sheet used for the 1968 episode "The Empath." As shown, the bridge of the "Enterprise" was on Stage 31, here still referred to as Stage 9. (Image courtesy of Rob Klein)

Ladies' Day (RKO, 1943)—Sox dressing room.

Rookies in Burma (RKO, 1943)—process shots involving an elephant and a jeep were on this stage.

Tender Comrade (RKO, 1943)—process shots of the wartime factory.

Alibi Baby (RKO, 1945)—short subject; the (Edgar) Kennedy living room.

The Bells of St. Mary's (RKO, 1945)—The St. Mary's church and vestibule were built here for this very successful sequel to *Going My Way* (1944). Oddly, only the first film was a Paramount picture.

Pan-Americana (RKO, 1945)—editorial office, game room, and patio sets.

The Spanish Main (RKO, 1945)—assorted.

Back to Bataan (RKO, 1945)—Most of this John Wayne war film was shot in Culver City. The famous "Bataan death march," however, was shot near LA's Mulholland Drive. This stage played the "Australian headquarters."

I Remember Mama (RKO, 1948)—process shots for train; also "Katrin's attic."

Gunplay (RKO, 1951)—bunkhouse.

Star Trek (TV, 1966–1969)—Most of the *Enterprise* sets stood here on this single stage. Billy Blackburn, who played a variety of roles during that series' production, once remarked how strange it was to walk across the familiar bridge and then around to the edge of the flats—and to see the bare plywood backs, the electrical wire hanging out of the machinery, and the lumber and sandbags holding up those walls. "It was fascinating," he remembers. "But part of me didn't want to see it. Part of me just wanted to look away."[55]

Little House on the Prairie (TV, 1974–1983)—assorted.

Angie (TV, 1979–1980)—A fire onstage on April 30, 1979, damaged the sets for this sitcom.

First Monday in October (1981)—The Supreme Court scenes were shot here and on Stage 32.

Amen (TV, 1986–1991)—assorted.

Wayne's World 2 (1993)—assorted.

Coneheads (1993)—assorted.

Indecent Proposal (1993)—assorted.

Addams Family Values (1993)—The second floor of the Addams mansion was built here.

Nick of Time (1995)—assorted.

A Very Brady Sequel (1996)—assorted.

Fired Up (TV, 1997–1998)—assorted.

Becker (1998)—assorted.

Community (TV, 2009–2015)—one of two stages used during the series run.

Shot on Stage 32:

Young Bride (RKO, 1932)—Allie's (Helen Twelvetree) room was shot here. Director William A. Seiter seems to have replaced William Dieterle sometime during production.

King Kong (RKO, 1933)—The ferocious sequence of Kong attacking an elevated train was shot here in December of 1932—some of the last footage taken for the film. It opened in March.

Rafter Romance (RKO, 1933)—office and attic interiors.

The Gay Divorcee (RKO, 1934)—assorted.

Roberta (RKO, 1935)—assorted.

Top Hat (RKO, 1935)—assorted.

Village Tale (RKO, 1935)—Summerville home, general store, and church sets built here.

Swing Time (RKO, 1936)—assorted.

Bringing Up Baby (RKO, 1938)—This was known as the "green set" during production, due to the one hundred green mats laid here to simulate grass during production.

The Mad Miss Manton (RKO, 1938)—"men's lounge."

Having Wonderful Time (RKO, 1938)—recreation hall and dining room sets.

Abe Lincoln in Illinois (RKO, 1940)—Process shots as seen from the Rutledge wagon were shot here for this moving biography of Abraham Lincoln, which, unfortunately for RKO, was not a financial success.

Citizen Kane (RKO, 1941)—The great hall of Xanadu was built here, as were several other auxiliary sets for what some people consider the greatest film ever made. It has been remarked more than once that *Kane* was, by the standards of its era, a modest picture, whatever that means. In fact, a great deal of time and money went into its production. *Citizen Kane* shot from July 22, 1940, all the way to December 20 of the same year. All of the resources of a major studio were lavished upon its creation. By contrast, *The Fargo Kid* (RKO 1940), a Tim Holt Western, started production on July 13 and wrapped on July 27. It was in theaters that December while *Kane* was still shooting.

In 1991 the prop "Rosebud" sled, courtesy of its owner, Steven Spielberg, returned to the stage for the film's fiftieth anniversary. Two of the film's surviving stars, Joseph Cotton and Ruth Warrick, also attended, along with director Robert Wise, who edited *Kane*.

Pretty Dolly (RKO, 1942)—Leon Errol short subject; as the "Errol Building" lobby.

Tender Comrade (RKO, 1943)—the luncheon.

The Falcon and the Co-eds (RKO, 1943)—campus sets.

Passport to Destiny (RKO, 1944)—German prison.

Isle of the Dead (RKO, 1945)—This was another Val Lewton thriller, based on a haunting Arnold Böcklin painting, featured under the titles. Albrecht's living room and the general's room were built here. The same sets were later in the production, inexplicably re-created on Stage 22.

Back to Bataan (RKO, 1945)—rice paddies.

It's a Wonderful Life (RKO, 1946)—The river with falling snow observed by a suicidal George Bailey (James Stewart) on Christmas Eve was created here.

I Remember Mama (RKO, 1948)—the Steiner home sets.

The Errand Boy (1961)—The scenes with the studio pool were shot here.

Star Trek (TV, 1966–1969)—assorted swing sets representing new life forms and new civilizations.

Chinatown (1974)—assorted.

Little House on the Prairie (TV, 1974–1983)—The interiors of the Olson General Store were shot here.

The Last Tycoon (1976)—Robert De Niro walks by the outside of the stage.

History of the World: Part 1 (Twentieth Century Fox, 1981)—The wonderfully tasteless "Inquisition" production number with the swimming nuns used the stage's pool, which apparently has not been used since.

First Monday in October (1981)—Supreme Court scenes were shot here and on Stage 31.

The Golden Child (1986)—assorted.

Duet (TV, 1987–1989)—assorted.

Dear John (TV, 1988–1992)—shot on this stage and Stages 20 and 27, at different times.

Open House (TV, 1989–1990)—sitcom set in a real estate office.

Naked Gun 2 1/2: The Smell of Fear (1991)—assorted.

Bob (TV, 1992–1993)—Bob Newhart as a cartoonist: "I'm hopeful the show will be a success. It sure feels good,"[56] Newhart told the studio newsletter. It would, in fact, last for only thirty-three episodes.

The Boys Are Back (TV, 1994–1995) —assorted.

Star Trek: Nemesis (2002) —assorted.

Dr. Phil (TV, 2002–   )—support stage.

Community (TV, 2009-2015)—one of two stages used by this cult comedy.

61 NORTH GOWER GATE

This anonymous-looking entrance was built for trucks and heavy equipment, and in previous eras, for RKO executives important enough to actually park on the lot—no small honor on such a compact campus. Because of its nondescript appearance, this spot became a popular location for films needing an establishing shot of an industrial site or a military compound, or even a movie studio.

The North Gower Gate as it looked in 1996. Stages 27 and 28 are on the right.

The Godfather (1972) is a good example of this entrance's relatively frequent on-screen appearances. For that film, a cheap sign was thrown up over the gate and shot "almost second unit," as director Francis Ford Coppola put it, using a double for actor Robert Duvall and an anonymous cinematographer, who Coppola only remembers was *not* Gordon Willis, who brilliantly shot the rest of the film. Coppola reportedly did not like the look of the gate, but was forced to use it anyway by Paramount, which was nearly bankrupt, and very uneasy about that expensive film's commercial prospects. Recently Warren Beatty shot scenes for *Rules Don't Apply* (Twentieth Century Fox, 2016) on the site, with facsimiles of the original RKO signage again marking the location.

South of the North Gower Gate was, not surprisingly, the South Gower Gate, also known as the Lower Gower Gate, still there today. It was usually kept locked and seldom used, then as now, except for the not-infrequent times when its northern cousin was being used as a film location.

62 STAGE 28 (1930)

WIDTH: 96 feet, 9 inches

LENGTH: 83 feet, 8 inches

HEIGHT: 34 feet

SQUARE FEET: 8,262

63 STAGE 27 (1930)

WIDTH: 127 feet, 3 inches

LENGTH: 83 feet, 6 inches

HEIGHT: 32 feet

SQUARE FEET: 10,625

Stage 28, aka, RKO Stage 6, and its nearby sister, Stage 27, alias RKO Stage 5, were built together in 1930 as sound-recording stages, similarly to how Stages 11 through 14 were constructed at Paramount. Curiously, Stage 26, which is effectively part of the same complex, had been built a little earlier in the first mad rush to create talking pictures.

Both stages were also updated in 1984 for another technical innovation, video production, although Paramount was very late to the table on that one. Earl Lestz, president of the Studio Group, a department organized to streamline studio operations in the 1980s, remarked in 1989 that "*Entertainment Tonight* and other shows were being produced at studios off the lot because Paramount did not have videotape capability. We were sitting here with empty stages and paying out rental that should have been coming to Paramount."[57] As part of the same update, elevated sound and control booths and bleachers for audience-participation TV shows were also added.

Shot on Stage 28:

Symphony of Six Million (RKO, 1932)—Riverside Drive Apartments.

Rafter Romance (RKO, 1933)—The Chinese restaurant set was shot here; the Warner Bros. New York backlot was also utilized.

Good Housewrecking (RKO, 1933)—short subject; as the (Edgar) Kennedy house.

Flying Devils (RKO, 1933)—cabin interiors, as well as wooded scenes.

The Son of Kong (RKO, 1933)—"temple where bear enters."

Strictly Fresh Yeggs (RKO, 1934)—short subject; the Stanton home and tunnel.

Top Hat (RKO, 1935)—The bridal suite, Dale's (Ginger Rogers) hotel room, and Hardwick's (Edward Everett Horton) apartment sets were on this stage.

Break of Hearts (RKO, 1935)—the apartment of Roberti (Charles Boyer).

Mary of Scotland (RKO, 1936)—also Stage 27.

Quality Street (RKO, 1937)—also Stage 27.

Room Service (RKO, 1938)—also Stage 27.

The Mad Miss Manton (RKO, 1938)—the Manton apartment.

Having Wonderful Time (RKO, 1938)—The "rainstorm in Buzzy's bunk" was shot here.

Abe Lincoln in Illinois (RKO, 1940)—Edward's home.

Hitler's Children (RKO, 1943)—cathedral.

This Land Is Mine (RKO, 1943)—One of Jean Renoir's relatively few American films used this stage for its prison set.

Tender Comrade (RKO, 1943)—assorted.

Passport to Destiny (RKO, 1944)—Berlin hotel bedroom sets.

Alibi Baby (RKO, 1945)—short subject; the (Edgar) Kennedy kitchen set.

Sleepless Tuesday (RKO, 1945)—This was another Edgar Kennedy short subject, which probably reused the same sets as above.

Pan-Americana (RKO, 1945)—Jo Anne's Mexican suite.

Man Alive (RKO, 1945)—most of film shot here.

The Locket (RKO, 1946)—DA's office; also the home of Dr. Blair's London flat.

Born to Kill (RKO, 1946)—Helen's (Claire Trevor) room.

Out of the Past (RKO, 1947)—One of the ultimate *films noirs*, due to its oppressive atmosphere and shadowy lighting. "We used to light the sets with our cigarettes," Robert Mitchum once wisecracked. Those sets on this stage included Whit's (Kirk Douglas) apartment and hallway, and also the Blue Sky Club.

Dick Tracy Meets Gruesome (RKO, 1947)—The door and stairs near "hangman's knot" is how the production paperwork colorfully, if cryptically, describes the scenes shot on this stage. Dick Tracy was played by Ralph Boyd, and Boris Karloff played Gruesome.

Mr. Blandings Builds His Dream House (RKO, 1948)—Jim's (Cary Grant) office, Simms's (Reginald Denny) living room and office.

The Miracle of the Bells (RKO, 1948)—rectory; Father Paul's (Frank Sinatra) school.

Mannix (TV, 1967–1975)—assorted.

The Godfather: Part II (1974)—assorted.

The Great Gatsby (1974)—Unknown; according to the studio, something from this film shot on this stage.

Best of the West (TV, 1981–1982)—assorted.

Entertainment Tonight (TV, 1981–2007 seasons)—primary set.

The Insider (TV, 2004–2007 seasons)—also known as *Omg! Insider*; shot adjacent to the *Entertainment Tonight* sets.

Big Time Rush (TV, 2009–2013)—assorted.

Shot on Stage 27:

Young Bride (RKO, 1932)—chop suey parlor.

Is My Face Red? (RKO, 1932)—fire escape and broadcast station sets.

Symphony of Six Million (RKO, 1932)—tenement set.

Flying Devils (RKO, 1933)—speakeasy sequences.

Of Human Bondage (RKO, 1934)—department store window.

Strictly Dynamite (RKO, 1934)—Moxie's (Jimmy Durante) apartment.

Hooray for Love (RKO, 1935)—The theater set was built and shot here.

Mary of Scotland (RKO, 1936)—also Stage 26.

Quality Street (RKO, 1937)—also Stage 26.

Room Service (RKO, 1938)—also Stage 26.

Bringing Up Baby (RKO, 1938)—process shots of the station wagon and Westlake jail scenes.

The Mad Miss Manton (RKO, 1938)—DA's office and the hospital room sets.

Three Sons (RKO, 1939)—Pardway family house sets.

The Fargo Kid (RKO, 1940)—the Winters family home; also on Stage 25.

Citizen Kane (RKO, 1941)—assorted *Chicago Inquirer* offices.

Cat People (RKO, 1942)—Alice's hotel lobby set.

Ladies' Day (RKO, 1943)—hotel lobby and Pullman car sets.

Tender Comrade (RKO, 1943)—Jo Jones's (Ginger Rogers) bedroom.

The Falcon in Hollywood (RKO, 1944)—The Falcon (Tom Conway) solves a case at "Sunset Studios."

The Falcon in San Francisco (RKO, 1945)—The Falcon investigates "Doreen's apartment."

The Bells of St. Mary's (RKO, 1945)—upper and lower hall; Patsy's mother's apartment.

It's a Wonderful Life (RKO, 1946)—George's (James Stewart) office in the Building and Loan; also the tollhouse on the bridge.

Out of the Past (RKO, 1947)—Whit's Tahoe place and library sets.

Return of the Bad Men (RKO, 1948)—saloon and Guthrie Bank.

The Arizona Ranger (RKO, 1948)—Tim Holt Western; Butler cabin.

Guns of Hate (RKO, 1948)—Tim Holt Western; Judy Jason's living room.

Gunplay (RKO, 1951)—Tim Holt Western; saloon.

Mission: Impossible (TV, 1966–1973)—assorted.

The Sterile Cuckoo (1969)—assorted.

The Godfather (1972)—This title is included here because the studio insists that something from the film was shot on this stage, and on Stage 30. Director Francis Ford Coppola, however, is adamant that only second-unit footage was shot on the lot, and that this footage consisted only of exteriors shot outside Stages 29–31, and on New York Street.

The Great Gatsby (1974)—As on

The Godfather (1972), little on the production of this film supports the supposition that scenes for this one shot on Stage 27. But the studio, again, tells us that it is so. Maybe Paramount knows more than we do.

Mork & Mindy (TV, 1978–1982)—Pam Dawber, who costarred with Robin Williams in this Boulder, Colorado-set series, has remarked that guests on the soundstage during production included Ginger Rogers, who would have known the stage well.

Entertainment Tonight (TV, 1981–2007 seasons)—used as office space, mostly.

Tortellis (TV, 1982)—short-lived *Cheers* spin-off.

Dear John (TV, 1988–1992)—shot on this stage, and Stages 20 and 32 at different times.

Down Home (TV, 1990–1991)—assorted.

Leeza (TV, 1994–2000)—assorted, along with Stage 26.

Baby Bob (TV, 2002–2003)—This comedy about a talking baby shot fourteen episodes on this stage, of which only nine were aired.

The Insider (TV, 2004–2007)—also known as *Omg! Insider*; secondary sets.

Dirty Sexy Money (TV, 2007–2009)—assorted New York settings.

Big Time Rush (TV, 2009–2013)—offices of Rocque Records, recording studio, and hotel bedroom scenes.

Mr. Sunshine (TV, 2011–2012)—primary sets for a less-than-successful Mathew Perry vehicle.

Happy Endings (TV, 2011–2013)—assorted, as Chicago.

The Thundermans (TV, 2013–)—Nickelodeon show.

Tabloid (TV, 2014–2015)—assorted.

64 STAGE 26 (1929)

WIDTH:	100 feet, 2 inches
LENGTH:	68 feet, 5 inches
HEIGHT:	28 feet
SQUARE FEET:	6,853

Originally RKO Stage 4, this stage, like several other RKO stages, was designed by art director Carroll Clark as the first actual sound-recording stage on their lot. In fact, the original RKO sound department, rehearsal hall, and scoring stage was next door in what was in the late 1960s part of Glen Glenn Sound and recording stages "E" and "G," and is now an audio-mixing and dubbing booth.

Stage 26 has a connecting door to the adjacent Stage 27, and shares some of the titles below with that stage.

Shot on Stage 26:

Symphony of Six Million (RKO, 1932)—Felix's (Ricardo Cortez) Park Avenue office set.

Hold 'Em Jail (RKO, 1932)—The sets built onstage here were doubled by exteriors taken outside and, as the production clerk described it, "beyond Director's Building."

What Price Hollywood? (RKO, 1932)—Polo field; also Max Carey's apartment sets.

King Kong (RKO, 1933)—The "cave set" was utilized here for one day, January 10, 1933, very late in the *Kong* production schedule, and long after the other jungle sequences were completed.

Of Human Bondage (RKO, 1934)— Reginald Owen's character's living room set. This was also Victoria station, and the medical classroom set.

Jalna (RKO, 1935)—Vaughn's (Nigel Bruce) home.

Top Hat (RKO, 1935)—The title number was shot here and on

Stage 27 next door. Madge's apartment (as played by Helen Broderick) was on Stage 26 only.

Break of Hearts (RKO, 1935)—Most of this early Katharine Hepburn vehicle was shot on this stage, although the daily production reports for the film repeatedly complained that she was late showing up for work.

Quick Money (RKO, 1937)— scenes were shot here under the working title *Taking the Town*.

Danger Patrol (RKO, 1937)—Goliath Club and Chinese restaurant interiors.

The Mad Miss Manton (RKO, 1938)—Lane and Thomas office.

Swing Vacation (RKO, 1939)—short subject; cosmetic company interiors were here.

Chicken Feed (RKO, 1939)—This Billy Gilbert short subject shot the "Downey home" sequences here.

Three Sons (RKO, 1939)—Ullman's apartment.

The Fargo Kid (RKO, 1940)—hotel room.

You'll Find Out (RKO, 1940)—the living room.

Citizen Kane (RKO, 1941)—"Susan's first apartment."

Cat People (RKO, 1942)—On August 8, 1942, producer Val Lewton and director Jacques Tourneur shot a scene on this stage involving a bus coming suddenly out of the dark, its air brakes hissing menacingly.

This scene makes audiences jump to this day. In fact, Lewton said later that he wanted to put at least one "bus"—a scene designed to startle audiences—in each of his films afterward.

The Magnificent Ambersons (RKO, 1942)—Morgan's library, ballroom interiors, hospital corridor, and the Amberson kitchen sets were all here.

Dear! Deer! (RKO, 1942)—For this Leon Errol short subject, this was the "Errol home."

Bombardier (RKO, 1943)—seashore and beach sets.

Ladies' Day (RKO, 1943)—the team's dugout.

Fight for Freedom (RKO, 1943)—Virginia Beach process shots.

Passport to Destiny (RKO, 1944)—Dietrich's office.

Curse of the Cat People (RKO, 1944)—The Reed home interiors were built here for this moody sequel to *Cat People* (1942). Some of the sets were reportedly cannibalized from those from *The Magnificent Ambersons* (1942).

Feather Your Nest (RKO, 1944)—This short subject was shot entirely on this stage.

The Falcon in San Francisco (RKO, 1945)—the Falcon's hotel room.

The Body Snatcher (RKO, 1945)—Gray's (Boris Karloff) stable and room; also the anatomy room.

Back to Bataan (RKO, 1945)—This stage was used as a "Jap warehouse."

It's a Wonderful Life (RKO, 1946)—Montage sequences were shot on this stage.

Born to Kill (RKO, 1946)—the Laury living room.

Dick Tracy Meets Gruesome (RKO, 1947)—Tracy's office.

The Miracle of the Bells (RKO, 1948)—Dunnigan's (Fred MacMurray) hotel room.

Mr. Blandings Builds His Dream House (RKO, 1948)—the Blandings living room.

Make Room for Daddy (TV, 1953–1964)—occasionally used by the classic sitcom.

The Naked Jungle (1954)—plantation interiors.

The Guns of Will Sonnett (TV, 1967–1969) —assorted.

Sextette (Crown International Pictures, 1977)—Mae West's bridal suite set was shot here. "Closed Set: No Visitors Please" proclaimed the call sheets circulated around the lot, about her return to her old studio.

Hard Copy (TV, 1989–1999)—primary set.

Leeza (TV, 1994–2000)—along with Stage 27.

The Insider (TV, 2004–2007)—also known as *Omg! Insider*; secondary sets.

True Jackson, VP (TV, 2008–2011) —assorted.

Supah Ninja (TV, 2010–2011) —assorted.

How to Rock (TV, 2012)—assorted.

Marvin Marvin (TV, 2012–2013)—Nickelodeon show.

The Paramount research department in its original location in the directors-writers building. Pictured is librarian Peggy Schwartz, whose expression here is priceless, 1928.

65 RESEARCH DEPARTMENT

For most of its long life the Paramount research library was in the directors-writers building. Only at the very end of its tenure was it over here, in the old RKO property building, near the original RKO library.

The Paramount library started as a file cabinet at Selma-Vine containing pictorial and textual materials which were used by writers and art directors and costumers for fact-checking and for inspiration on period films. Eventually the collection expanded as a resource for getting the proper look for films set in foreign lands, foreign cities, army bases, hospitals, Georgia chain gangs, cavalry forts, rubber plantations, circus tents, airports, alleys, artists' colonies, coliseums, casinos, castles, casbahs, barbershops, bordellos, bingo parlors, barnyards, submarines, subways, South Sea islands, starships, sewers, railyards, and occasionally even Hollywood studios.

According to publicity for *Reap The Wild Wind* (1942), for example, the research department consulted 444 books, 177 periodicals and newspapers, and 28 dictionaries, glossaries, and encyclopedias, ultimately compiling a bibliography filling 312 mimeographed pages. The fact that these numbers came from the publicity department would have made them highly suspicious, had the bibliography not turned out to be an actual document that was made available to schools for consultation.

What came to be known as the Paramount Research Library was established in 1915 by Elizabeth B. McGaffney and managed from the early 1930s to the early 1960s by Gladys Percey. Among the anonymous and sometimes mole-like studio librarians, Percey was often (but not always) the only one credited on-screen for her contributions. She had a close, if contentious, relationship with C. B. DeMille, who seemed to respect her tenacity at discovering minutiae about bygone eras, which he always seemed happy to disregard if fiction proved to be more dramatic or visually interesting than Percey's meticulously documented truths. In 1959 she wrote a memo regarding Marlon Brando's anachronistic dialogue in the script of *One-Eyed Jacks*. A reader can practically hear the disdain in her voice regarding Brando as she remarks that "I didn't for one minute think he'd change a word, but I felt with a stupendous production such as this, he might like to be protected by knowing—like Mr. DeMille."

DeMille was in fact responsible for the largest single subject covered in the studio library: Moses and the Exodus. Ever since his original *Ten Command-ments* in 1923, C. B. had continued to collect, and to encourage the Paramount library to collect, materials on that era. This hobby continued throughout the 1930s and 1940s, even before DeMille admitted to his interest in a remake. In fact, the lead researcher on the subject, Henry Noerdlinger, published a book called *Moses and Egypt* (1956) based on what the department had amassed on Moses' lost years. DeMille happily wrote the introduction.

According to Percey, "one of the most dog-eared volumes in the department's collection, one that is widely used by members of the art department as a choice text, is *American Homes of Culture*, illustrating the horror-architecture of the last century. The book was acquired from Goodwill for twenty-five cents."[58]

By the close of the studio era, the library—now under the management of one Elizabeth. Higgason—encompassed the entire spectrum of accumulated and combined visual knowledge within its collection.

Unfortunately, the close of the studio era also meant, ultimately, the close of the research library. In 1969, the studio closed the department, which had been operating out of this office in the old Desilu Property Building. The staff of two, which had been as many as sixteen in the 1940s, was sent home. The library remained on the lot in same location for over a decade, but was finally packed up and moved to an off-lot warehouse in the early 1980s.

Enter Debbie Fine. Debbie had worked at the library during the last year of its operation. When that job ended in 1969 she eventually moved on to a position, in 1978, with producer George Lucas. "George wanted a library to be part of a complex he was building in Marin County. He gave me a generous budget to buy books and periodicals. But I knew we could never match the original studio libraries—

The interior of the old RKO prop storage building in 2013. In 1968 the research department materials were being stored here as well.

particularly the huge clipping/picture files in nearly 100 file cabinets. I told George about the Paramount Library I had someday hoped we could acquire."

Lucas' film, *Raiders of the Lost Ark* (1981), was fortunately a Paramount picture. Debbie was permitted access to the collection during production, which she found in some disarray. "I told George of my concern about the library's future, and my hope we could make an offer before it may be broken up and sold off, although we had no physical space for the library at that time," she recalls.

"It wasn't until late 1987 that the right circumstances came together for an offer. I had heard the library had been packed up in boxes and moved off the Paramount lot, and we now had space for it.

There was a meeting at Skywalker Ranch with George, myself, and Paramount execs, one of whom remembered me and I him. I think that helped give them a sense of trust in us to be good guardians of the library. A deal followed. The day the library arrived at the ranch, I was on cloud nine. After close to twenty years of worrying about what would happen to it, this was one of the great moments of my life. I can never thank George enough for the magnificent act of saving the library."[59]

Ironically, in 1987 Lillian Michelson, who had been managing an independent research library based on the Samuel Goldwyn collection, moved her files to the Mae West Building (which had been built in 1930) at Paramount, to operate the library as an independent contractor on the lot. She later moved to an editorial building on Twelfth Street, next to Stage 16. Eventually the collection migrated to DreamWorks Animation Studios in Glendale, but that didn't last long either.

The original RKO collection meanwhile is now safely, if improbably, preserved at director Francis Ford Coppola's vineyard in Napa Valley. According to Marc Wanamaker, the owners had wanted to liquidate it and Coppola, fortuitously, had purchased it "at a distressed price."

The golden era of the studio research libraries and research librarians is long past. Those still intact have all struggled to survive for decades. Fortunately, due to George Lucas and Debbie Fine, the Paramount Library, with its myriad spirals of files on pharaohs and pirates and pageants and passenger pigeons, and on perhaps hundreds of thousands of other topics, survives today. It survives as a quaint relic of a lost, pre-Internet era, as a symbol of all that we have learned, and, perhaps, of all that we have forgotten.

66 TRANSPORTATION DEPARTMENT

The original transportation department, which maintained and repaired both production-related and -photographed vehicles, was a long narrow shed on the northeast corner of the lot near the Lemon Grove gatehouse. In 1941 the studio had to rent a garage just outside of that gate for the department to use temporarily when their own quarters were being used to store sets. In *The Blue Dahlia* (1946) and other movies, the transportation department itself was used as a set, usually as a garage.

With the Desilu merger, the offices were moved into the RKO transportation building, originally part of the Gower Mill, but at the time, sharing with the property department overflow items. During this era the department was open from seven a.m. to seven p.m., and included cars, trucks, tractor-trailers, generator trucks, insert camera cars, and a twenty-one-passenger bus, all billed out at $2.00 to $4.00 an hour for the vehicle and $5.00 to $5.50 per hour for the driver.

Today, the same department, now located in the Lemon Grove parking structure across the street from its original location, offers many of the same services, although the buses they provide now carry up to thirty-two people. (The drivers make more money, as well.)

ABOVE LEFT: The Paramount transportation department, in a sense, can be traced back to this 1913 location trip to the San Fernando Valley for *The Squaw Man*. Directors Cecil B. DeMille and Oscar Apfel, seated on alternate sides of the truck, and leading man Dustin Farnum, center, are surrounded by local color. ABOVE RIGHT: The RKO mill, now known as the Gower mill, once housed part of the RKO transportation department as well. It included a narrow opening from which flat pieces of scenery could be removed. The outline of that slot is still visible on this wall today, 2013.

67 STAGE 25 (1921)

WIDTH: 169 feet

LENGTH: 75 feet, 2 inches

HEIGHT: 28 feet

SQUARE FEET: 12,703

The southern wall of Stage 25 looks onto the park and originally consisted of ladies dressing rooms and wardrobe storage areas, 2016.

Stage 25 (RKO Stage 3) seems to have often been used for special effects and montage and rear-projection process shots during the RKO era, just as Stage 2 was utilized for similar sequences next door at Paramount. The stage was reportedly very popular with actresses during this era due to the convenient row of dressing rooms along Stage 25's southern wall. In fact, Lucille Ball, who was not important enough to have a dressing room in this building during her RKO days, moved in to these offices when she bought the lot. Lucy and Desi quickly modernized Stage 25 for three-camera audience shoots, adding 157 bleacher seats on the southern wall and an elevated sound/control booth.

In fact, Lucy's *The Lucy Show* (TV, 1962–1968) was initially filmed on Stage 25, although it moved to Stage 21 after the first two seasons. Later, as Lucy's relationship with Charles Bluhdorn, and Paramount, frayed, she eventually moved that successful program yet again, this time to Universal Studios.

Stage 25 also includes a 17-foot-by-19-foot pit.

Shot on Stage 25:

Bird of Paradise (RKO, 1932)—The "Mahumahu's hut" scenes were filmed here for this erotic South Seas adventure, as were assorted pickup shots. The film also shot on Stage 23, at the RKO Pathé backlot, on another stage at Warner Bros., out on Catalina Island, and on a very rare (and expensive) location trip, in Hawaii.

The Most Dangerous Game (RKO, 1932)—The exterior of the cliff, the "chateau," and process shots were done here, and on Stage 20. Most of this film was shot at Pathé. "Cooper's tree," named after producer Merian C. Cooper, was on Stage 12 at that other lot, and was used immediately thereafter for *King Kong*, particularly the memorable scene where Kong shakes the frightened sailors off that log.

Symphony of Six Million (RKO, 1932)—Jessica's (Irene Dunne) room.

Hold 'Em Jail (RKO, 1932)—The "broadcast cell" set for the Wheeler and Woolsey comedy was built here.

What Price Hollywood? (RKO, 1932)—Mary's (Constance Bennett) garden.

King Kong (RKO, 1933)—Willis O'Brien's unit used Stage 3 at RKO to shoot many of the animated scenes (called "technical scenes" by the production). Most of the shots with the big Kong head and hands, used when full-size people had to interact with Kong, were shot on this stage as well, although the grisly scenes—long censored, with Kong stepping on natives—were shot on Stage 32. Some of the rear-projection material, including miniature rear projections, was also composed on Stage 3. These compositions, which were used to place full-size people into miniature sets, were more sophisticated than anything ever attempted up to that time, and in fact, for years afterward.

Many of *Kong*'s live-action scenes were shot at Pathé. The native village, salvaged from *Bird of Paradise* (RKO, 1932), was on the backlot there, as were settings for some of the New York sequences and the great wall, a redressed set from DeMille's *The King of Kings* (Pathé, 1927).

Off-lot locations also included Nichols Canyon on January 10, 1933, Bronson Canyon, and the San Pedro beach on August 19, 1932. Scenes of Kong's memorable Broadway debut were filmed at LA's Shrine Auditorium, also in August. New York City, photographed by co-director Ernest B. Schoedsack and cinematographer Edward Linden, played itself, thanks to a second-unit trip.

The Son of Kong (RKO, 1933)—Studio memos somewhat cryptically refer to the sequences shot on this stage for the *Kong* sequel as involving "big hand," "earthquake," "storm at sea," and the "ship's rail and wheelhouse."

Emergency Call (RKO, 1933)—ambulance process shots.

Flying Devils (RKO, 1933)—process shots from an airplane.

Rafter Romance (RKO, 1933)—process shots, as seen from inside a taxicab.

Of Human Bondage (RKO, 1934)—taxi process shots.

Strictly Dynamite (RKO, 1934)—auto process shots.

Where Sinners Meet (RKO, 1934)—more auto process shots.

Top Hat (RKO, 1935)—process shots involving the hotel.

Jalna (RKO, 1935)—"cliff" and "clearing" sets.

The Arizonan (RKO, 1935)—cemetery process shots.

Break of Hearts (RKO, 1935)—process and montage shots involving a train and an Italian villa.

Hooray for Love (RKO, 1935)—process shots of Gene Raymond's estate.

High Flyers (RKO, 1937)—"exteriors near estate" scenes for Wheeler and Woolsey comedy.

Having Wonderful Time (RKO, 1938)—Emil's (Jack Carson) store and Teddy's (Ginger Rogers) place.

Bringing Up Baby (RKO, 1938)—Susan's (Katharine Hepburn) apartment.

The Hunchback of Notre Dame (RKO, 1939)—On April 21, 1939, Creighton Chaney, also known as Lon Chaney Jr., tested on this stage for the role of Quasimodo, the same part his father had played in an earlier (1923) version of the same story. Charles Laughton eventually played the role. RKO paid $389.50 to film young Chaney's unsuccessful screen test, which unfortunately has not survived. Chaney was not the only future name who didn't make it onto the *Hunchback* cast list. Jose Ferrer, Martha Scott, and Uta Hagen also lost out on roles.

The Fargo Kid (RKO, 1940)—stagecoach set process shots.

You'll Find Out (RKO, 1940)—the main entrance to Bellcrest Manor.

Call Out the Marines (RKO, 1942)—parade grounds, rifle range, and barracks.

Cat People (RKO, 1943)—the tearoom set.

Tender Comrade (RKO, 1943)—"Menzies shots," meaning sequences designed by production designer William Cameron Menzies, who was uncredited on this film.

Nevada (RKO, 1944)—Assorted taverns and saloons were shot here; star Robert Mitchum drinks at all of them.

The Falcon in Hollywood (RKO, 1944)—taxi process shots.

A Game of Death (1945)—Rainsford's room, Ellen's room, and the trophy room sets were here for this second-rate remake of *The Most Dangerous Game* (RKO, 1932), shot on the same stage. Noble Johnson plays the same brutish servant role in both films.

West of the Pecos (RKO, 1945)
—fiesta!

Pan-Americana (RKO, 1945)—process shots for Mexican taxicab sequence.

The Body Snatcher (RKO, 1945)—MacFarlane's Pub.

The Spanish Main (RKO, 1945)—prison set; also the "Inn of the Sea Turtle."

Betrayal from the East (RKO, 1945)—assorted.

The Locket (RKO, 1946)—Dr. Blair's reception room and office.

The Falcon's Adventure (RKO, 1946)—hotel room.

Riff-Raff (RKO, 1947)—Dan's (Pat O'Brien) building and office.

Dick Tracy's Dilemma (RKO, 1947)—assorted sets for a film shot under the title *Dick Tracy vs. the Claw* (which they should have kept).

Out of the Past (RKO, 1947)—Sonora Pass Café, Jeff's Mexican hotel, the Sterling Club, and some process shots involving a terrace and Jeff's car were all shot here.

Night Song (RKO, 1947)—Cathy's studio (process).

Mystery in Mexico (RKO, 1948)—assorted process shots.

If You Knew Susie (RKO, 1948)—The dressing room and Washington, DC, park scenes were shot here. Both the script and the star, Eddie Cantor, felt a little old-fashioned in 1948, and even more so today.

She Couldn't Say No (RKO, 1954)—Doc's lower-floor set.

The Lucy Show (TV, 1962–1968)—See above.

Taxi (TV, 1978–1983)—This stage served as the location of this somewhat bittersweet sitcom for the first season only, after which it would move to Stage 23.

Bosom Buddies (TV, 1980–1982)—primary location.

Cheers (TV, 1982–1993)—One of the best-remembered of all sitcoms features an iconic bar set (designed by Oscar winner Richard Sylbert), supposedly based on an actual pub in Boston, the Bull & Finch, a relationship which that bar, established in 1969, has not failed to take advantage of since then. The Bull & Finch has, in fact, been subtly redesigned to look more like the Hollywood *Cheers* set, and in 2002, it was officially renamed "Cheers Beacon Hill." Life imitates art.

After *Cheers* lifted its last glass of suds in 1993, the set moved up the road to the Hollywood Entertainment Museum on Hollywood Boulevard. After the museum closed in 2006, it was reclaimed by CBS and eventually rescued by television memorabilia collector James Comisar, who enlisted the help of series co-creator James Burrows in rescuing and restoring the by then badly damaged artifact, with the intention of establishing a permanent home in a museum, hopefully in Los Angeles. "These artifacts need to be exhibited, celebrated, and discussed here in Hollywood," Comisar has pointed out. Sadly, the museum has yet to materialize. Ted Danson, when informed about the bar's post-*Cheers* adventures, agreed that the museum should happen and that it should happen in LA. "What a great home for the bar. We're all beginning to feel like museum pieces," he said in 2014.[60]

Kelsey Grammer played Dr. Frasier Crane in *Cheers* for 204 episodes, from the 1984 season on.

Frasier (TV, 1993–2004)—Kelsey Grammer returned as Dr. Frasier Crane for an additional 263 episodes and eleven years in this beloved *Cheers* spin-off, set in Seattle. If anyone is keeping count, this is probably a record for a single actor to play the same character on the same stage in a prime-time series.

Out of Practice (TV, 2005–2006)—assorted.

Dreamgirls (2006)—unknown sequences.

My Boys (TV, 2006–2010)—assorted.

True Jackson, VP (TV, 2008–2010)—assorted.

How to Rock (TV, 2012)—assorted.

Marvin Marvin (TV, 2012–2013)—another Nickelodeon kids' show.

The Paramount Gower entrance was an old RKO walk-in gate. Seen here in 2012, it would close in 2015.

During the long RKO era, the famous walk-in entrance on Gower was how a starlet auditioning for a role, or an exhibiter in Hollywood for a convention, would have entered from the street. The visitor would have been checked in by a receptionist prior to crossing "Fifth Avenue" in order to walk across a sidewalk dissecting a lawn to the RKO administration building, where that studio's constantly changing cavalcade of executives awaited them. (At RKO the streets were named Fifth Avenue, Broadway, and Park Avenue running north-south and numbered Forty-Second to Forty-Sixth Streets going east-west, a very cosmopolitan touch.)

The building through which one entered, or tried to enter, RKO was long known as administration building A (administration building B is the current Chevalier Building). It was built in 1929. A small screening room was added to the third floor in 1946. Studio chairman Sherry Lansing once had her office on the other side of the window looking into the park, on the building's eastern side.

Today, because of its proximity to this park, this structure is known as the Ball Building, after Lucy, of course. The Ball Building is also considered by employees, many of whom work lonely night details for the security department, to be one of the most haunted structures on the lot.

On December 30, 1993, an incident was entered into the security record concerning the Ball and Chevalier Buildings. Because the holiday season has always been a slow production period, only two security guards, a veteran officer and a trainee, were patrolling the park and the buildings surrounding it. The trainee noticed "someone" watching them from the second floor of the Ball Building. Neither man had a pass key, however, so they had to call the main security office to send someone who could get them inside. By the time they got the door open the intruder had vanished; when searched, the building was completely deserted. Many employees of the same building also tell stories of an old lady often sighted on that same second floor who vanishes into thin air when confronted!

Across Gower Avenue and this gate, a 950-car parking structure at Gower Street and Waring Avenue was constructed in 1990.

The walk-in Gower entrance was closed in 2015 and moved north between the Ball and Lasky Buildings to the north, so that people entering the lot from Gower would not disturb the tenants inside.

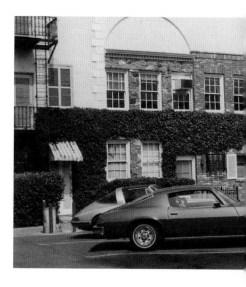

69 (LUCY) PARK

This park area surrounded by the RKO star dressing rooms, writers' offices, and administration buildings marks one of the studio's most beloved spots. Despite our tendency to romanticize them, movie studios are primarily industrial sites, with little room for aesthetics. This area, however, always boasted at least the appearance of gentility which most of the rest of that (or any) studio long lacked.

Looking east into the complex there was a green lawn with rosebushes, shade-producing trees, and sidewalks leading into the old RKO administration complex. Stages 25 and 26 are on either side, covered with genteel looking offices and dressing rooms, so the building on the other side of that lawn, strikes a visitor as somewhat academic—not collegiate, exactly, but certainly public school-worthy. The structure was long covered with shady arched entranceways which made the area seem even more like an inspired place to ponder the meaning of

ABOVE: Lucy Park and the old RKO administration building in 1976.
RIGHT: The park as Jefferson High School in the TV series *Happy Days*. Henry Winkler, pictured, actually was afraid of motorcycles.

art, and, more likely, the art of the deal. Actually, the building is no more substantial than any of the sets and many of the screenplays that came out of RKO, and these entranceway columns were made, set-like, out of lumber with stucco troweled on top.

The administration building with those columns portrayed both Fillmore Junior High School in *The Brady Bunch* (TV, 1969–1974) and Jefferson High School in *Happy Days* (TV, 1974–1984). In *The Falcon's Adventure* (RKO, 1946), the same location served as the front of the Palms Hotel. In *Clash by Night* (RKO, 1952) a young Marilyn Monroe was eyeballed by a line of bug-eyed husbands as she crossed the park. In the 1968 *Mannix* episode, "The Silent Cry," it was the home of one of Mannix's clients. In *The Last Tycoon* (1975), John Carradine, giving that studio tour of the lot, walks through the park, pointing out the "administration building" to his star-struck guests. Recently, the scene in the monster-on-the-loose movie *Cloverfield* (2008), where the beast is rampaging across Central Park, was filmed in this neighborhood as well.

This administration building, now named after Maurice Chevalier, was built in 1921 by FBO as administration building B, and originally opened onto Gower Avenue itself. It hasn't changed much in the decades since, although the

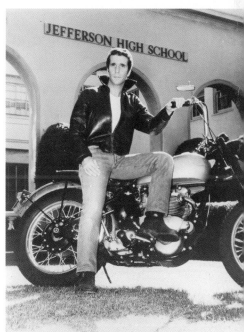

interior was renovated in 1987 for producer Frank Mancuso Jr. Those graceful arches in front of the building have been removed as well. This occurred when it was discovered that the wood underneath the stucco exterior was infested with termites.

Nominally, at least, this was where Howard Hughes reigned when he bought the studio in 1948. Hughes apparently went onto the lot only on occasion during the five years he was the sole owner, preferring to run the studio from rented offices on the Samuel Goldwyn lot up the road. A possibly apocryphal story reveals that he only visited RKO once, and his sole order regarding the place was to "paint it."

Hughes actually fidgeted and interfered with RKO's production pipeline to the extent that profits dipped by 90 percent in the first year of his eccentric reign. He ultimately sold the company in 1955 to the General Tire and Rubber Company for $25 million. Lucille Ball proceeded to buy the lot in 1957, as well as RKO's Culver City plant, for just over $6 million.

Lucy's dressing room/office, built with Stage 25 in 1921, was on the northern side of the park behind an odd-shaped facade with irregularly shaped doors and windows and elaborately varied brick and stone. A studio story, perpetuated on the current Paramount tour, holds that part of it was decorated to look like Lucy's home at 1000 North Roxbury Drive, in Beverly Hills, so that footage of the happy couple frolicking at home with their children could be faked on-lot for the media. Unfortunately, the Lucy home they are referring to, which the Arnaz family moved into midway through the run of *I Love Lucy* (1951–1957), was white stucco, not brick or stone.

At the edge of the park is a square of cement containing the handprints of *Cheers* (TV, 1982–1993) stars Ted Danson and Woody Harrelson, with Harrelson helpfully printing in the square that he was "naked" at the time. An on-lot urban legend maintains that the two of them lost a bet and had to streak around the lot as a consequence, stopping only long enough to leave their names in some conveniently wet cement along the way.

During the filming of an episode of *My Favorite Martian* (TV, 1963–1966), Ray Walston, shooting a scene in the park with costar Bill Bixby, was bitten in the face by a monkey who was appearing with them in the episode. Fast action on the part of Walston's stand-in, Billy Blackburn, got Walston to the first-aid department and then to a plastic surgeon in time to avoid permanent facial damage.

Since 1986, the Paramount Child Care Center has been in front of the Chevalier Building as well.

70 STAGE 24 (1927)

WIDTH: 169 feet, 6 inches

LENGTH: 74 feet, 6 inches

HEIGHT: 28 feet

SQUARE FEET: 12,628

RKO's old Stage 2, built by Robertson-Cole, was occasionally, depending on production needs, divided into Stages 2A and 2B, with 2B, to the west, being the larger of the two. With the knocking down of the wall between RKO and Paramount, 2B became Stage 24 and the former 2A was renamed 24A. RKO often used 2A as a recording studio; in fact, Glen Glenn Sound occupied this space in the early 1970s before the wall between the stages was finally taken down permanently in the 1990s. During the television era, elevated sound/control booths and bleachers were added for three-camera TV shoots. The stage also has an 18-foot-by-18-foot pit in the floor, although the studio no longer rents out the pit to outside clients.

Stage 2 was built by FBO and converted to sound by RKO in 1929; the stage was divided for the first time during this conversion. The interior was modified again in the television era to include an elevated sound/control booth and bleachers. In the 1990s the stage was occasionally used as a support stage for other productions, and even as warehouse space to store equipment and sets.

Like Stage 25, which it faces from the other side of Lucy Park, Stage 24 has offices on one wall. In this case those offices originally contained the RKO story department. This building with these offices is now known as the Marx Bros. Building (or as the "Mark Brothers" Building, as an unidentified but knowledgeable film historian who copy-edits the Paramount website insists on calling it).

Shot on Stage 24:

Ghost Valley (RKO, 1932)—Interior scenes for a tunnel were constructed here. The exteriors utilized Bronson Cave in LA's Griffith Park, which has played virtually every cave needed in every movie and TV series since then.

Is My Face Red? (RKO, 1932)—The office of gossip columnist Ricardo Cortez was on Stage 2B.

Symphony of Six Million (RKO, 1932)—Blind students' classroom sets were built on Stages 2A and 2B (as well as on 1B).

Hold 'Em Jail (RKO, 1932)—office sets on 2B.

King Kong (RKO, 1933)—Many live-action sequences were shot here, including mayhem involving Kong's full-size foot, the entrance to the Empire State Building, the cabin and the deck of the *SS Venture*, the police station, and the "lunchroom in hotel"—which presumably refers to where Fay Wray is talked into joining the fateful expedition.

Good Housewrecking (RKO, 1933)—short subject; living room hallway and study sets.

The Son of Kong (RKO, 1933)—miniatures shot on 2A.

Of Human Bondage (RKO, 1934)—front lawn; also "Bohemian Restaurant."

A Night at the Biltmore Bowl (RKO, 1935)—For this short subject with Betty Grable, only sound recording seems to have been done on this stage.

Top Hat (RKO, 1935)—The bandstand set was on Stages 2A and 2B.

Village Tale (RKO, 1935)—Old Ike's (Edward Ellis) place.

Quick Money (RKO, 1937)—Dining room and kitchen scenes were shot on Stage 2B.

Bringing Up Baby (RKO, 1938)—Vance Stables were shot on stage 2B.

Gunga Din (RKO, 1939)—The telegraph office scenes, as well as the sergeant's and the colonel's office sets, were built on Stage 2B. Exteriors for this very expensive George Stevens picture were shot at Lake Sherwood, Lone Pine, and at the RKO Ranch.

Chicken Feed (RKO, 1939)—Billy Gilbert short subject; "plumbing shop and office" on 2B.

You'll Find Out (RKO, 1940)—The scenes with Kay Kyser's band were shot and recorded on 2A. Stage 1B next door was the broadcast studio.

Citizen Kane (RKO, 1941)—The scene in Susan Kane's bedroom where Kane throws a tantrum and, nearly, a precious snow globe, was born on Stage 2B, as were the scenes in the *Chicago Inquirer* city room, the sequence inside a tent in the Everglades, and some other bits and pieces. Over on 2A, on December 2, 1940, Bernard Herrmann recorded *Kane*'s legendary score with thirty-five studio musicians. Two additional scoring days, the last on January 8, followed.

The Magnificent Ambersons (RKO, 1942)—Morgan office set.

Rookies in Burma (RKO, 1943)—Burmese tavern.

Fight for Freedom (RKO, 1943)—Johnnie's Place (bar).

The Falcon and the Co-eds (RKO 1943)—The undertaker's parlor and workroom were on 2B; 1B next door contained the cottage interiors.

Show Business (RKO, 1944)—assorted bars.

Curse of the Cat People (RKO, 1944)—schoolroom on 2A.

Nevada (RKO, 1944)—assorted interiors on 1B; Comstock game room on 2B.

A Game of Death (RKO, 1945)—"lodge" set was on Stage 2B.

West of the Pecos (RKO, 1945)—Brazos's Bar on Stage 2B; "hotel room" on 1B.

The Spanish Main (RKO, 1945)—the "Don's Palace" set.

The Falcon's Adventure (RKO, 1946)—assorted sets.

The Farmer's Daughter (RKO, 1947)—Loretta Young nabbed an Oscar for this one. Hotel sets were on 2B.

Dick Tracy Meets Gruesome (RKO, 1947)—police hospital and autopsy room.

Design for Death (RKO, 1947)—Oscar-winning documentary (written by Dr. Seuss!), mounted here and on Stage 28. No director is credited, although Richard Fleischer's name is listed in that capacity in the studio archives.

Riff-Raff (RKO, 1947)—airplane scenes (process).

Out of the Past (RKO, 1947)—Mexican hotel lobby and street.

Television Turmoil (RKO, 1947)—short subject; "cut-rate appliance store" on 2B.

Follow That Music (RKO, 1947)—band leader Gene Krupa's short subject; 2A and 2B.

Mr. Blandings Builds His Dream House (RKO, 1948)—corner of an office on 2B.

The Miracle of the Bells (RKO, 1948)—Dr. Jennings's office (process); also hospital room.

Punchy Pancho (RKO, 1951)—Leon Errol short subject; hotel lobby and jewelry store on Stage 2B.

Family Ties (TV, 1982–1989)—The beloved sitcom shot here, except for the pilot, which shot off-lot, and the first season, which filmed on Stage 28. Michael Gross, one of the stars, once reflected that working on the lot made him feel like he was part of Hollywood history. "I'd roam the property past darkened soundstages or through the streets of the old backlot, imagining 'The Marx Brothers worked here,' 'Bing Crosby may have stood on this spot,' or 'Mae West could have taken on the entire USC football team in this very dressing room.' "[61]

A view looking south past Stages 22 and 24, 1991.

American Dreamer (Warner Bros., 1984)—unknown.

Home for Christmas (1991)—assorted.

Bran Flakes commercial (shot June 24, 1991)—the entire commercial.

Mommies (TV, 1993–1995)—assorted.

Sister, Sister (TV, 1994–1999)—assorted.

Girlfriends (TV, 2000–2008)—assorted.

Barbershop (TV, 2005)—assorted.

Dirty Sexy Money (TV, 2007–2009)—assorted New York settings.

My Boys (TV, 2008–2010)—assorted.

Men of a Certain Age (TV, 2009–2010)—assorted.

Supah Ninjas (TV, 2010–2011)—assorted.

The Girl with the Dragon Tattoo (Columbia/MGM, 2011)—assorted.

71 STAGES 22 AND 23 (1928)

WIDTH: 169 feet, 6 inches

LENGTH: 74 feet, 8 inches

HEIGHT: 28 feet

SQUARE FEET: 12,657

The old RKO Stage 1 was constructed as one stage. Like Stage 24, it was apparently first divided, temporarily, in 1929 when it was converted for sound usage. It was still two stages (1A and 1B) when Paramount acquired the property, and until 1995, when the wall between them was (permanently?) taken down. Like on Stage 24, the largest section was the western (Stage 23) side, which during the RKO era was known as 1B; the smaller, eastern side (Stage 22) was Stage 1A. In the 1970s the stage was partially converted for live-audience television filming, although recently—except for three internal dressing rooms, which have always been welcome in that medium—the stage has not specifically been marketed as a television stage.

Today, there is no Stage 22 at Paramount. The entire building is known as Stage 23.

Shot on Stages 22 and 23:

Ghost Valley (RKO, 1932)—hotel scenes.

Symphony of Six Million (RKO, 1932)—The classroom for the blind was built on Stage 1B.

Is My Face Red? (RKO, 1932)—Mildred's cabin stood over on 1B.

Young Bride (RKO, 1932)—house and hall.

The Most Dangerous Game (RKO, 1932)—The chart-room sets and yacht scenes at the beginning of the film were on Stage 1B.

Bird of Paradise (RKO, 1932)—On RKO Stage 1B a tank was utilized for underwater scenes, yet today, Stage 23 is one of the comparatively few on the lot that does not have such a tank. Has it been filled in? Or is it still there, under the floor, forgotten and awaiting rediscovery?

What Price Hollywood? (RKO, 1932)—exteriors of Grauman's Chinese Theatre were on 1B.

Hold 'Em Jail (RKO, 1932)—warden's office on 1B.

The Son of Kong (RKO, 1933)—miniatures shot on 1A.

Strictly Fresh Yeggs (RKO, 1934)—short subject; wrecked car and house exteriors.

Of Human Bondage (RKO, 1934)—"Mildred's last home" was here. Mildred, of course, was played by Bette Davis, in a role that made her a star.

Strictly Dynamite (RKO, 1934)—Stage 1A housed Georgie's inner office; Georgie was played by William Gargan, but Jimmy Durante was the whole show.

A Quiet Fourth (RKO, 1935)—A young Betty Grable was the star of this short subject; Stage 1A played the "Johnson Home."

Jalna (RKO, 1935)—shot on RKO Stage 1A.

The Arizonan (RKO, 1935)—The "Paradise Saloon" was built on Stage 1B for this Richard Dix vehicle.

Break of Hearts (RKO, 1935)—The backstage and dressing room sets were on Stage 1A.

Sock Me to Sleep (RKO, 1935)—short subject; Edgar Kennedy's home.

The Informer (RKO, 1935)—McPhillip's kitchen was on Stage 1A; "Bogey's hole" was on 1B.

Danger Patrol (RKO, 1937)—Rocky's office, Gabby Donovan's home, and Easy's living room sets were on Stage 1B. Rocky is played by Frank M. Thomas, Donovan by Edward Gargan, but despite what the production paperwork asserts, there is no character named "Easy" in the existing film, which was shot under the title *Highway to Hell*.

Twenty Girls and a Band (RKO, 1938)—short subject; dormitory interiors on Stage 1A.

Stage Fright (RKO, 1938)—Leon Errol short subject; theater interiors on Stage 1A.

Russian Dressing (RKO, 1938)—short subject; "boy's room" and "hotel room" on 1A.

The Mad Miss Manton (RKO, 1938)—The Lane living room and Henry Fonda's office sets were on Stage 1B.

The Fighting Gringo (RKO, 1939)—The living room and barbershop were on 1A; the border cantina was built on 1B.

You'll Find Out (RKO, 1940)—Kay Kyser's room was on 1B.

Come on Danger (RKO, 1942)—The Ramsey office, sheriff's office, and closet for this Tim Holt Western were on Stage 1A. The jail corridor and the Manzanita bar were on 1B.

The Magnificent Ambersons (RKO, 1942)—boardinghouse sequences.

Rookies in Burma (RKO, 1943)—"shell hole" and Captain Tomura's office.

Show Business (RKO, 1944)—San Francisco hotel room.

The Falcon in San Francisco (RKO, 1945)—"club car, night" on Stage 1B; second-unit scenes *were* shot in San Francisco.

First Yank Into Tokyo (RKO, 1945)—Tanahe's office on stage 1B.

The Bells of St. Mary's (RKO, 1945)—"Mr. Breen's apartment" was on Stage 1A.

Pan-Americana (RKO, 1945)—the editor's private office on 1A.

The Body Snatcher (RKO, 1945)—"Hobbs's Pub" on 1B.

Man Alive (RKO, 1945)—"Waterfront Drive" and "Connie's dressing room."

It's a Wonderful Life (RKO, 1946)—Makeup, hair, and wardrobe tests were performed on Stage 1A for this film's leading ladies, Donna Reed and Gloria Grahame. Stage 1B was the home of Uncle Billy's place.

Born to Kill (RKO, 1946)—"Kraft hall and living room" on 1B.

Wall Street Blues (RKO, 1946)—short subject with Edgar Kennedy, on 1A.

Dick Tracy Meets Gruesome (RKO, 1947)—science hall office and lab, 1B.

The Farmer's Daughter (RKO, 1947)—rooming house, hall, and other sets.

Mind over Mouse (RKO, 1947)—short subject, again with Edgar Kennedy, on 1A.

Television Turmoil (RKO, 1947)—short subject, yet again with Edgar Kennedy, on 1A.

Host to a Ghost (RKO, 1947)—1A. Another short subject with Edgar Kennedy.

No More Relatives (RKO, 1948)—1A. Another short subject with, yes, Edgar Kennedy. Why has no one ever nicknamed this the "Edgar Kennedy Stage?"

The Arizona Ranger (RKO, 1948)—Tim Holt Western; "rawhide ranch interiors" on 1B.

Mighty Joe Young (RKO, 1949)—This Oscar-winning sort-of follow-up to *King Kong* was mostly shot on the Pathé lot. Only the animated sequences of Joe, a good-natured gorilla, were shot on this lot, between June 22 and December 20, 1948. Willis O'Brien, who had earlier masterminded *Kong*, here largely had to rely on his assistants, Ray Harryhausen and Pete Peterson, to perform most of the actual animation, while O'Brien worked out the technical details.

She Couldn't Say No (RKO, 1954)—radio station set.

Star Trek (TV, 1966–1969)—occasional.

The Mod Squad (TV, 1968–1973)—assorted.

Blansky's Beauties (TV, 1977) —assorted.

Taxi (TV, 1978–1983)—This series was shot on Stage 23, except for the first season, which shot on Stage 25.

The Cavanaughs (TV, 1986–1989) —assorted.

Day by Day (TV, 1988–1989) —assorted.

Sister, Sister (TV, 1994–1999) —assorted.

Goode Behavior (TV, 1996–1997)— This Sherman Hemsley vehicle was the last original show produced by MTM (Mary Tyler Moore Productions), which would soon be bought, and absorbed, by Fox.

Girlfriends (TV, 2000–2008) —assorted.

Dirty Sexy Money (TV, 2007–2009)— assorted New York settings.

My Boys (TV, 2008–2010)—assorted.

Men of a Certain Age (TV, 2009– 2010)—Paramount has plaques on all of their soundstages with the titles of notable shows shot inside. Someone, allegedly Ray Romano, didn't like the idea that Paramount did not consider his new show "notable," so he used a label maker to add his project to these plaques. Today *Men of a Certain Age* does indeed have a plaque on all of the stages on which it shot on the lot. Maybe the label maker helped?

Supah Ninjas (TV, 2010–2011) —assorted.

The Girl with the Dragon Tattoo (Columbia/MGM, 2011)—assorted.

72 STAGE 21 (1935)

WIDTH:	97 feet, 2 inches
LENGTH:	91 feet, 8 inches
HEIGHT:	35 feet
SQUARE FEET:	8,907

Until 1935 this area on the southwest corner of three RKO lots was a parking lot with a few sets and temporary buildings. But in 1935, even though RKO was suffering from a lingering bank-controlled receivership, the studio went ahead with its long-planned construction of three new stages, 11, 12, and this one, 14, on the corner, which would also include an enormous, real-life version of their logo: a beeping water tower astride the globe. When lit, this titanic edifice could be seen from miles away. A little girl who one day in the future would be known to the world as Marilyn Monroe used to look at this globe at night from her bunk at the nearby Hollygrove Orphanage and dream of stardom.

Another little girl who would never grow up, Heather O'Rourke, supposedly haunts this stage, and Stage 19. Heather played "Carol Anne" in the Poltergeist series before dying at the age of twelve in 1988. Some maintain that a "little

bit" of these films were shot on Stage 21, which would explain the apparition, although no one actually seems to know whether or not she ever worked on this stage. O'Rourke did act in a few *Happy Days* episodes on Stage 19, however.

Stage 21 as seen from Melrose and Gower in 1937, and in 1991.

When Desilu and Paramount acquired RKO, they painted over this globe and took the radio tower down. They probably would have removed the globe as well, but engineers sent to poke about in the rafters above the stage informed executives that the entire roof would have to be pulled apart in order to remove the previous studio's trademark. So the globe stayed. Eventually it was even painted to reflect its appearance during the RKO era.

In 2012 the studio announced its "Paramount Pictures Hollywood Project," which was a comprehensive twenty-five-year plan to renovate old buildings and create new ones on the lot. Among the buildings scheduled for demolition was Stage 21. Fortunately, the plan was put on hold in 2016 due to a power struggle between the studio and Viacom. In fact, Paramount Pictures recently spent Viacom money to restore the globe and the stage under it, which they had recently announced they intended to demolish.

For many years Stage 21 was leased to KCAL-TV (originally KHJ) as part of a long-standing RKO contract. KCAL redesigned the interior extensively in 1989 to create a high-tech newsroom. They moved off-lot to Studio City in 2002. Their adjacent offices, next door to Stage 21, are now the home of Paramount's security, environmental, health and safety, and tour departments.

Shot on Stage 21:

Twenty Girls and a Band (RKO, 1938)—short subject; café scenes.

Gunga Din (RKO, 1939)—Assorted scenes were shot here, including the porch, the house where Cary Grant romances Joan Fontaine, and the dungeon snake-pit sequences.

Call Out the Marines (RKO, 1942)—the "Shore Leave Café."

Cat People (RKO, 1943)—the Serbian restaurant and the pet shop.

Hitler's Children (RKO, 1943)—commandant's office.

This Land Is Mine (RKO, 1943)—freight office, warehouse, Lambert's office.

Passport to Destiny (RKO, 1944)—Reich Chancellery corridor; Hitler's office.

The Falcon in San Francisco (RKO, 1945)—Carl's room and Loomis's bedroom; Loomis, uncredited, is played by Jason Robards Sr.

It's a Wonderful Life (RKO, 1946)—Mr. Potter's library was built here, for $3,000 (the estimate RKO had given production was $1,500, later adjusted to $2,100). Also, Martini's roadhouse, which in the fantasy scenes becomes Nick's Place, and part of Bailey Park was built on this stage.

Dick Tracy Meets Gruesome (RKO, 1947)—"Inspiration Point."

Heading for Trouble (RKO, 1947)—Edgar Kennedy short subject, shot almost entirely on this stage.

Return of the Bad Men (RKO, 1948)—Vance's (Randolph Scott) office.

The Thing from Another World (RKO, 1951)—The electrocution of the Thing was shot here.

She Couldn't Say No (RKO, 1954)—boardinghouse.

The Lucy Show (TV, 1962–1968)—1968 season only.

The Greatest American Hero (TV, 1981–1983)—unidentified 1982 episode.

Lemony Snicket's A Series of Unfortunate Events (2004)—assorted.

Entourage (TV, 2004–2011)—assorted.

Community (TV, 2009–2015)—The exterior of the Greendale Community College Library was constructed around the exterior of the stage.

The Girl with the Dragon Tattoo (Columbia/MGM, 2011)—assorted.

73 STAGE 20 (1935)

WIDTH: 153 feet, 4 inches
LENGTH: 98 feet, 9 inches
HEIGHT: 35 feet
SQUARE FEET: 15,141

RKO Stage 12 was built along with its sisters, Stages 14 and 11, in 1935. Because of these stages' proximity to the street, it was easy to bring in audiences for filmed sitcoms, so popular series like *Laverne & Shirley* (1976–1983) and *Webster* (1983–1987) could conceivably keep the same artists employed in the same stage for decades. To this end, an elevated sound/control booth and bleachers (210 seats) have been permanently added to the stage.

Shot on Stage 20:

What Price Hollywood? (RKO, 1932)—the movie stairway set.

The Most Dangerous Game (RKO, 1932)—The exterior of the cliff, as well as the "chateau" and process shots, were done here, and on Stage 25.

Danger Patrol (RKO, 1937)—Montages and scenes involving a truck transporting nitroglycerine were shot here.

Stage Fright (RKO, 1938)—Leon Errol short subject; "Errol home interiors."

The Mad Miss Manton (RKO, 1938)—apartment and Chez Louis nightclub sets.

Having Wonderful Time (RKO, 1938)—Teddy's bunk.

Russian Dressing (RKO, 1938)—"Pierre's Club," "living room," and "bandstand" scenes were shot here for this short subject. The bandstand was also re-created outside on the studio lawn.

Swing Vacation (RKO, 1939)—short subject; "Club Lido Café" scenes.

Call Out the Marines (RKO, 1942)—Blake's (Paul Kelly) office; the washroom.

The Magnificent Ambersons (RKO, 1942)—Process shots for the Morgan auto factory were done here.

The Falcon and the Co-eds (RKO, 1943)—assorted.

Ladies' Day (RKO, 1943)—The "Wacky Waters" hotel room and St. Louis airport scenes were here; Wacky is played by Eddie Albert, opposite Lupe Velez.

Show Business (RKO, 1944)—as "an RKO stage," in 1932, before the stage was built.

Curse of the Cat People (RKO, 1944)—The creepy "Farren" home interiors were shot here. The exterior was a real (and really creepy) Victorian mansion, located at 900 West Adams in downtown LA.

Beat the Band (RKO, 1947)—bandstand.

Night Song (RKO, 1947)—Carnegie Hall.

Return of the Bad Men (RKO, 1948)—camp set.

I Remember Mama (RKO, 1948)—camp.

The Window (RKO, 1949)—roof.

She Couldn't Say No (RKO, 1954)—desert and roadhouse scenes.

My Three Sons (TV, 1960–1972)—filmed here only until 1967 season.

That Girl (TV, 1966–1971)—assorted.

The undisputed king of 1970's television. Garry Marshall, surrounded by some of his subjects, Ron Howard, Penny Marshall, Robin Williams, Cindy Williams, Pam Dawber and Henry Winkler, at the side entrance of Paramount's Hart Building, 1978.

Laverne & Shirley (TV, 1976–1983)—Creator Garry Marshall created this very popular *Happy Days* spin-off, which starred Cindy Williams and Penny Marshall, Garry Marshall's sister. Unlike its parent, however, which had a congenial family atmosphere, the *Laverne & Shirley* set was stressful and very noisy. "I overheard someone say that the cast of *Happy Days* puts cups up to the wall so they can hear Penny and Cindy screaming at the writers," Marshall once admitted.[62]

Webster (TV, 1983–1987)—primary set for the popular sitcom.

Flesh+Blood (Orion, 1985)—The studio makes otherwise unsubstantiated claims that part of director Paul Verhoeven's first English-language film was shot here. Perhaps they are thinking of a 1979 TV movie, *Flesh & Blood*, which did shoot here?

Dear John (TV, 1988–1992)—shot on this stage and Stages 32 and 27 at different times.

Dead Again (1991)—Kenneth Branagh evokes the ghosts of earlier Hollywood thrillers in the same spot where many of them were shot.

Addams Family Values (1993)—The first floor of the creepy house and the conservatory were built here.

Star Trek: Voyager (TV, 1995–2001)—unidentified sequences.

Primal Fear (1996)—Edward Norton got an Oscar nomination for his film debut, made here.

Claude's Crib (TV, 1997)—assorted.

Yes, Dear (TV, 2000–2006)—The pilot was shot at CBS in Studio City; the last season was shot here.

We Were Soldiers (2002)—Mel Gibson's Vietnam war film shot here and in Georgia.

Dirty Sexy Money (TV, 2007–2009)—assorted New York settings.

Forgetting Sarah Marshall (2008)—assorted.

The Girl with the Dragon Tattoo (Columbia/MGM, 2011)—assorted.

The New Normal (TV, 2012–2013)—assorted.

Instant Mom (TV, 2013–2015)—another Nickelodeon sitcom.

74 STAGE 19 (1935)

WIDTH:	153 feet
LENGTH:	97 feet, 7 inches
HEIGHT:	35 feet
SQUARE FEET:	14,930

RKO's Stage 11 was for many years a feature-film stage, although single-camera situation comedies were occasionally filmed inside its walls during the 1960s The current configuration of the stage, which includes an elevated sound/control booth and bleachers for 193 audience members, was added to the stage in 1971, for *The Odd Couple.*

This stage is believed to be haunted by Lucille Ball's one-time wardrobe lady. Who this spectral costumer was—and how the victims she haunts know that this is what she was in life—has not been determined.

Shot on Stage 19:

High Flyers (RKO, 1937)—"Arlington house" sets for this Wheeler and Woolsey comedy.

Twenty Girls and a Band (RKO, 1938)—short subject; principal's office, lower hall, and party room scenes.

The Mad Miss Manton (RKO, 1938)—the Manton building lobby and elevator.

Three Sons (RKO, 1939)—minister's home and flophouse; also process shots as seen from the window of the taxi.

Abe Lincoln in Illinois (RKO, 1940)—Rutledge bedroom, post office, engine room, senate corridor, Lincoln's office, first class hotel, etc.

Citizen Kane (RKO, 1941)—The city room of the *Chicago Inquirer*, Kane's newspaper, was constructed here.

Come on Danger (RKO, 1942)—Ramsey ranch.

Hitler's Children (RKO, 1943)—German courtroom.

The Falcon and the Co-eds (RKO, 1943)—the Falcon's (Tom Coway) apartment.

The Spook Speaks (RKO, 1947)—Leon Errol short subject; his house, in the movie, was here.

Out of the Past (RKO, 1947)—the gaming room.

Bet Your Life (RKO, 1948)—Leon Errol short subject; again, his house, in the movie, was here.

The Window (RKO, 1949)—condemned building.

When Worlds Collide (1951)—Hendron's (Barbara Rush) office.

She Couldn't Say No (RKO, 1954)—trout pool and farmhouse.

My Three Sons (TV, 1960–1972)—shot here only until the 1967 season.

Donovan's Reef (1963)—The Boston-set scenes filmed here.

Star Trek (TV, 1966–1969)—This stage was used occasionally for this series; for example, the mission set for the classic "City on the Edge of Forever" episode was built here.

That Girl (TV, 1966–1971)—assorted New York interiors.

The Odd Couple (TV, 1970–1975)— This show, one of the most popular Paramount sitcoms in syndication, was canceled at the end of every one of its five seasons. The show would then be renewed for the fall, when the network would unfailingly see the ratings spike up during the summer rerun season, at which point stars Jack Klugman and Tony Randall would renegotiate their contracts. ABC, certain the show would never make it into syndication, even gave the duo a piece of the syndication rights. "It turned out to be a very good thing for us. That 'piece' sent both of my kids to college," Klugman has recalled.[63]

The show shot on Stage 19 for its entire run, although it seems the pilot used Stages 4 and 1 as well. That pilot and the entire first season was shot with a single camera using sets salvaged from the feature-film version. For season two, the set was opened up so that a studio audience could watch the action being recorded with three cameras.

Old Blue Eyes Is Back (TV, 1973)— Frank Sinatra returned from his 1971 "retirement" with this TV special, also known as *Magnavox Presents Frank Sinatra*, which was seen by an estimated audience of forty million people. Gene Kelly guest-starred.

Happy Days (TV, 1974–1984)—As on *The Odd Couple*, *Happy Days* was originally shot like a feature film, using a single camera. But in its third season, *Happy Days* switched to a studio-audience format, as well, making it in this instance less cinematic, but oddly, much more successful, ratings-wise. The exterior of Arnold's Drive-In, which in the pilot was called Arthur's, was constructed in these early seasons on the lot and was a frequent location. When the show moved indoors, stock footage of this set, which had been demolished, was reused shamelessly to represent the exteriors.

A *Happy Days 30th Anniversary Reunion Special*, made in 2004, re-created the interior of Arnold's. Unfortunately that later program was shot on a stage at CBS.

Producer Garry Marshall was responsible for both *Happy Days* and *The Odd Couple*—fourteen years of continuous employment on Stage 19.

Mr. President (TV, 1987–1988)— George C. Scott, a most unlikely sitcom star, played the title role.

Ghost (1990)—assorted.

Wings (TV, 1990–1997)—Another popular sitcom, the stage here played Nantucket Memorial Airport.

Some inside jokes are perhaps *too* inside. In *Wings*, actor William Hickey occasionally played a character called "Carlton Blanchard." In the 1927 Paramount film *Wings*, a different actor, also named William Hickey, played a different character, also named "Carlton Blanchard." It could also be a coincidence.

Rules of Engagement (2000)—assorted.

Kath & Kim (TV, 2008–2009)—assorted.

Fresh Beat Band (TV, 2009–2013)—assorted.

See Dad Run (TV, 2012–2014)—Scott Baio, from *Happy Days* and *Joanie Loves Chachi*, returned to Paramount for the Nickelodeon series, this time playing the dad.

[1] Kent Black. "Married . . . with Chutzpah," *Los Angeles Times*, August 19, 1981.

[2] "First Person: Jerry Zucker," *Variety*, July 15–21, 2002.

[3] Interview: Cecilia de Mille Presley, January, 2016.

[4] Yvonne De Carlo, with Doug Warren. *Yvonne: An Autobiography*. New York: St. Martin's Press, 1987.

[5] Interview: Larry Jensen, March, 2016.

[6] Frank Westmore. *The Westmores of Hollywood*. Philadelphia and New York: L. P. Lippincott, 1976.

[7] Charles Higham and Joel Greenberg. *The Celluloid Muse: Hollywood Directors Speak*. Chicago: Henry Regency Company, 1969.

[8] Westmore, *The Westmores of Hollywood.*

[9] Joseph Giovannini. "L.A.'s Movie Kremlins," *Los Angeles Herald Examiner,* December 12, 1979.

[10] "The Two-Hour Tour," *Inside the Gate,* Vol. 2, Issue 2, April–May, 2006.

[11] "After 50 Years, He Can Call Paramount Home," *Los Angeles Herald Examiner,* August 25, 1983.

[12] Steve Lasky. "Inside Security at Hollywood's Paramount Pictures," *Security Technology Executive Magazine,* May 8, 2009.

[13] Barry Williams and Chris Kreski. *Growing Up Brady: I Was a Teenage Greg.* New York: HarperCollins, 1992.

[14] Interview: Bill Warren, May, 2016.

[15] DVD: *The War of the Worlds—Special Collector's Edition* (1953).

[16] Interview: Leonard Maltin, May, 2016.

[17] DVD: *The War of the Worlds.*

[18] Interview: Jensen.

[19] Interview: Randal Kleiser, April, 2016.

[20] Higham and Greenberg. *The Celluloid Muse.*

[21] Interview: Richard Lindheim. March, 2016.

[22] "Behind the Scenes—A Studio Group Production," *Paramount News,* March/April, 1989.

[23] Interview: Lindheim.

[24] John Burlingame. "Paramount's Stage M Closes," *Film Music Society* (online at www.filmmusicsociety.org/news_events/features/2006/082906.html, August 29, 2006).

[25] "Paramount Landmark Number Two," *Paramount Parade,* Vol. No. 3, January, 1937.

[26] Ibid.

[27] Interview: Jensen.

[28] Jesse Lasky. *I Blow My Own Horn.* New York: Doubleday, 1957.

[29] Williams and Kreski, *Growing Up Brady.*

[30] Ibid.

[31] Ronald L. Davis. *The Glamour Factory: Inside Hollywood's Big Studio System.* Dallas, TX: Southern Methodist University Press, 1993.

[32] Interview: Presley.

[33] Scott Eyman. *Empire of Dreams: The Epic Life of Cecil B. DeMille.* New York: Simon and Schuster, 2010.

[34] Interview: Presley.

[35] Davis, *The Glamour Factory.*

[36] Edward Dmytryk. *On Film Editing.* New York: Focal Press, 1984.

[37] Interview: Presley.

[38] George Takei. *To the Stars.* New York: Pocket Books, 1994.

[39] Davis, *The Glamour Factory.*

[40] Ibid.

[41] Ibid.

[42] Interview: Lindheim.

[43] Ruth Ryon. "At 75, Paramount Still Building," *Los Angeles Times*, August 23, 1987.

[44] Grace Kingsley. "Universal to Picture World," *Los Angeles Times,* June 3, 1926.

[45] Dan Morain. "Universal May Get DeMille Barn," *Los Angeles Times*, February 21, 1982.

[46] Ron Haver. *David O. Selznick's Hollywood*. New York: Alfred A. Knopf, 1980.

[47] DVD: *The War of the Worlds*.

[48] Takei, *To the Stars*.

[49] Jim Arnold. "Backlot New York Rises Again: Behind the Facade," *Paramount News*, September/October, 1991.

[50] Josh Gajewski. "Windy City Wannabe," *Los Angeles Times*, August 7, 2006.

[51] Interview: Kleiser.

[52] William Thut. "Paramount's Sky," *Los Angeles Times*, September, 10, 1989.

[53] Interview: Jensen.

[54] "Remembrance of Things Past," *Paramount Parade*, Vol. 2, September, 1938.

[55] Interview: Billy Blackburn, January, 2016.

[56] "Bob," *Paramount News*, September/October, 1992.

[57] "Behind the Scenes—A Studio Group Production."

[58] Rudy Rolland. "A Study in Research," *Paramount Parade*, October, 1948.

[59] Interview: Debbie Fine, March. 2016.

[60] Bryn Elise Sandberg. "Cheers' Bar Finally Finds a Museum Home," *Hollywood Reporter*, August, 7, 2014.

[61] Marley Brant. *Happier Days: Paramount Television's Classic Sitcoms 1974–1984*. New York: Billboard Books, 2006.

[62] Garry Marshall. *My Happy Days in Hollywood: A Memoir*. New York: Crown Archetype, 2012.

[63] Jack Klugman. *Tony and Me: A Story of Friendship*. West Linn, OR: Good Hill Press, 2005.

RIGHT: The smiles on the stars look less forced than those worn by the executives for this 1969 study taken during some of the studio's darkest days. Top row; Rock Hudson, John Wayne, and Yves Montand. Bottom row; Lee Marvin, Robert Evans, Barbra Streisand, Paramount VP of Production Robert Donnenfield, and Clint Eastwood. OPPOSITE RIGHT: Adolph Zukor, 95 years old, on one of his rare ceremonial visits to the studio he built. His driver is veteran security guard Fritz Hawkes, 1968.

CHAPTER 4
Knocking Down the Gate

This studio is where everything happened so long ago,
and it's still here, just as it was.

—Faye Dunaway

*I*n 1967 Robert Evans and his hatchet men found a studio moribund, and stricken with indecision. The eighteen-member board of directors in New York was grumbling that the beleaguered Paramount should be sold off, either intact, or piecemeal.

In fact, Gulf+Western was about to create, in 1969, a new company—Paramount Studio Properties, Inc.—just for the purpose of selling off the lot, if not the company. Paramount Studio Properties severed Paramount film production from Paramount real estate, with the intention of selling at least half the property, reportedly to the cemetery from which it had originally been carved. Author Bernard F. Dick has astutely pointed out that this restructuring created, for the first time, a subtle distinction between "the studio lot and the movie studio. The movie studio was intact; the lot, negotiable."[1]

In 1969, Evans, seeing his new kingdom slipping away, talked director Mike Nichols into shooting a promo reel to present to the board of directors. Upon his arrival in New York, film in hand, Evans promised to resign and waive the $300,000 it would cost to buy out his contract if they would just watch that film.

261

The studio in decline. Although at least some of the executive's cars are still nice, 1973.

The board accepted his proposal. A projector was wheeled in and the lights were dimmed. This little movie, which still survives, and which Evans credits with saving the studio, opens with Evans saying, "I'm here at the studio borrowing a set from *The Young Lawyers*, and that's where we are now. As a matter of fact, I don't even have an office at the studio anymore. Last year we packed up our gear, cut down our staff, tightened our belts, moved into small offices, little offices in Beverly Hills. The money we spend is not going to be on extravagances. The money we spend is going to be on the screen. And speaking of the screen, well, that's the reason we're here today."[2]

Evans then proceeded to promote upcoming Paramount pictures, including *Love Story* (1970), and *The Godfather* (1972), both of which, as Evans pointed out, had been developed as novels at Paramount, and both of which, as he couldn't have known, would go on to become two of the biggest hits in history.

When the movie was over and the lights brought back up, the board of directors sent Evans back to his "small office," located at 202 North Cannon Drive, with the company intact—for the moment.

Evans, surprisingly, turned out to be just what the studio needed at that particular juncture in its history. Only thirty-nine in 1969, he shook the cobwebs out of the backlot and immediately started producing "relevant" entertainment which would appeal to the Woodstock generation and to their children—if not to their parents. The films he and his associates made revived the company and once again made movies, in general, an instigator in rather than a reflection of popular culture.

Love Story and *The Godfather* were encircled by other hits as well, including *Romeo and Juliet* (1968), *The Odd Couple* (1968), *Rosemary's Baby* (1968), *True Grit* (1969), *Death Wish* (1974), *The Godfather: Part II*, and *Chinatown* (1974). Note, however, that several of these blockbusters came out *before* Evans's impassioned plea to keep the studio open, which is perhaps proof as to how much that stoic board of directors really did want out of Hollywood.

On the commercial front, Paramount went from being number nine at the box office (out of only seven studios!) to number one in 1972. At the Gulf+Western takeover, Paramount made up only 5 percent of the parent company's volume. Later, Evans recalls that "they didn't even have to show it on the books of the stockholders, because when you're under 5 percent, you don't have to show it. When we left, Paramount Pictures was over 50 percent of their volume."[3]

Another threat was still very much pending, however. In mid-1970, Paramount Studio Facilities, now renamed Marathon Studio Facilities, went ahead with a deal to sell half of the studio property—not to the Cemetery, but to a shady Italian conglomerate, Società Generale Immobiliare (SGI)—in exchange for a stock swap and seat for Bluhdorn on the SGI board. SGI presumably had the intention of building houses or offices on their half of the fifty-two-acre lot.

The sale did not happen. The Securities Exchange Commission turned out to be very interested in both SGI and in Gulf+Western's practice of transferring assets, including the studio, into subsidiaries and then reporting gains on those assets separate from the parent company.

So the lot, like Paramount itself, survived the turmoil and the threats from within and without. The truth was, however, that with the demise of the studio system, a physical studio was, as Jaffe cynically implied, somewhat superfluous. From a business standpoint, it would have been cheaper to rent production facilities elsewhere than to keep them on hand and ready on the lot. Hollywood was now about the deal, and about the package. The actual dirty work of production had somehow become an afterthought, almost an anachronism. This is true even today. Yet the product had to be made somewhere, and in the 1970s, and again, to a lesser degree today, "somewhere" was usually in Los Angeles. Still, there was little benefit, other than convenience, to making that product in a studio that was actually owned by the company.

In this new, upside-down world, the overhead of maintaining a city-sized factory in Hollywood was suddenly not a way to maximize revenue, but was now, in fact, perceived as being potentially crushing to those all-important profits. For every project mounted, post-studio-system, the entire assembly line to realize that project had to be created, from scratch, and from the ground up. Everyone, from the actors to the accountants, was now hired by the job, for the job, and then sent home when that job was done—only to be rehired, in theory, to do the same thing for the very next project.

Even more dire for the studio was Hollywood's new accounting system, in which every service on that studio's lot was now charged to production. And the office from which that production was mounted was no longer a central "Production Department"—on staff and managing every Paramount picture—but rather an independent entity built from scratch to operate not in service of the studio, but in service of that one picture only.

Once there was no longer an incentive from a cost perspective to shoot a Paramount movie at Paramount, producers—who were often on the lot for a single project themselves, and felt no incentive to support the studio—could save money by shopping around and using a rival studio's facilities, or they could decide to shoot in an independent "rental" lot, like Raleigh Studios, just across the street, and whose cheaper stages were tantalizingly visible to these producers just through the black wrought-iron Bronson Gate.

During this same era, outside or independent producers making non-Paramount product, who couldn't have even gotten a formal meeting at Paramount, suddenly found those same iron gates thrown wide open to them. Just as in-house producers were now free to go elsewhere, outside productions were now courted to fill those suddenly empty soundstages, often at fire-sale prices, when no internal tenants could be booked.

These outside productions often included the sleaziest type of *Day of the Locust* bottom-feeders. Peter Bart, an executive on the lot at the time who later wrote a book about his experiences, maintains that "within weeks after the shady Italian financiers of Immobiliere SGI acquired a principal stake in the Paramount backlot on Melrose Boulevard, its mammoth soundstages were being rented out to porn producers. On the same soundstage where Roman Polanski had labored with Mia Farrow on *Rosemary's Baby*, pornmeisters were shooting hard-core scenes."[4]

Eventually, to try to bring Paramount back to Paramount, the studio's operations department took to providing 35,000 square feet of stage space free to internal clients, but, rather astonishingly, the suffocating studio overhead still managed to make it more expensive to film in-house than to rent facilities elsewhere.

In this unfriendly and inexplicable environment, what's surprising is not that Hollywood's decades-old existence was threatened, but that Paramount or any studio still exists today. As mentioned, RKO has largely been out of physical production since 1957. Twentieth Century Fox sold off hundreds of acres of backlot to develop a business community called Century City in 1963. Universal opened a successful theme park on their backlot in 1964. Columbia moved out of their old digs at Sunset and Gower to cohabitate with Warner Bros. in 1972. MGM has not been in possession of a physical studio lot since 1986.

Yet Paramount survives today, intact.

There are two reasons why Paramount was ultimately able to successfully combine the patterns of old and new Hollywood. The first is practical. As noted, the product had to be made somewhere. With soundstage space rapidly disappearing in Los Angeles, Evans, or someone, realized that like Raleigh Studios, Paramount could make a consistent, if slender, profit renting their still-peerless facilities to their own (and other studios') projects, along with independent productions, sleazy as they might have been. Television productions—their own, and those of outside studios—also provided a stable income for the company that could potentially continue for decades inside a rented soundstage occupied by a single successful series.

The other reason is more surprising because it involves, astonishingly, sentiment. The self-centered, self-indulgent, and self-important mob of twenty- and thirty-something invaders who wrestled Hollywood out of the aged hands of its creators in the 1970s were, significantly, the first generation who had grown up at the movies, and watching movies on television. These baby-boomers, instead of going out to get jobs to feed their families like their hard-scrabble, Depression-era parents had, had gone to the movies. Instead of working on family farms or going into their parents' businesses, they had gone to the movies. Instead of winning wars, or starting them, they had gone to the movies.

Although the term *movie brats* was coined to describe film school graduates like Francis Ford Coppola, Brian De Palma, George Lucas, and Steven Spielberg, it also applies to the young lawyers, hustlers, and business school graduates who had gone to the movies and then found themselves running the factories that made those movies.

For this generation that had been raised watching Paramount pictures and seeing Paramount Studios as a foil for Gloria Swanson and Jerry Lewis, it somehow seemed sacrilegious to have successfully raided the temple of their childhoods, only to topple that temple in a DeMille-like display of empty spectacle. When one worked *for* the studio, one also wanted to work *at* the studio.

The zeitgeist of the movie brats was perfectly captured by Michael Tolkin in his novel *The Player*, in which his young carpetbagger protagonist expresses gratitude about working at a studio that still "had property, with soundstages and backlots, where you could point to a building and say 'That was Alan Ladd's dressing room,' or 'Over here we made *Bringing Up Baby*' . . . he wanted to say, how can you make a movie in an office building?"[5]

So the studio and the studio lot somehow survived. The flamboyant Robert Evans, Hollywood's most prominent raider and romantic, would keep his job until 1974. Presumably by this time he had his own office on the lot again. He would also continue to occasionally produce films for the studio, until 2003's *How to Lose a Guy in 10 Days*.

Richard Sylbert, Evans's handpicked replacement, was an Academy Award–winning art director, and as odd a choice as Ernst Lubitsch had been. Given more time, Sylbert could have become a very creative executive indeed; unfortunately, Bluhdorn pulled him from the big chair after less than three years.

In the 1970s there was a brief nostalgia craze which led to a perceived interest among the public for classic Hollywood. Among the pictures which 1970s Hollywood produced to feed this supposed appetite was *Nickelodeon* (Columbia, 1975), *The Wild Party* (AIP, 1975), *Inserts* (United Artists, 1975), *Hearts of the West* (MGM, 1975), *Gable and Lombard* (Universal, 1976), *Silent Movie* (Twentieth Century Fox, 1976), *W. C. Fields and Me* (Universal, 1976), *Valentino* (UA, 1977), and *The World's Greatest Lover* (Twentieth Century Fox, 1977). Paramount's contribution to this trend was *The Day of the Locust* (1975), *Won Ton Ton: The Dog Who Saved Hollywood* (1976), *The Last Tycoon* (1976), and, to a lesser degree, *The Godfather* (1972).

Oddly, a vein of self-hatred, uncommented upon at the time by audiences or critics, is also evident in the overall tone of most of these films. Perhaps this was part of an unintended plea by the movie brats about their inherited world and about its values. Perhaps it was a cynical and self-loathing way of making money. Perhaps it was mere coincidence.

While few of these movies achieved anything approaching significance at the box office, their sheer number meant they left a lasting residue of memories with audiences who did not pick up on the cynicism in these films. Ultimately, even more so than the films they were inspired by, these movies established in the minds of those audiences what Hollywood was like in the "Golden Age."

Paramount's *The Day of the Locust*, based on Nathanael West's classic novel, is perhaps the grimmest Hollywood movie ever made. To say that none of the characters are sympathetic would be an understatement as grotesque as the world of cockfights and stag films these characters inhabit. In fact, both the film and the book seem intent on depicting Hollywood as a hell heap, which everyone either aspires to claw to the top of, or is too dim-witted to escape. The climax of *Day of the Locust* takes place at Grauman's Chinese Theatre at the premiere of DeMille's *The Buccaneer* (1938). This premiere, which in real life was reportedly uneventful, as depicted here almost literally goes to hell when a frenzied, star-obsessed lynch mob sacks and burns the city in the name of hatred and misguided star worship.

Unlike in *The Godfather*, and other films where the studio played itself under an alias, *Locust*, in contradiction of the source novel, is set at a recognizable Paramount, which is repeatedly identified by name. A scene in which a poorly built set collapses, killing hordes of hapless and grasping extras inside of a soundstage, was changed from a scene set on a backlot in the book, probably to accommodate Paramount's lack of outdoor sets at the time. But the self-loathing result is exactly the same. As a gag, William Castle—the legendary exploitation producer-director famous for his cheap sets—played the director on the camera crane in this sequence, one of the few humorous moments in the film. Of course, the audience would not have been in on the joke. The final effect of *Day of the Locust*—the film, if not the book—is to leave the viewer wondering if the venom in the screenplay (by Waldo Salt) is being directed toward the film's audience of "locusts," or toward the studio itself.

The Last Tycoon (1975), based on F. Scott Fitzgerald's unfinished novel, is, by contrast, almost a valentine to the lost studio system—gone, but still fondly remembered by its survivors in the 1970s. Robert De Niro plays a movie-obsessed studio executive, based, according to movie-obsessed scholars, on MGM's

The Day of the Locust (1974) was Paramount's attempt to mine its own history. Star William Atherton does look hopeful.

movie-obsessed Irving Thalberg. "This studio will fall without me," De Niro's character, Monroe Stahr, says at one point. Whether true or not, this statement separates him dramatically from *Locust*'s sideshow of bottom-feeders, who would never have been able to get past that studio's Bronson Gate, let alone into Monroe Stahr's carpeted office. The truth is, the studio can indeed survive without producers like Stahr, just as MGM survived Thalberg's passing in 1936.

At the end of *Tycoon*, Stahr, his brilliant career now very much in doubt, walks down an unoccupied studio street and into an empty soundstage. Are we supposed to mourn the end of an era, or the end of an executive?

In 1974 an executive named Barry Diller would become the new CEO of Paramount. Diller had a television background, and famously hired many other executives, also mostly from television, who would later head their own studios or networks. Most significantly for Paramount, these "Killer Dillers" (yes, that's what they were called) included Michael Eisner, Dawn Steel, Jeffrey Katzenberg, and Don Simpson, all of whom would hold upper management positions at Paramount and then run other studios.

Out of Diller's successful reign would materialize hits like *Looking for Mr. Goodbar* (1977), *Saturday Night Fever* (1977), *Grease* (1978), *Heaven Can Wait* (1978), *Airplane* (1980), *Raiders of the Lost Ark* (1981), *Terms of Endearment* (1983), *Footloose* (1984), and *Beverly Hills Cop* (1984). During this same period, Diller and his staff also revitalized the television division, which had come a long way since the Desilu days, and which would come to rule the medium in the 1970s and '80s, when the company was grinding out an impressive thirty hours of television a week.

In 1987 Paramount chairman Frank Mancuso, who was a real filmmaker rather than a bureaucrat, and who was sincerely interested in the studio's history, announced that he was renaming twenty-seven buildings on the lot in recognition of many "who have contributed significantly to Paramount's longevity and success . . . a lasting tribute to their achievements here."[6]

The newly christened buildings were named after Adolph Zukor, Charles Bluhdorn, Bob Hope, Barney Balaban, Clara Bow, Maurice Chevalier, Gary Cooper,

W. C. Fields, the Fleischer Brothers, the Marx Bros., William S. Hart, Jesse Lasky, Jerry Lewis, Carole Lombard, Dean Martin, Josef von Sternberg, Preston Sturges, Gloria Swanson, Hal Wallis, Mae West, Billy Wilder, Bing Crosby, Edith Head, Lucille Ball, B. P. Schulberg, and Ernst Lubitsch. Cecil B. DeMille also had his old building formally and forever designated in his name.

Bronze plaques have been placed on the buildings with their new monikers, but in spite of Mancuso's insistence that the buildings would be associated with the people they were being christened for, there seemed ultimately, to be little rhyme or reason as to whose name ended up on which building. Historian Marc Wanamaker, who had painstakingly researched and selected all the names, unfortunately was unable to stop an internal Paramount committee from dropping those names onto any building they saw fit.

LEFT: Gary Cooper was one of twenty -seven stars to have a building on the lot named in their honor in 1987. BOTTOM: *Star Trek* Producer Gene Roddenberry also had, in 1991, a building dedicated in his honor, 1993. RIGHT: Western Costume Company at Bronson and Melrose Avenue— Western Costume was Paramount's long-time neighbor—and very briefly, one of its subsidiaries, 1990.

A few other buildings have been named after Paramount alumni since this mass christening. Producer A. C. Lyles had his office, aptly enough, in the Hart Building (built in 1936), but it was the mailroom, attached to Stages 13 and 14, which was named after Lyles in 1988. In 1991, producer Gene Roddenberry also had a (newly constructed) building named in his honor, although Roddenberry's office, like Lyles's, had been in the Hart Building. Art director Hans Dreier in 1994 had an office suite named in his honor, as has actor Ray Milland, who had his name placed above the longtime security building.

Just outside the gate, other changes were afoot as well. Mike Levee, a former Brunton Studios executive, had founded the United States Prop and Costume Company in 1926, but since 1930, their offices, in front of Paramount and facing Melrose Avenue, had been the massive and labyrinthine headquarters of Western Costume. Western could trace its roots back to L. L. Burns and Harry Revier, who co-owned the barn in which DeMille had shot *The Squaw Man*. Burns in particular had been collecting Native American trinkets and costumes as a hobby, and had started renting these objects out for Westerns, from which had come the "Western Costume" moniker.

In 1988, Western Costume, which had been co-owned by several studios over the years, was sold in its entirety to Paramount. Paramount did not want Western Costume at all, as it turned out, but rather its building, a five-story monolith which they wanted to tear down in order to extend the lot out to Melrose Avenue. To that end they sold Western to the Trinity Group, which had been organized by three entities (one of which was author Sidney Sheldon), while keeping the building. Western moved to North Hollywood, where it remains today.

With Western out of the way, and after some other purchases, the studio now controlled all of the real estate south of Marathon Street to Melrose Avenue.

The reconstruction of Paramount's Melrose frontage as it all looked in May, 1993.

Only KCAL Television, which was a leased-from-Paramount holdover from the RKO/Desilu era, kept them from Melrose Avenue across the entire front of the lot. That lease finally ended in 2002, at which point the total size of the lot equaled sixty-five acres. Unfortunately, Paramount angered some preservation societies when they tore down Western's historic building, which was, after all, the reason they had purchased it to begin with. The building, while undoubtedly historic, was also not terribly attractive, so the furor was short-lived.

First up after the expansion, the studio rebuilt into offices the so-called Valentino Building, named after an apartment building, the Valentino Arms, built on that site in 1926 just outside the lot to capitalize on the tumult caused by the matinee idol's unexpected demise. Valentino, despite many printed accounts to the contrary, did in fact work on the lot, but only in the pre-Paramount era.

272

The Marathon Office Building, left, and the Paramount Theater, right, were two of the many expansions and improvements to the lot in the 80s and 90s.

His dressing room was on the eastern side of the current plant, near Van Ness Avenue. For years stories circulated about Valentino having a tunnel built from this building to the administration building, for easier entry. The stories, of course, are untrue, but the tunnel itself may have had at least a thin basis in fact. Allegedly this tunnel was built not by Valentino, but by Zukor or other executives, in order to spirit their mistresses in and out of the lot.

During this period the studio also added a park, additional parking, and the lavish 516-seat Paramount Theater, which boasts an impressive 21-foot-by-54-foot screen and 35mm, 70mm, and digital projection capabilities. The lobby for this theater has also appeared (as a hotel) in *Clear and Present Danger* (1994). The Pickford Building, formally a bank at the mouth of Valentino Place, came out of the expansion as well. Mary Pickford might have driven by once. Finally, in 1993, the Marathon Office Building was dedicated near the corner of Van Ness and Melrose.

A pleasant walkway, Paramount Plaza, was installed at this time across the front of the Bronson Gate, and east-west across the lot, with cobblestones, a fountain, and a gift shop on the route, making the Paramount experience more genteel than it has ever been. The studio also has installed a park bench along the plaza, which they would like visitors to believe was used in their beloved blockbuster, *Forrest Gump* (1994), although the actual prop resides in the Savannah, Georgia, History Museum.

In 1988 the studio also added a new gate at the mouth of Melrose that mimicked, on a larger scale, the iconic Bronson Gate. In fact, many tourists visiting the studio, or driving by, often mistake this copy for the original, which, with the expansions, is now well inside the lot. The fountain further obscures any public view of the world's most iconic entrance, which is no longer an entrance at all, and is much too small for modern vehicles to enter through anyway.

South of the Bronson Gate the studio tore out a warren of garages and apartments, and in 1992 replaced much of this real estate with a grassy area called Marathon Park, across from the Redstone Building. Some of these offices had

ABOVE LEFT: The Windsor Gate, seen here under construction in 1988.
ABOVE RIGHT: Unlike the more-famous Bronson Gate, the Windsor Gate actually faced traffic on Melrose Avenue, and so was designed specifically to mimic its more famous sister. A clear case of giving the public what they want to see, 1991.

been the home of KTLA Television, in which Paramount had owned a minority stake from 1947 until 1964, when cowboy star Gene Autry had purchased the company for $12 million. Unlike nearby KCAL, KTLA had actually been a subsidiary of Paramount—although many people who worked for KTLA had always felt they were second-class citizens due to the competition between film and television, and that they were kept (just) off the lot for that very reason. KTLA is now based at the nearby Sunset Bronson Studios. KMEX, a Spanish-language station, later occupied the property. Part of the Bronson parking lot is on the space now.

In an irony too sublime to ignore, all of these loving studio improvements and renovations were overseen by none other than Stanley R. Jaffe, who in 1970 had advocated for "getting rid of" that very same studio.

Charles Bluhdorn died in 1983. His successor Martin Davis was, unlike Bluhdorn, an entertainment industry veteran, albeit a New York one, whose preferred arena was the boardroom rather than the backlot. Perhaps Davis was a bit *too* veteran to be considered a movie brat; by 1983 he had already worked at Samuel Goldwyn and Allied Artists before joining Paramount, back in 1958.

Unlike his predecessor, however, Davis realized that "Paramount" was a more valuable and resonant name among generations of consumers than the almost comically monolithic Gulf+Western. In fact, Mel Brooks had mocked that moniker in his film, *Silent Movie* (Twentieth Century Fox, 1976), calling it "Engulf and Devour." So one of Davis's first actions as CEO was to start selling off most of the company's non-entertainment-related assets. He renamed the new parent company off of one of its subsidiaries, Paramount Communications. Even the publishing division, which included Simon & Schuster and Pocket Books, would thereafter be known as "Paramount Publishing."

Davis also fired the ambitious Diller in 1984. Diller would launch an unsuccessful bid to purchase the company, which instead went to Viacom for $10 billion in 1993. Viacom (which stood for Visual and Audio Communications) was originally the television syndication division of CBS. The company was spun off from its parent in 1971, although the two companies would merge in 1999.

Sumner Redstone, the head of Viacom, was, like many of his earliest predecessors, a former film exhibitor.

In 1992 Davis hired Sherry Lansing, who had become the first female head of production in Hollywood history (at Twentieth Century Fox in 1980), and installed her as chairman of Paramount's motion picture group. Lansing's successful, levelheaded, twelve-year tenure would include hits like *Forrest Gump* (1994), the studio's highest-grossing movie to date, *Braveheart* (1995), *Mission: Impossible* (1996), and *Titanic* (produced with Twentieth Century Fox, 1997), one of the most popular films in history.

Also in 1984, the studio implemented a $16 million renovation project on their stages in order to entice TV productions shot on video, an increasingly common practice during the era, onto the lot. The project was a success, and both *Solid Gold* (1980–1988) and *Entertainment Tonight* (1981–2007 seasons) would ultimately move onto these modernized stages.

In 2002, for the company's ninetieth anniversary, Lansing (or her publicist) found a moment to reflect nostalgically on the ghosts of an era she was not personally there to remember:

> The weight of the past can be both exhilarating and rewarding. When I first came to Paramount as an independent producer, I was given a charming office overlooking a park. It had been Lucille Ball's office, and the park had been created for her use. I parked my car where Moses once parted the Red Sea. I strolled by soundstages that have been the scene of everything from *Sunset Boulevard* to *Star Trek*.
>
> To get to my current office I walk by offices formerly occupied by Alfred Hitchcock, and by the screening rooms used by such greats as Gloria Swanson, Alan Ladd, and Billy Wilder, and then through hallways lined with photographs from their classic films. My own office once belonged to Adolph Zukor, one of the very founders not just of this company, but of the entire industry.[7]

The lot as it looked in 1985, just before the expansion.

277

In 2005, Viacom and CBS were again split into two companies, with some Paramount assets, including the studio, drifting over to the "new" Viacom, and some to CBS. Brad Grey and Gail Berman ended up with Lansing's position. The following year Grey purchased DreamWorks SKG for $1.6 billion. DreamWorks had been an unsuccessful attempt to create an eighth studio, the first such attempt in decades, although DreamWorks's successful animation division was not included in the deal, and DreamWorks itself relaunched as an independent in 2008.

In this era of international conglomerates and transglobal production, it seems appropriate to wonder about the place of a traditional studio in the twenty-first century, and about whether or not the physical property in Hollywood today even constitutes "Paramount" as an entity in any way beyond the symbolic.

Modern production is done all over the world, with the physical studio now functioning more as a headquarters than as a factory in the traditional sense. The components involved in the creation of "filmed" entertainment, as well as the method of delivering those components to audiences, can now be assembled and delivered from behind a desk.

Scott Billups of PixelMonger, a Hollywood visual effects boutique, points out that virtual backlots, with vast libraries of locations and environments, are already available and can be plugged in faster than an equivalent set could be constructed or an equivalent location booked, rendering obsolete much of the hundred-year-old business model Hollywood created and used to operate by. "Movie studios don't want to actually make movies," he points out. "The process of production—however much is done using actual people and actual sets, and wherever that process is carried out—is still messy and arduous. But once another business—the gaming industry, perhaps—proves that virtual, or augmented, reality is a viable and reproducible concept, then Hollywood will embrace and evolve along with that concept. Wait and see."[8]

"The real threat to Hollywood as a factory town has not been the ability to create sets inside a computer," Richard Lindheim asserts. "The real threat

After the renovations. Paramount as it looked in 2013.

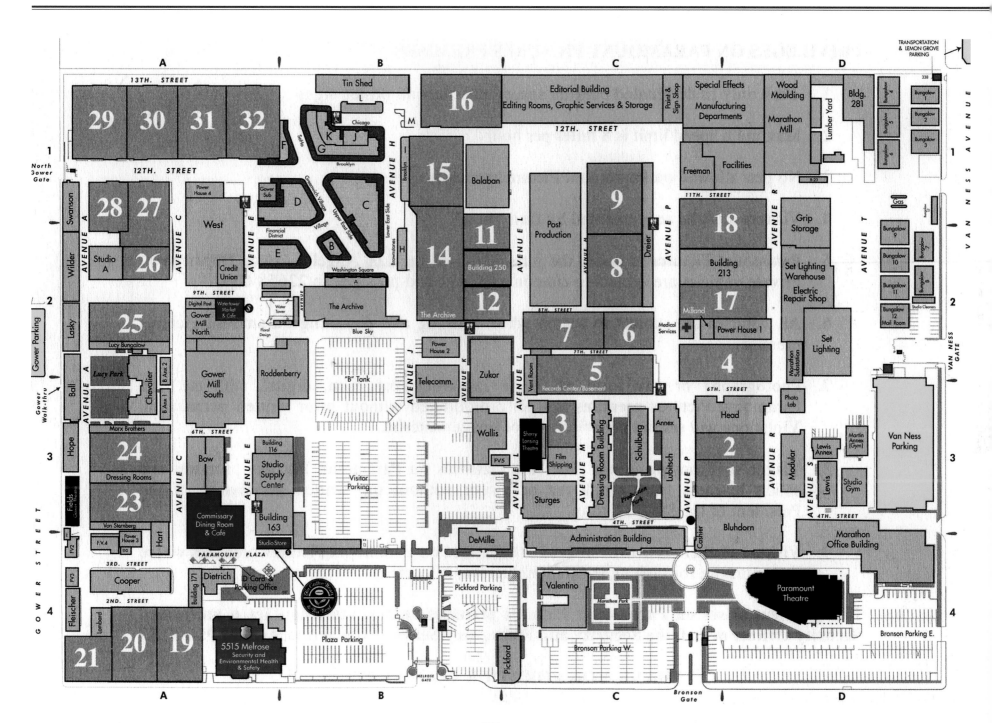

actually came years ago when movies started to be made on location. Originally, an actor drove to the same studio every day and parked in the same parking space and went to the same dressing room and then the same soundstage. Location trips were rare, because the equipment was huge and cumbersome, especially if you were shooting in Technicolor, where the lights had to be so hot that takes were ruined because they would melt the makeup right off of the actors' faces. But with the arrival of lightweight equipment, Africa could suddenly play Africa." Those actors, and Hollywood, thus left the soundstage.

"The problem with location shooting was that it was (and is) expensive, and impractical," Lindheim continues. "The sound recorded on location is never usable; it always has to be re-created in ADR. And suppose when you get there, the weather doesn't want to cooperate? Creatively, locations were also frustrating in that you always had to accept what you found when you got to that location. You could never quite find the Africa you imagined in preproduction."[9]

Lindheim and Billups point out that all of this has started to spin the wheel back to that same soundstage again. A new invention spearheaded by Billups,

Paramount's 75th anniversary in 1987 brought together 62 celebrities who gathered in front of the Bronson Gate for this once in-a-lifetime photograph. Later anniversaries, specifically the 90th in 2002, and the 100th in 2012, would attempt to recapture the same magic, but this is the one for the ages. Featured: Top row: Ali MacGraw, Burt Lancaster, Scott Baio, Bruce Dern, James Cann, Glenn Ford, Fred MacMurray, Shelly Long, James Stewart. Second row: William Shatner, Peter Graves, Molly Ringwald, Rhea Perlman, Dorothy Lamour, Olivia Newton-John, Ted Danson, Cindy Williams, Lou Gossett Jr., Matthew Broderick, Gene Hackman, Walter Matthau, Robin Williams. Third row: Jane Russell, Mike Connors, Anthony Perkins, John Travolta, Robert Stack, Janet Leigh, Mark Harmon, Charles Bronson, Faye Dunaway, Buddy Rogers, Charlton Heston, Gregory Peck, Ryan O'Neil, Rhonda Flemming, Timothy Hutton, Leonard Nimoy. Fourth row: Andrew McCarthy, Olivia de Havilland, Henry Winkler, Kevin Costner, Cornel Wilde, Don Ameche, DeForest Kelley, Tom Cruise, Penny Marshall, Bob Hope, Debra Winger, Victor Mature, Elizabeth McGovern, Robert De Niro. Fifth row, seated: Martha Raye, Dana Andrews, Elizabeth Taylor, Frances Dee, Joel McCrea, Harry Dean Stanton, Harrison Ford, Jennifer Beals, Marlee Matlin, and Danny DeVito.

called the "Smart-Stage," enables actors on the set to see, in real time, the "location" which has been digitally created and with which they are interacting. Lasky and Zukor, and especially DeMille, would have been thrilled.

In 2012 Paramount celebrated its hundredth anniversary. For the occasion, the studio corralled and cajoled 116 stars, everyone from Kirk Douglas to Justin Bieber, for a group shot on Stage 18, photographed by Art Streiber on January 13. The studio had wanted to take the picture in front of the Bronson Gate, but Annie Leibovitz had used the gate as a backdrop for the ninetieth anniversary portrait in 1992, and earlier, the seventy-fifth anniversary photograph had been taken there as well.

The hundredth anniversary attracted a tremendous amount of attention in the popular press. On *CBS Good Morning*, correspondent Lee Cowan interviewed Brad Grey while he was walking across the lot.

"When you're here late at night, do the ghosts of the old studio haunt you a little bit?" Cowan asked the CEO.

Grey smiled and nodded. "Yeah, I think there are ghosts all over this lot, to be honest with you," he said.

The unasked question, of course, was whether those ghosts were the specters of the people who made the movies, or of the movies themselves.

[1] Bernard F. Dick. *Engulfed: The Death of Paramount Pictures and the Birth of Corporate Hollywood*. Lexington: University Press of Kentucky, 2001.
[2] Robert Evans. *The Kid Stays in the Picture*. New York: Hyperion, 1994.
[3] Todd McCarthy. "The Way They Were, Baby," *Variety*, July 15–21, 2002.
[4] Peter Bart. *Infamous Players: A Tale of Movies, the Mob (and Sex)*. New York: Weinstein Books, 2001.
[5] Michael Tolkin. *The Player*. New York: Grove Press, 1988.
[6] "Paramount Retags 27 Buildings After Some of Brightest Lights," *Variety*, July 29, 1987.
[7] John Douglas Eames and Robert Abele. *The Paramount Story: The Complete History of the Studio and Its Films*. New York: Simon & Schuster, 1985, 2002.
[8] Interview: Scott Billups, April, 2015.
[9] Interview: Richard Lindheim. March, 2016.

Appendix: Other Gates

I used to do extra work over on Long Island. The studio's closed now.

—Ann Darrow (Fay Wray) in *King Kong* (RKO, 1933)

The purpose of this book, contrary to whatever the publisher might insist, is to prove that Paramount is not a thing, not a company, not an entity, not a state of mind, and not, despite what human resources might insist, made up of its people. Paramount, rather, is a *place*, just like Rome, Italy, Nacogdoches, Texas, Ontario, Canada, Mount Everest, the Empire State Building, or even Hollywood are, in fact, places.

For generations people have been saying that Hollywood is a state of mind, and it is—for whatever that's worth. But more importantly, Hollywood, and Paramount, are actual tangible, sometimes terrible, entities that exist beyond and apart from their products and legacy and people. Paramount is a place haunted with ego and hubris and genius, and perhaps even with actual ghosts. It deserves to be recognized for what it is, not just for why it is. It deserves to be recognized not just as a symbol or a logo, or as a metaphor, not as a Camelot or a Shangri La, but as a vessel for whatever we put into it, just as is New York or the Taj Mahal or the Mississippi River. We don't treat the Golden Gate Bridge as *only* a metaphor. But Hollywood—Paramount—has never before gotten its due as a part of the world.

That said, although Paramount is first and forever a place, it is not only *one* place. The "other" Paramounts—namely, the Astoria, New York, lot and the ranch property in the Santa Monica Mountains, have gotten short shrift in this book and elsewhere. A third studio, in Joinville, France, and a few other, lesser properties are interesting, but didn't last long enough to make much of an impact. Likewise, the Selma-Vine lot, and before that, the little barn in which Hollywood was born, as well as the Lasky Ranch, while important, were each more gestation spots for the property that has been the subject of this study. The main body of the text and the photographs hopefully tell the story to the satisfaction of most readers.

If not, there is at least one more book to be written on this subject, and hopefully, another author to write it.

Here, then, is the tale of the other Paramounts . . .

THE PARAMOUNT RANCH

Paramount, under the subsidiary of Paramount Land Corporation, purchased the 2,745 acres of property in Agoura, near Malibu, on July 1, 1927, from the Waring family for $42,500. Earlier the studio had leased the property from the Warings, so they would have already been aware of its suitability for outdoor scenes.

Actually, the sale was brokered by something called the "Central Motion Picture District," which was doing the same thing for what became the Mack Sennett Film Studios in Studio City at about the same time. Whatever the details, the Warings—Bruce, known to the locals as "Jigs," and his wife Madge—had owned the property, one of the largest ranches in southern California, since 1917, although how much "ranching" was actually performed on the site is debatable. It is known that the Warings used their unexpected windfall of movie money to abandon ranching altogether and buy themselves an elegant urban home in Los Feliz.

The Ranch was adjacent to Cornell Road, just south of Ventura Boulevard in the Santa Monica Mountains. For the official opening of the property under Paramount's

LEFT: The surviving ranch property as it looked in 1986. RIGHT: *The Old-Fashioned Way* (1934) brought W.C. Fields to the Ranch.

stewardship, starlet Mary Brian was driven out from Hollywood across the various bumpy access roads to have her photograph taken with various workmen and cowboys, who were clearing out the area where sets were to be constructed.

The Ranch had several advantages over the Hollywood lot in that it was studded with unobstructed views of the mountains, water, hills, and wooded areas. It could double as a thousand different places, including the American frontier, which even in those days Hollywood was having some trouble doing.

The first structure built on the lot by Paramount was a kitchen-bunkhouse called the Longhorn. A caretaker was installed to watch over the place. Local cowboys, of which there were a great many in those wild days, provided cheap labor and could do stunt work for the cameras as needed. The first Western town built on the site was near Sierra Creek Road and Kanen Road. This set is long gone, and should not be confused with later Paramount Western locations which came down the trail in later years. Some sets were also moved from the Lasky Ranch to the Paramount Ranch.

Under the Tonto Rim (1928) was, according to probably unreliable publicity, the first film shot on the Paramount Ranch after the purchase. By 1937 there were multiple standing sets on the grounds, including Asian and European settings to complement the Western locales. Outside producers like David O. Selznick and Samuel Goldwyn also built sets on the property, which Paramount was then able to utilize themselves, or to rent to other studios. In 1938 the studio could boast of the following standing sets on the property:

Corral: Used both as a set and as a holding area for livestock working elsewhere on the property.

Bunkhouse: Again, used as a set and also as actual living quarters for wranglers who were working on Westerns being filmed at the Ranch.

ABOVE LEFT: The Marco Polo set, as used, aptly enough, on *The Adventures of Marco Polo*, 1938. ABOVE RIGHT: *Rose of the Rancho* (1936) is seen utilizing the ranch's elaborate hacienda set.

Bull Ring: First used in the film *The Trumpet Blows* (1934); the stucco walls gave it a Mexican feeling.

Fort Stockade: Built around 1928. Frances Farmer, the doomed starlet whose life later became the subject of a movie, was photographed on the set during a publicity junket in 1935.

Medea Creek Bed: An actual natural location which was seized upon by film-makers as a way to add a bit of scenic interest to a setting. Used dozens of times over the years in films like *The Virginian* (1929), *Only the Brave* (1930), *A Man from Wyoming* (1930), *The Thunder Below* (1932), *Holiday Inn* (1942), and *California* (1958). For *The Adventures of Tom Sawyer* (UA, 1937), the creek was dammed so as to suggest the Mississippi River.

Marco Polo Set: As China, constructed for *The Adventures of Marco Polo* (UA, 1938), which starred Cary Cooper in the title role. Cooper was no stranger to the Ranch, although his previous films there had all been Westerns. The set continued to be used into the 1940s.

Hacienda Set: Built for *The Thunder Below* (1932), although frustratingly, *The Border Legion* (1930) appears to include sets which resemble the Hacienda (perhaps built from the same blueprints?). Regardless, this Mexican-style rancho was later used in *Woman Trap* (1936), *Rose of the Rancho* (1936), and many others.

German Street / Austrian Street: Probably built for Lubitsch's *Broken Lullaby* (1932); reused in *Till We Meet Again* (1936), this time as Austria; *The Maid of Salem* (1937), this time as Massachusetts; and others.

***Ebb Tide* (1937) Set:** Built in 1937 as a tropical island location. Costar Francis Farmer again visited the Ranch for location scenes.

Taylor Ranch: A frequent Western location. *The Santa Fe Trail* (1930) seems to be one of its earliest appearances, although the origin of the set's name is still debated.

Mexican Village: Built for *The Wolf Song* (1929), with Gary Cooper, who, along with Francis Farmer, sometimes must have felt like he lived on the property during this era.

San Francisco Street: Probably built in 1936 for DeMille's (and Gary Cooper's) *The Plainsman* (1936), where it played Abilene, Kansas, not San Francisco. Later used (again, not as San Francisco) in *The Texans* (1938). For *Wells Fargo* (1937), a different set merged with this earlier version and did play the city on the bay. *The Parson of Panamint* (1941) and others followed.

Western Town Street: At one time more than forty buildings were clustered in this elaborate frontier re-creation. Films shot on the set include *Stairs of Sand* (1929), *The Light of Western Stars* (1930), *Only the Brave* (1930), *The Conquering Horde* (1931), *Caught* (1931), *Make Me a Star* (1932), *Ghost Valley* (RKO, 1932), *Lone Cowboy* (1933), *Melody in Spring* (1934), *Arizona Mahoney* (1936), and countless others.

The German-Austrian Street, as New England in *The Maid of Salem* (1937).

Tom Sawyer Street: Originally a part of the Western Town Street set, it became a sleepy Missouri village in *The Adventures of Tom Sawyer* (UA, 1937). The residential section of the street seems to have been created, or very much expanded upon, for this film. In *The Miracle of Morgan's Creek* (1944), the village was brought up to date for World War II, giving the district a fusion of period and modern architecture which was similar to many actual American small towns of the time.

French Village Set: Actually more of a chateau with outlying buildings, built for the Pola Negri vehicle *Barbed Wire* (1927). This movie was apparently actually filmed at the Lasky Ranch, although the sets seem to have been moved, or rebuilt at the Paramount Ranch, because they appear in another World War I drama, *A Man from Wyoming* (1930), and a comedy, *Anybody's War* (1930).

In addition to these standing sets, the Ranch also boasted a wide variety of support buildings, including a fire station, mill, lumberyard, mess hall (being that this was a ranch, it seems wrong to call it a commissary), garage for storing and maintaining vehicles, prop room, bunkhouse, water tank, and a caretaker's house where the foreman and caretaker resided, directing all of the maintenance on the site.

Many of the notable pictures shot at the Ranch used no particular sets at all. The property with its trees, plains, and hills was perfect for outdoor pictures like the Hopalong Cassidy films with William Boyd, *Only the Brave* (1930) and *Fighting Caravans* (1931), both with Gary Cooper, as well as *The Vanishing Frontier* (1932), *Buck Benny Rides Again* (1940), *The Roundup* (1941), and *Fancy Pants* (1950).

Movies with primarily foreign locations, in addition to those mentioned above, like *Morocco* (1930) and *A Farewell to Arms* (1932), both with Gary Cooper, as well as *The Last Outpost* (1935), *So Proudly We Hail!* (1943), Charlie Chaplin's *Monsieur Verdoux* (UA, 1947), and *Golden Earrings* (1947), among others, also cast the ranch as a range of places from Maine to Marrakesh.

Modern, primarily urban-set films like *It's a Gift* (1934), *Car 99* (1935), *Murder with Pictures* (1936), *These Three* (UA, 1936), *Nothing Sacred* (UA 1937), *The Arkansas Traveler* (1938), *Dr. Cyclops* (1940), *Remember the Night* (1940), *Caught in the Draft* (1941), *I Married a Witch* (1942), *High Explosive* (1943), and *Dynamite* (1949) also found the ranch useful.

DeMille used the set for *The Plainsman* (1936), *Union Pacific* (1939), *North West Mounted Police* (1940), *The Story of Dr. Wassell* (1944), and *Unconquered* (1947). Gary Cooper was in four out of the five.

In 1943, however, due to a downslide in production and an upturn in real estate prices, the studio sold the property. The buyer was a working rancher, Eiser Wickholm, who in spite of what he had assured Paramount—that he intended to lease the land back to the studio as needed—turned around and sold the same land off in parcels. Eventually the "Wickholm Ranch" consisted of only 336 acres. In 1952 William B. Hertz bought these acres as an investment and for recreation purposes. During this period many of the original sets described above were destroyed. But a new Western town was constructed, which Paramount and other studios and television producers continued to use. In 1959 the site was sold yet again, to a company which intended to race sports cars on the property. Fortunately for them, *The Devil's Hairpin* (1957) had, in fact built a race-track on the property, which was still there, and was adapted to that purpose by the new owners.

In the late 1970s, Historian and consultant Marc Wanamaker was brought in by the National Park Service to write a feasibility study and historical report regarding the acquisition of the property. Based on this report, in June of 1980 the Park Service purchased the ranch. Fortunately the Western set, by then the only backlot still standing, was maintained, and rebuilt extensively for the TV series *Dr. Quinn: Medicine Woman* (1993–1998).

Other projects shot at the ranch in recent decades include *Helter Skelter* (TV, 1976), *Charlie's Angels* (TV, 1976–1981), *The Dukes of Hazzard* (TV, 1979–1985), *Reds* (1981), *MacGyver* (TV, 1985–1992), *Diagnosis Murder* (TV, 1993–2002),

Scream (Dimension, 1981), *CSI* (TV, 2000–2015), *Carnivale* (TV, 2003–2005), *The O.C.* (TV, 2003–2007), *Weeds* (TV 2005–2012), *The Lake House* (Warner Bros., 2006), *Van Helsing* (Universal, 2008), *American Sniper* (Warner Bros., 2014), and *Bone Tomahawk* (RLJ, 2015).

ASTORIA

Opened on September 20, 1920, as an East Coast production hub at a time when New York still had many such studios, Astoria was located at Pierce and Sixth Avenue in Long Island.

Zukor, who preferred the East Coast, was a big fan of the facility; Lasky, the Californian, never understood this. "Though the Astoria studio [was definitely needed] as an adjunct to our facilities in the West," he wrote, "it was always a headache to the production department. Overhead was higher in the New York area, the studio was limited in size and utility, weather destroyed sets on the backlot time and again, and locations for exteriors were more of a problem than amid the scenic variety of the West."[1]

In fact, in 1926 the studio was closed due to these very reasons, and due to the general redundancy involved in operating a second lot at all. Astoria might have become merely a footnote, like Joinville, in the Paramount saga, had it not been for the arrival of sound. The studio was unlocked and the lights were turned back on in 1928 because suddenly actors were required to speak for the cinema.

This other Paramount studio soon developed its own house style, perhaps due to its proximity to Broadway. Many an actor working on the Great White Way in the evenings could now shoot a movie in the daytime at Astoria. *The*

ABOVE: The Astoria studio as it looked in 1919. RIGHT: The interior of one of the Astoria stages, 1929.

French Star Welcomed By Paramount

Paramount Studio News

"THE WHOLE SHOW"

Three
Pictures
Started
This Week

Leaders
To Confer
In N.Y.
Next Week

VOL. 2   OCTOBER 18, 1928   No. 20

LONG ISLAND STUDIO ACTIVE

PLANS FOR
SEASON TO
BE DRAWN

Pep Club Fete
Annual Banquet Tonight

Bebe Turns Interviewer

BROADWAY
STARS FOR
N. Y. FILMS

Despite this optimistic 1928 studio newspaper headline, the recently reopened Astoria Studio would again be closed in 1932. (Image courtesy Hollywood Heritage)

Letter (1929) would be the first talkie shot on the lot, and would make good use of its star, Broadway actress Jeanne Eagels, who would go on to win a posthumous Oscar nomination. (Eagels, who died of drug-related causes the same year, would later become the subject of a biopic.)

Likewise, the Marx Brothers shot their first film, *The Cocoanuts* (1929), in the daytime while performing onstage in *Animal Crackers* at night. After filming *Animal Crackers* itself in 1930, they would move west. Their contemporary W. C. Fields eventually made nine movies at Astoria before going to Hollywood in 1931. *Applause* (1929) starred Helen Morgan (who, like Eagels, would later have her life transformed into a movie), but, more importantly, was directed by another Broadway vet—Rouben Mamoulian, who, like the Marx Brothers and Fields, would soon be Hollywood-bound.

Gloria Swanson, however, believed that the studio was more than just a way station to California. "It was certainly not just another Hollywood. The place was full of free spirits, defectors, refugees, who were all trying to get away from Hollywood and its restrictions. There was a wonderful sense of revolution and innovation."[2]

It didn't last. In 1932, Zukor, during the bankruptcy procedure, unhappily agreed to once again shutter Astoria, and consolidate Paramount's production activities in California. Only the lavish Paramount Theater on Broadway and Forty-Third Street, which had been built in 1926 and also housed company offices, would remain in New York.

The property was eventually leased to the Eastern Service Studio for independent producers. In 1942 the US Army purchased the lot for $500,000, and it became the Signal Corps Photographic Center (SCPC).

In 1970 the studio was declared "surplus property" by the US government and was leased, unsuccessfully, by LaGuardia Community College. In 1975 the planning division of the city of New York, which was considering purchasing the studio from the government, brought in Marc Wanamaker as a consultant regarding dispensation of the property, which ultimately led to the studios again being utilized as a production facility. In 1982 real estate developer George S. Kaufman assumed control of the lot and renamed the property the Kaufman Astoria Studios. This latest incarnation of the Astoria lot has been a successful one. The TV series *Sesame Street*, from 1993 on, has been a longtime tenant. Among Kaufman Astoria's seven stages is the massive "Stage E," which remains the largest soundstage in the United States, east of Hollywood.

[1] Jesse Lasky. *I Blow My Own Horn*. New York: Doubleday, 1957.
[2] Gloria Swanson. *Swanson on Swanson*. New York: Random House, 1980.

Bibliography

Books

Adamson, Joe. *Byron Haskin: Directors Guild of America, Series 1*. New York: Scarecrow Press, 1995.

Affron, Charles, and Mirella Jona Affron. *Sets in Motion: Art Direction and Film Narrative*. New Brunswick, NJ: Rutgers University Press, 1995.

Bart, Peter. *Infamous Players: A Tale of Movies, the Mob (and Sex)*. New York: Weinstein Books, 2001.

Berg, A. Scott. *Goldwyn: A Biography*. New York: Riverhead (Penguin) Books, 1998.

Birchard, Robert S. *Images of America: Early Universal City*. Charleston, SC: Arcadia Publishing, 2009.

Bradbury, Ray. *A Graveyard for Lunatics*. New York: Alfred A. Knopf, 1990.

Brant, Marley. *Happier Days: Paramount Television's Classic Sitcoms 1974–1984*. New York: Billboard Books, 2006.

Brownlow, Kevin. *The Parade's Gone By*. New York: Alfred A. Knopf, 1968.

Crafton, Donald. *The Talkies: American Cinema's Transition to Sound, 1926–1931*. Oakland: University of California Press, 1999.

Davis, Ronald L. *The Glamour Factory: Inside Hollywood's Big Studio System*. Dallas, TX: Southern Methodist University Press, 1993.

———. *Just Making Movies: Company Directors on the Studio System*. Oxford: University Press of Mississippi, 2005.

De Carlo, Yvonne, with Doug Warren. *Yvonne: An Autobiography*. New York: St. Martin's Press, 1987.

DeMille, Cecil B. *The Autobiography of Cecil B. DeMille*. New Jersey: Prentice Hall, 1959.

Dick, Bernard F. *Engulfed: The Death of Paramount Pictures and the Birth of Corporate Hollywood*. Lexington: University Press of Kentucky, 2001.

Dmytryk, Edward. *On Film Editing*. New York: Focal Press, 1984.

Eames, John Douglas, and Robert Abele. *The Paramount Story: The Complete History of the Studio and Its Films*. New York: Simon & Schuster, 1985, 2002.

Evans, Robert. *The Kid Stays in the Picture*. New York; Hyperion, 1994.

Eyman, Scott. *Empire of Dreams: The Epic Life of Cecil B. DeMille*. New York: Simon & Schuster, 2010.

Fernett, Gene. *American Film Studios: An Historic Encyclopedia*. Jefferson, NC: McFarland, 1988.

Fitzgerald, F. Scott. *The Last Tycoon*. New York: Charles Scribner's Sons, 1941.

Friedrich, Otto. *City of Nets*. New York: Harper & Row, 1986.

Gabler, Neil. *An Empire of Their Own: How the Jews Invented Hollywood*. New York: Doubleday, 1988.

Gmuer, Leonhard H. *Rex Ingram: Hollywood's Rebel of the Silver Screen*. Berlin: Druck and Verlag, 2013.

Higham, Charles, and Joel Greenberg. *The Celluloid Muse: Hollywood Directors Speak*. Chicago: Henry Regency Company, 1969.

Haver, Ron. *David O. Selznick's Hollywood*. New York: Alfred A. Knopf, 1980.

Irwin, Will. *The House That Shadows Built*. New York: Doubleday, Dorian & Company, Inc., 1928.

Jensen, Larry. *Hollywood's Railroads, Volume One: Virginia and Truckee.* Washington: Cochetopa Press, 2015.

Jewell, Richard B. *RKO Radio Pictures: A Titan Is Born.* Los Angeles: University of California Press, 2012.

Klugman, Jack. *Tony and Me: A Story of Friendship.* West Linn, OR: Good Hill Press, 2005.

Lasky, Betty. *RKO: The Biggest Little Major of Them all.* New Jersey: Prentice-Hall, Inc., 1984.

Lasky, Jesse. *I Blow My Own Horn.* New York: Doubleday, 1957.

Leonard, Sheldon. *And the Show Goes On: Broadway and Hollywood Adventures.* New York: Limelight, 1994.

Marshall, Garry. *My Happy Days in Hollywood: A Memoir.* New York: Crown Archetype, 2012.

Mordden, Ethan. *The Hollywood Studios.* New York: Fireside Books, 1988.

Pawlak, Debra Ann. *Bringing Up Oscar: The Story of the Men and Women Who Founded the Academy.* Glendale Heights, IL: Pegasus, 2011.

Presley, Cecilia de Mille, and Mark A. Vieira. *Cecil B. DeMille: The Art of the Hollywood Epic.* Philadelphia: Running Press, 2014.

Pye, Michael, and Linda Myles. *The Movie Brats: How the Film Generation Took Over Hollywood.* New York: Harry Holt and Company, 1984.

Rosenberg, Bernard, and Harry Silverstein. *The Real Tinsel.* New York: Macmillan, 1970.

Sanders, Coyne Steven, and Tom Gilbert. *Desilu: The Story of Lucille Ball and Desi Arnaz.* New York: Quill, William Morrow, 1993.

Schwartz, Sherwood. *Inside Gilligan's Island: From Creation to Syndication.* Jefferson, NC: McFarland, 1988.

Shapiro, Melany. *Bonanza: The Unofficial Story of the Ponderosa.* Las Vegas: Pioneer Books, 1993.

Stephens, E. J., Michael Christaldi, and Marc Wanamaker. *Images of America: Early Paramount Studios.* Charleston, SC: Arcadia Publishing, 2013.

———. *Images of America: Paramount Studios 1940–2000.* Charleston, SC: Arcadia Publishing, 2016.

Swanson, Gloria. *Swanson on Swanson.* New York: Random House, 1980.

Takei, George. *To the Stars.* New York: Pocket Books, 1994.

Taylor, Troy. *Bloody Hollywood.* Decatur, IL: Whitechapel Press, 2008.

Thompson, David. *The Whole Equation: A History of Hollywood.* New York: Alfred A. Knopf, 2005.

Tolkin, Michael. *The Player.* New York: Grove Press, 1988.

West, Nathanael. *The Day of the Locust.* New York: New Directions, 1939.

Westmore, Frank. *The Westmores of Hollywood.* Philadelphia and New York: L. P. Lippincott Company, 1976.

Williams, Barry, and Chris Kreski. *Growing Up Brady: I Was a Teenage Greg.* New York: HarperCollins, 1992.

Yarbrough, Tinsley E. *Those Great Western Movie Locations.* Greenville, NC: Tumbleweed Press, 2008.

Zukor, Adolph, with Dale Kramer. *The Public Is Never Wrong: The Autobiography of Adolph Zukor.* New York: G. P. Putnam's Sons, 1953.

Periodicals

"After 50 Years, He Can Call Paramount Home," *Los Angeles Herald Examiner,* August 25, 1983.

Arnold, Jim. "Backlot New York Rises Again: Behind the Façade," *Paramount News,* September/October 1991.

"Behind the Scenes—A Studio Group Production," *Paramount News,* March/April 1989.

Black, Kent. "Married . . . with Chutzpah," *Los Angeles Times*, August 19, 1981.

"Bob," *Paramount News*, September/October 1992.

Burlingame, John. "Paramount's Stage M Closes," *Film Music Society* (online at www.filmmusicsociety.org/news_events/features/2006/082906.html), August 29, 2006.

Burrough, Bryan. "The Siege of Paramount," *Vanity Fair*, January 31, 1994.

Davis, Charles Jr. "Richard Arlen Repaid for Nice Gesture of Three Decades Ago," *Los Angeles Times*, June 23, 1963.

"The Day the Dream Factories Woke up," *Life*, February 27, 1970.

Dick, Bernard F. "Citizen Zukor," *Variety*, July 15–21, 2012.

"Dr. Hugh J. Strathearn," *Paramount Parade*, Vol. IX, No. 4, August 1944.

"Famous Players Moves to New Los Angeles Studio," *Motion Picture News*, May 15, 1915.

"Federal OK Limits Gulf & Western's Desilu Acquisition," *Los Angeles Times*, July 26, 1967.

"First Person: Jerry Zucker," *Variety*, July 15–21, 2002.

"Flames Damage Desilu and Paramount Studios," *Los Angeles Times*, October 30, 1965.

Gajewski, Josh. "Windy City Wannabe," *Los Angeles Times*, August 7, 2006.

Giovannini, Joseph. "L.A.'s Movie Kremlins," *Los Angeles Herald Examiner*, December 12, 1979.

Girsone, M. R. M. "Further Enlargement of Paralta Plant Proposed," *The Dramatic Mirror*, March 9, 1918.

"Hollywood Barn Will Be Studio Museum," *Canyon Crier News*, November 24, 1982.

Jaffe, Sam, as told to Sam Locke. "The Night Paramount Burned," *Los Angeles Magazine*, October 1990.

Kingsley, Grace. "Universal to Picture World," *Los Angeles Times*, June 3, 1926.

Lasky, Steve. "Inside Security at Hollywood's Paramount Pictures," *Security Technology Executive Magazine*, May 8, 2009.

Leigh, Alan. "Gated Community," *The Hollywood Reporter*, Special Issue, July 2002.

———. "Show Starting," *The Hollywood Reporter*, Special Issue, July 2002.

McBride, Joseph. "Par Dusting Off Its Heritage," *Variety*, April 27, 1990.

McCarthy, Todd. "The Way They Were, Baby," *Variety*, July 15–21, 2002.

Morain, Dan. "Universal May Get DeMille Barn," *Los Angeles Times*, February 21, 1982.

Mungon, Donna. "Sam Jaffe: Looking Back at Hollywood by One Present at the Creation," *Los Angeles Times*, March 19, 1995.

Murphy-Burke, Jeanmarie. "From Rugs to Relics," *Paramount News*, March/April 1987.

———. "Working Out at Work: The Gym Then and Now," *Paramount News*, November/December 1987.

"New Paralta Studios Near Completion," *Motography*, April 20, 1918.

"Paramount Landmark Number One: The DeMille Barn," *Paramount Parade*, Vol. I, No. 2, November 25, 1936.

"Paramount Landmark Number Two," *Paramount Parade*, Vol. I, No. 3, January 1937.

"Paramount Modeler Honored," *Paramount Parade*, May 1951.

"Paramount Retags 27 Buildings After Some of Brightest Lights," *Variety*, July 29, 1987.

"Powerhouse," *Paramount Parade*, Vol. IX, No. 6, November 1945.

"Remembrance of Things Past," *Paramount Parade*, Vol. II, September 1938.

"Reopening of Paramount Studio's Main Hollywood Gates Symbol of New Era," *Paramount World*, Vol. X, No. 10, October 1964.

Rolland, Rudy. "A Study in Research," *Paramount Parade*, Vol. 12, Issue 6, October 1948.

Ryon, Ruth. "At 75, Paramount Still Building," *Los Angeles Times*, August 23, 1987.

Sandberg, Bryn Elise. "'Cheers' Bar Finally Finds a Museum Home," *Hollywood Reporter*, August 7, 2014.

Schreger, Charles. "History on the Move: Original DeMille Studio Will Get New Life as Museum," *Milwaukee Journal*, September 27, 1979.

Sederberg, Arelo. "Gulf & Western's Chairman Admits He Loves Lucy, Too," *Los Angeles Times*, July 27, 1967.

"Shoot the Works," *Paramount Parade*, Vol. V, No. 2, April 1941.

Simon, Richard. "Dispute Over Studio Logo Scales Heights," *Los Angeles Times*, December 2, 1982.

"The Studios of Hollywood Call the Roll of Honor," *Motion Picture Herald*, March 25, 1944.

"The Two-Hour Tour," *Inside the Gate*, Vol. II, No. 2, April/May 2006.

Thut, William. "Paramount's Sky," *Los Angeles Times*, September 10, 1989.

Wanamaker, Marc. "Historic Hollywood Movie Studios, Part 1," *American Cinematographer*, March 1976.

———. "Historic Hollywood Movie Studios, Part 2," *American Cinematographer*, April 1976.

———. "Historic Hollywood Movie Studios, Part 3," *American Cinematographer*, May 1976.

"Wilshire Phantom House Soon To Be Only Memory," *Los Angeles Times*, February 24, 1957.

Winters, Don. "The Dream Factory," *Los Angeles* magazine, August 2012.

Wyatt, Martin. "Martin Davis, 72: Created Modern Paramount," *New York Times*, October 6, 1999.

Websites

Bison Archives (www.bisonarchives.com)

Blog: The *Cheers* Set . . . by Ken Levine (kenlevine.blogspot.com/2006/09/cheers-set.html)

Blog: Dear Old Hollywood (dearoldhollywood.blogspot.com)

Blog: Matte Shot—A Tribute to Golden Era Special FX (nzpetesmatteshot.blogspot.com)

Chaplin-Keaton-Lloyd Film Locations (and more) (silentlocations.wordpress.com)

Film & TV Studio Backlots and Ranches (groups.yahoo.com/group/StudioBacklots)

Film Music Society (www.filmmusicsociety.org)

Haunted Hollywood by Troy Taylor (www.prairieghosts.com/hollywood.html)

Hollywood's Railroads (www.cochetopapress.biz)

Kaufman Astoria Studios (www.kaufmanastoria.com)

Moviemaking Locations (www.movielocationsplus.com)

Paramount Studio (www.paramountstudios.com)

Seeing Stars in Hollywood (www.seeing-stars.com)

Star Trek Comprehensive Reference Site (memory-alpha.wikia.com/wiki/Portal:Main)

Western Costume Company (westerncostume.com/about-us/history)

Interviews

Billups, Scott. April, 2015.

Blackburn, Billy. January, 2016.

de Mille Presley, Cecilia. January, 2016.

Fine, Debbie. March, 2016.

Greco, Mike. December, 2015.

Jensen, Larry. March, 2016.

Kleiser, Randal. April, 2016.

Kohn, Barbara Jaffe. December, 2015.

Lasky, Betty. December, 2015.

Lindheim, Richard. March, 2016.

Maltin, Leonard. May, 2016.

Phillips, Ed. February, 2016.

Wanamaker, Marc. assorted.

Warren, Bill. May, 2016.

Ziarko, Charles. May, 2013.

Other

Heumann, Leslie, with Richard Adkins, Bill Ellinger, Ruthann Lehrer, Christy McAvoy, and Marc Wanamaker. "Los Angeles Conservancy Paramount Studios Tour" script. February 9, 1992.

Wanamaker, Marc. *A History of the Paramount Ranch 1769–1989*. Agoura, CA: National Park Service, June 1, 1990; updated February 28, 1996.

Videos

The Godfather—DVD Collection (1972)

Island of Lost Souls—*Criterion Collection Edition* (1932)

Rear Window—*Collector's Edition* (1954)

The Six Degrees of Helter Skelter (2009)

Sunset Boulevard—*Special Collector's Edition* (1950)

The Ten Commandments—*Special Collector's Edition* (1957)

Vertigo—Collector's Edition (1958)

The War of the Worlds—Special Collector's Edition (1953)

Index

Note: page numbers in italics indicate a photo, illustration, etc.